THE GAME
BELIEVES
IN YOU

HOW DIGITAL PLAY CAN MAKE
OUR KIDS SMARTER

GREG TOPPO

palgrave
macmillan

The great thing, then, in all education, is to make our nervous system our ally instead of our enemy.

—William James, *Habit*

THE GAME BELIEVES IN YOU
Copyright © Greg Toppo, 2015
All rights reserved.

First published in 2015 by PALGRAVE MACMILLAN® TRADE
in the United States—a division of St. Martin's Press LLC, 175 Fifth
Avenue, New York, NY 10010.

Palgrave® and Macmillan® are registered trademarks in the United
States, the United Kingdom, Europe and other countries.

ISBN: 978-1-137-27957-6

Library of Congress Cataloging-in-Publication Data

Toppo, Greg.
   The game believes in you : how digital play can make our kids
smarter / Greg Toppo.
      pages   cm
   ISBN 978-1-137-27957-6 (hardback)
   1. Video games in education. 2. Video games and children. 3. Video
games—Study and teaching. 4. Education—Effect of technological
innovations on. I. Title.
LB1028.75.T66   2015
794.8—dc23

                                                          2014040335

Design by Letra Libre, Inc.

First edition: April 2015

10 9 8 7 6 5 4 3 2 1

Printed in the United States of America.

CONTENTS

PROLOGUE

Hard Fun

Early one April afternoon at Charles W. Raymond Elementary School near the heart of Washington, D.C., word spread quietly that JiJi was in the building. Lunch had just ended and virtually all 450 students were back in class. But a fortunate few, clutching bathroom passes or notes from the office, had caught a fleeting glimpse of the enormous velour-skinned penguin as he—she?—trundled, cross-eyed, through the echoing tiled hallways, a cluster of adult minders following closely behind.

JiJi in the building? How could it be? For most of the students, she (we'll use the pronoun "she" for simplicity's sake, though JiJi's gender is an enduring mystery) was an abstraction, an animation, a befuddled two-inch-high drawing on their laptop screens. Mute and poker faced, all she had ever really done was stare at them stupidly and, at key moments, walk across the screen. They might see her hundreds of times a day and never, ever exchange a word. JiJi never wavered, but she also never waved, never blinked, never offered a fish or applause or a fins-up. She planted the occasional flag at key moments, but that was about the limit of her enthusiasm. She was a flat little cartoon character, perhaps a few thousand pixels on a screen. But she was, to these children, as recognizable as Mickey Mouse, and more beloved.

JiJi was the hapless little mascot of a math game they played most days, one that showed the students, through simple animations, whether they got a problem right or wrong. Each time they were right, the software instantly built a smooth little road and JiJi appeared, tottered across the screen from left to right, and disappeared off the edge. The player's reward was another, harder problem. Whenever the solution was wrong, the game blocked JiJi's way and she bumped up against the barrier, then quickly retreated. Her little walk was both the reward for a thousand jobs well done and the incentive to try again, for as long as it took to get it right. She was a bit of computer code with a simple message: *Never give up.*

It was the spring of 2014, and a few days earlier, she had helped the Raymond students post some of the largest math gains of any elementary school in the city. The school, like many in D.C., serves mostly poor kids—at Raymond, 99 percent of students in 2014 qualified for free lunches under the federal government's poverty guidelines. They still had a long way to go if they were going to match suburban kids—41 percent of Raymond students were learning to speak English and many still struggled with basic skills. In the long-running Testing Wars that our schools have been fighting for more than a decade, these children were, depending on your point of view, either faithful foot soldiers or cannon fodder. Either way, they came to school each day under enormous pressure to improve. But that April, city data showed, a larger percentage of Raymond students had moved into the "proficient" and "advanced" math skills categories than at nearly any other elementary school, rich, poor, or in between, in all of D.C.[1] JiJi, all two inches of her, had quietly motivated the Raymond kids to do more math, remember what they learned, and keep going.

As soon as the large, live-action JiJi began appearing in Raymond classrooms that afternoon, everything stopped. Students yelled her name, put down their pencils, and sat in a kind of delighted awe. Her creator, a forty-one-year-old neuroscientist and computer engineer named Matthew Peterson, stood next to her, dressed in jeans and a suit jacket and looking like he hadn't gotten quite enough sleep. He explained that they were visiting because JiJi had heard about how hard the students were working. He asked the students to stand at their desks if they had played through all of the game's levels; in most classes, about one in three students stood, even though two months still remained in the school year. In a few classes, it was as many as half. They proudly rose as the adults clapped and JiJi waved, then did a little dance. Though these kids had lots to do each day, finishing the long, seemingly never-ending game was clearly on their minds. At one point during the visit, as JiJi and her entourage walked between classrooms, a student ran by and yelled, "I'm at 83 percent!"

In class after class, Peterson answered students' questions—JiJi was about to turn seventeen, he said, and yes, she'd come in a car. A second-grader asked him, "Why do the problems keep getting harder?" Without pausing to think or strategize about how to diplomatically answer this fraught question, Peterson said, "Because hard things are the *most fun* things to do." Then he invited everyone to gather around JiJi for photos. The adults pulled out cell phones and the kids crowded together, even the fourth graders who, by all rights, should have been too old to get excited about a group photo with a person in a penguin suit. They froze in their places as adults fumbled with camera buttons. They stood up straight and smiled, the tallest of them still a full foot shorter than JiJi. In a few classes, one or two students wrapped their arms around her, snuggled into her velveteen fur, closed their eyes and just took a moment, photos be damned. One first-grade teacher, standing beside her class, told them, "You all have to tell JiJi, *'Thank you!'* right?" They replied in unison, *"Thank you, JiJi!"*

If you haven't visited a school lately, the sight of children doing math with the help of a digital cartoon penguin might surprise you. It shouldn't. For many kids, JiJi and creatures like her have become a part of their school day, as normal and natural as retractable pencils and low-fat chocolate milk. After decades of ambivalence, suspicion, and sometimes outright hostility, educators are beginning to discover the charms of digital games and simulations, in the process rewriting centuries-old rules of learning, motivation, and success.

Technology has always pushed to take the focus off teachers and put it on students—what is a chalkboard but a bit of paint on a wall that invites students to step forward, draw letters, lines, and numbers, and take control of their learning?[2] But digital technology, and games in particular, go even further. Because games *look so little like school,* they force us to reconsider our most basic assumptions about how children learn: What is school for and what should students *do* there? Where should kids get their content and how? How important is it that they *like* what they're doing? What is our tolerance for failure and what is our standard for success? *Who is in control here?*

This is the story of a still-unfolding drama, the tale of a small, mostly unconnected group of visionaries who, for the past forty years, have been pushing hand controllers—and control—to students. Starting with rudimentary borrowed equipment in the 1970s, they've searched for ways to make learning more rigorous, more sticky, and more fun. To many researchers who have spent years investigating games and learning, the "If?" question has morphed into "How?" Asking if schools can accommodate games, according to University of Wisconsin scholar Kurt Squire, is like asking 500 years ago if universities could accommodate books.[3] As our understanding of cognitive science and game design advances, said Paul Howard-Jones, the British neuroscientist who leads the University of Bristol's NeuroEducational Research Network, games will become central to schools. "I think in thirty years' time, we will marvel that we ever tried to deliver a curriculum without gaming."[4]

This may all seem like a new idea, but actually it's not. Teachers have long used pencil-and-paper games, cards, dice, and board games to teach and reinforce key concepts. Even the electronic versions of games have a history dating back two generations. The eighth graders who shot buffalo in the first rudimentary version of *The Oregon Trail* on a teletype in a Minneapolis classroom in 1971 are now old enough to be grandparents. The movement's *de facto* vision statement emerged exactly twenty-five years ago, when an eight-year-old boy in an after-school program at MIT's Media Lab was showing off a bit of handiwork he'd created with LEGOs and a rudimentary computer program. Asked about the usefulness of the project, he told a skeptical TV reporter, "Yes, this is fun, but it's *hard fun*."[5]

What this small group of tinkerers found is that games focus, inspire, and reassure young people in ways that school often can't. Then as now, they believed, if you are a young person, games give you a chance to learn at your own pace, take risks, and cultivate deeper understanding. While teachers, parents, and friends may encourage and support you, these natural resources are limited. Computers work on a completely different scale and timetable. They're "infinitely stupid and infinitely patient," according to game designer Michael John.[6] Your teacher may be overwhelmed, your friends wish you'd finish your homework, and your mom just wants to go to bed. But as JiJi demonstrates, a well-designed game sits and waits . . . and waits. It doesn't care if that wearisome math problem takes you fifteen seconds or four hours. Do it again. Take all day. The game believes in you.[7]

Increasingly, it also *knows* you, or at least your abilities, better than anyone. At exactly the same time that schools have taken the questionable path of implementing more high-stakes standardized tests keyed to the abilities of some imaginary bell-curved student, games have gone the opposite route, embedding sophisticated assessment into gameplay, in the process becoming complex learning tools that promise to deflate the tired "teach to the test" narrative that weighs down so many great teachers and schools.

In virtually all commercial games, from the simplest connect-the-dots iPhone app to the most elaborate multiplayer console role-playing game, the learning *is* the assessment. One of the pleasures of these games is, quite simply, the luxury they afford us to learn, to see instantly how well we've learned, and then to try again without fuss or interruption until we succeed. "Think about it," linguist and games researcher James Paul Gee said recently. "If I make it through every level of *Halo*, do you really need to give me a test to see if I know everything it takes to get through every level of *Halo?*"[8]

The implications for school are, in a way, staggering. Imagine if every morning, in every school, every child showed up and worked as hard as he or she could. Students would eagerly accept challenges that they *know* are not only suited to their abilities but beyond them, trying repeatedly in the face of failure after failure, so engaged that at the sound of the final bell, they'd look up and wonder where the day had gone. What if schools, from the wealthiest suburban nursery school to the grittiest urban high school, thrummed with the sounds of deep immersion? That may sound a bit idealistic, but this is how educators in this field routinely talk about their work. They even have a name for the thing that happens when students are immersed in work that is perfectly suited to their abilities: *flow*. "It's not so much that we want them to be having fun all the time," said Arana Shapiro, co-director of Quest to Learn, a New York City public middle and high school built around play, "but more, 'Can we make the learning so engaging and so interesting and so hands-on that you have the feeling that you lose yourself in it?' And that's a different kind of fun."[9]

"We play to unlock our future selves," said game theorist and designer Nicole Lazzaro.[10] Developmental psychologists have long extolled the importance of play, saying it is essential to children's physical and psychological well-being and a key component of learning. Brain science confirms that from birth, people learn with their hands, manipulating the stuff of the world in order to understand it. "Play is the work of children," said educator Friedrich Froebel,[11] who is credited with inventing kindergarten. Growing up in Chicago in the 1930s, longtime kindergarten teacher and author Vivian Gussey Paley remembered, school was "serious business," but it never interfered with opportunities to play. "The odd thing was, no one thought we played too much. It was what children were supposed to do, and when we didn't play our mothers would feel our foreheads to see whether we were sick."[12]

Kids make mud pies and paper airplanes, they climb trees and play the piano. The entire time they're exploring and learning about the world. As neurologist Frank Wilson said, "A hand is always in search of a brain and a brain is in search of a hand."[13] We celebrate play and even fight for children's right to do more of it once they're in school. Yet we're quick to jettison play when we feel it's not up to the serious task of moving large amounts of material into our children's minds, especially when they're older. This book proposes that we rethink that belief. Let's consider a broader application of play in children's lives, one that holds out the possibility that more play and playful thinking could, ironically, make our schools more serious, productive places. As astrophysicist Jodi Asbell-Clarke, who is leading a team developing science and math games, once told me, "We're not trying to turn your students into gamers. We're trying to turn your gamers into students."[14]

Much of the challenge behind Asbell-Clarke's daring proposition boils down to this: we don't know what's happening in kids' heads when they're playing games. Actually, we *think* we know what's happening and we don't like it. This book offers a peek beneath the hood, showing that what's happening is often exactly the opposite of what it looks like. What looks like escapist fun is actually deep concentration. What looks like instant gratification is, in fact, delayed gratification in clever disguise. What looks like spectacle is a system that is training players to *ignore* the spectacle and focus on the real work at hand. What looks like anything-goes freedom is submission to strict rules. What looks like a twenty-first-century, flashy, high-tech way to keep kids entertained is in fact a tool that taps into an ancient way to process, explore, and understand the world.

Unlike many previous education movements, this one seems to defy easy labels. It is neither conservative nor liberal, neither wholly traditional nor wholly experimental. Games, it turns out, have a little something for everyone. For the crunchy and student-centered, games scratch an essential itch, sucking kids into a deep stream of engagement and teaching them to think, negotiate, imagine, and problem-solve. Games give children autonomy and agency, helping them design their own solutions, collaborate with friends, and create natural "affinity groups" that help bring learning alive outside the classroom. For the skills-and-assessment type, games scratch an equally essential itch: they frontload massive amounts of content, offer focused and efficient drill-and-practice, build on prior knowledge, strengthen grit, and, at the end of the day, deliver a personalized performance data stream that would make the most hard-assed psychometrician smile. If this were a soccer league, everyone wouldn't get a trophy. Everyone would get a spreadsheet detailing his or her role in the game—every pass, every kick, every missed opportunity.

This is mostly because a good game doesn't reward just showing up or watching from the sidelines—it requires players to *act,* to give it their best shot, to assess what went wrong and come back next time with a better plan. Commercial video games, after all, began life as machines that ate all the quarters in your pocket. They were designed to lead users to certain failure, but in a pleasurable way that kept them coming back for more. They had to be hard but not too hard, brief but not too brief. Coin-operated chess, for instance, might be thrilling, but it wouldn't make its creator rich, since a quarter might purchase an hour's playtime.

Since their coin-op days, of course, games have gotten more ambitious, epic, and complex. Since the rise of the first sophisticated home video-game systems in the early 1980s, games have gotten longer and more challenging because there's an economic incentive to do so. That incentive exists because our brains *like* to be challenged, wrote science author Steven Johnson. If our brains really liked mindless entertainment, "then the story of the last thirty years of video games—from *Pong* to *The Sims*—would be a story of games that grew increasingly simple over time." Exactly the opposite has occurred, he said. "The games have gotten more challenging at an astounding rate."[15]

In 1967, media critic Marshall McLuhan predicted that within two decades, technology would make school unrecognizable. "As it is now, the teacher has a ready-made audience," he wrote. "He is assured of a full house and a long run. Those students who don't like the show get flunking grades." But if students were given the choice to get their information elsewhere, he predicted, "the quality of the experience called education will change drastically. The educator then will naturally have a high stake in generating interest and involvement for his students."[16]

McLuhan was right about one thing: students can now get much of their information elsewhere. Many young people "are now deeply and permanently technologically enhanced," said business and education consultant Marc Prensky[17]—his observation will hit home to anyone who has watched teenagers sit in a Starbucks, wait in line at a Walgreens checkout stand, or attend a family function. But in school, those who don't like the show still get flunking grades. However, these students have a vision of something different. They now have the experience, outside of school, of diving into worlds that are richer and more relevant than anything they get in school. There's a technical term for this phenomenon, in which someone sees the possibilities that lie just out of reach but must spend time doing lesser things. It's called *boredom,* or as theologian Paul Tillich once described it, "rage spread thin."

In spite of our teachers' heroic efforts, our schools are fighting a losing battle with boredom. Indiana University's High School Survey of Student Engagement finds that 65 percent of students report being bored "at least every day in class." Sixteen percent—nearly one in six students—are bored in *every class*.[18]

Perhaps school, for all its efforts, simply isn't challenging enough. In a 2006 study of high school dropouts, eight in ten said they did less than an hour of homework per night. Two-thirds said they would have worked harder if more had been demanded of them.[19] When American journalist Amanda Ripley in 2013 surveyed hundreds of exchange students from around the world, she found that nine out of ten international students who spent time in the United States said classes were easier here; of the American teenagers who had studied abroad, seven out of ten agreed. "School in America was many things, but it was not, generally speaking, all that challenging," she wrote. "The evidence suggests that we've been systematically underestimating what our kids can handle, especially in math and science."[20]

This is all happening at what is probably the worst time for our fortunes as a nation. Recent high-profile international comparisons show that our kids are falling behind others in places like Finland and Singapore in skills and knowledge. But in the long run, our kids care less about competing with Finland than about having schools that challenge them and engage their interest. While games haven't yet improved schools in any kind of systematic way, that could soon change. A generation of teachers who learned division with *Math Blaster,* history with *The Oregon Trail,* and the principles of urban planning with *SimCity* now see games as just another tool, like a calculator. Each spring, Baby Boomer teachers are retiring by the thousands. Their young replacements, born in the late 1980s and early 1990s, well after the dawn of the home video-game console, have never known a world without video games. Among students, only 3 percent *don't* play games.

The shift has happened quietly, but it has been complete. When she went to college in the fall of 1990, journalist Megan McArdle believed that any freshman who brought his game system with him "would have been essentially announcing that he did not plan to have sex for the next four years. Now the consoles proudly sit in the living rooms of thirtysomething homeowners."[21]

How different is the present moment? In 2012, the Educational Testing Service, the folks who bring you the SAT, formed a partnership with, among others, the video game giant Electronic Arts, the folks who bring you *Madden NFL, Mass Effect,* and *Battlefield 3.* The result is an experimental nonprofit dubbed the Games, Learning and Assessment Lab, or GlassLab, which is creating educational versions of commercial video-game titles with deep learning analytics under the hood. Based at Electronic Arts' Silicon Valley headquarters and funded by the Bill & Melinda Gates Foundation and the John D. and Catherine T. MacArthur Foundation, GlassLab is bristling with PhD-level learning scientists and assessment experts who are experimenting with ways to combine game mechanics with academic content. The effort's ultimate aim is essentially to do away with standardized testing as we know it. The group has already created a software tool that gathers data from gameplay and translates it into instant reports that teachers, parents, and administrators can use to see how well students are doing against established learning standards. GlassLab has also mined textbooks to develop a tool that teachers can use to replace chapter assignments with games that cover the same content.

The U.S. Department of Education and the National Science Foundation are investing millions of dollars into gaming experiments. Deep-pocketed philanthropies like the Gates and MacArthur foundations have committed to spending upward of $100 million to promote educational gaming. In 2011, publishing giant Pearson LLC joined forces with Gates to push for more education-related games, and President Obama, at the urging of several experts, invited a video-game scholar to be a senior policy analyst in the White House Office of Science and Technology Policy.

Obama also launched his Digital Promise effort that seeks to push for more research into, among other things, educational games. At a White House event that fall, sharing the stage with White House deputy policy director Tom Kalil was, improbably, Gabe Newell, co-founder of a company called Valve. If you are not a gamer, you have never heard of him or his company, but if you are, you know exactly who Newell is. He's the developer of the beloved *Half-Life* and *Portal* video game series. The former is a ground-breaking, sci-fi-themed first-person shooter. The latter is a dryly comic, devilishly difficult series of logic puzzles that invites players to escape from a concrete-slab, maze-like laboratory by strategically blasting dimensional holes into the walls. "It's really about science," Newell said of *Portal* a few months earlier. "It's about spatial physics, it's about learning reasoning."[22] Looking a bit bored by the White House proceedings, Newell sat staring out from behind little round John Lennon glasses, a guy in a golf shirt surrounded on all sides by suits, his arms folded across his broad chest. If he'd had a portal gun at that moment, he'd have surely blasted his way out of the building. But he sat patiently and eventually promised to share *Portal*'s code with science teachers so they could use it to teach physics.

U.S. educators have spent a decade studying Finland for its educational secrets, but the Finns these days might offer a few surprising insights: they've found, for instance, that Finnish boys routinely outscore girls on English tests. Since boys play video games more frequently, and since the games are mostly in English, they've concluded that the games are teaching English. Meanwhile, Rovio, the Finnish company behind the *Angry Birds* games, is developing a preschool curriculum built around free play. Created in conjunction with the University of Helsinki, *Angry Birds Playground* covers all of the basic subjects, including math, science, language, music, physical education, and arts and crafts, and offers "a healthy balance between rest, play, and work," according to the company.[23]

Each year, Keith Devlin, the popular Stanford University math researcher, observes an unusual little ritual. He is invited annually to address the National Council of Teachers of Mathematics, and each time he asks teachers to raise their hands if they are gamers. By 2010, he'd been posing the question for five years, and each year the results were the same: just a few hands went up. Then, in 2011, at the group's annual meeting in Indianapolis, he saw something different: nearly every hand in the room went up.

Devlin mostly attributes this to a generational shift (also, the iPad had first appeared in the spring of 2010). But he said nearly all teachers are realizing that games are here to stay. "Nobody would think of being a teacher if they could not read," he said. "Well, video games and other digital media are new literacies."

According to Devlin, teachers have a responsibility to learn about kids' interests. "It's not the students' responsibility to put themselves in *our* place. As teachers, it's *our* responsibility to put ourselves in the students' place. And if they are in a digital world, where they will invest many hours solving difficult, challenging problems in a video game, it would be criminal if we didn't start where they are and take advantage of the things they want to do. That's the world they live in, that's the world they're going to own and develop. As teachers our job is to help them on that journey. We have to start where they are, and if they're in video games, we need to start there."[24]

ONE

A KIND OF ULTIMATE DECADENCE

How I Got Curious about Video Games

Robert Frost said that a poem begins as a lump in the throat. This book began as a sharp pain between the eyes. About twelve years ago, I asked my then-eleven-year-old daughter to name her favorite book. She looked at me as if she'd just noticed I had fins and gills—the question seemed that unusual to her—and I wondered, Do kids *have* favorite books anymore? Do books even register?

This was a child who was practically perfect in every way. She got straight A's, was crazy about playing the cello. A happy, gifted math whiz who could read several years above grade level, she was confident and college bound, the fifth grader that America wishes it could clone. If this kid didn't like reading, what chance did reading have?

She'd grown up in a house with books in every room, including the kitchen and each of the bathrooms. I'd been a teacher for the first few years of her childhood, so I'd collected cases of children's books. They lined the shelves in her room and her little sister's room. At least one Sunday a month found us at the local Barnes & Noble, eating, drinking, and browsing the shelves and bringing even more books home. This was a house where you couldn't eat dinner until someone cleared the newspapers and magazines off the kitchen table. We had more overdue library books than most people had books. To be fair, perhaps we overdid it. But given a choice after six years of schooling, my daughter might never again have picked up another book. She was not alone. One survey found that one-third of high-school graduates never read another book— *for the rest of their lives.*[1] I'm a journalist, so I started looking for someone to blame.

Nearly every daily influence in her life seemed a culprit: parents, teachers, friends, TV, music. Maybe it was her evolutionary birthright as a member of a race of restless hunter-gatherers. Or maybe, just maybe, reading—sustained, focused, calm, contemplative reading—had simply become too much trouble. I began researching relentlessly and found that kids were as steeped in books as ever—in 1954, public-school libraries had three books for every student. By 2000 they had seventeen.[2] But even as the number of books increased, reading seemed to have lost its appeal. Seventeen-year-olds' reading skills were essentially unchanged over more than forty years, even as nearly all other indicators of well-being rose. Meanwhile, between 1984 and 2012, the proportion of seventeen-year-olds who said they "never" or "hardly ever" read for fun had grown threefold.[3] *Never? Hardly ever?* Gilbert and Sullivan jokes aside, this was bleak.

I was, it turned out, not the only one wondering what was going on. Tech writer Nicholas Carr noticed that his newish habit of surfing the World Wide Web, with its hyperlinks and hunts for information, had rendered him practically incapable of finishing a book. He worried that we'd "evolved from being cultivators of personal knowledge to being hunters and gatherers in the electronic data forest."[4] The artist and writer David Trend, looking for the source of his eight-year-old daughter's "mysterious problem with the written word," came face-to-face with this: "In most of her life, she doesn't need reading," he said. Her world was driven by images, media, and interactive technologies, all so inviting and easy to access that learning to read "feels like a conspiracy invented by grown-ups and school."[5]

Most research on reading habits by then had found that upper-income, well-educated Americans read more than others, but even this statistic was in danger of fraying. By 2005, Northwestern University sociologist Wendy Griswold was beginning to talk about the emergence of a small, elite "reading class," much like a "leisure class" or "chattering class," that considers books very important, even as millions of Americans each year drop reading from their daily lives. It wasn't clear, she wrote, whether as a result reading would become a prestigious, rarefied skill or an "increasingly arcane hobby,"[6] like needlepoint or playing the autoharp. Griswold found that while educated people still read the most, younger educated people's reading had declined much the same as that of their less-educated peers. She foresaw an entire generation who *can* read but choose not to. The effect, she said, is the same as if millions *couldn't* read.

Was it the teaching? Yes, said longtime educator Kelly Gallagher, who in 2009 coined the grim term "readicide" to describe what he saw happening in schools nationwide. Like many of his colleagues, he was distressed at how schools were putting test prep before authentic learning. But he also saw that teachers, beyond the reach of administrators, were both "overteaching" and "underteaching" important books—when they weren't removing them altogether. Teachers were covering material too quickly and drowning students in "a sea of sticky notes, marginalia, and double-entry journals."[7] As a result, he said, kids' love of reading was being starved in the one place where it should be nourished. "Intentions are not the problem," he wrote, "our practices are the problem."[8]

The odd thing was that this crisis seemed to be hitting just as children's books were enjoying a rare moment in the sun. At the time, you couldn't help but look around and see that kids were reading and enjoying *massive* books, hardback novels of the sort that my generation would have considered uncool. The Harry Potter series and, a few years later, the *Twilight* books grabbed kids' imaginations and didn't let go. In 2008, the Harry Potter books occupied seven of the top nine spots on the "Top Books" list of my employer, *USA Today*. By 2010, the *Twilight* titles had spent two years in four of the top spots. When I met the great children's novelist M. T. Anderson, he told me that he'd worked in children's publishing in New York in the 1990s, and that if he had suggested a series of 700-page children's novels, he would have been laughed out of midtown Manhattan. "The prevailing wisdom was, 'No kid will ever read that book. That is a *ludicrous* thing to do.'" Now, he said, books of 700 and 800 pages are international bestsellers. "Vast series, taking up thousands of pages, are read by *every child*."[9]

So given the right books and social cues, kids could ingest large quantities of print. Were they really "reading less"? The question was tricky. Depending on how you asked it, you got different results. What did it even *mean?* How did you measure it? Minutes of reading? Pages consumed? Pounds of wood pulp whipped into vampire novels?

Eventually, a more interesting question emerged: *What are kids paying attention to these days?*

What I found was that they were paying attention to pretty much *everything:* books, music, movies, television, fashion, dance, science, history, economics, politics, photography. And they were paying attention to *each other*. Everything but school and the ways it was asking them to slice and dice academic disciplines. The amazing devices in their lives had given them access to a whole new world, as well as a different way of thinking about the world. We were living in what educator Will Richardson called a "moment of abundance"[10] that granted our kids access to virtually everything, all the time, on their own terms. School seemed to be struggling to keep up.

Video games typified this abundance better than almost anything else. Soon, everywhere I looked I saw that games were becoming a kind of cultural force that couldn't be ignored. They presented a way for young people to spend time together, to challenge each other, to blow off steam, to learn new things, and, in the end, figure out where they stood socially. In many cases kids loved the games themselves, in others they embraced the groups that formed around them to talk and write about the game, share hacks and news, and challenge each other to design new levels that were often jaw-droppingly difficult. Game designer Robin Hunicke has noted that Facebook is actually a complex, massively multiplayer online game, with challenges, rewards, and levels just like any other. Think about it for a second and you'll realize that the rules are simple: be the most fun, intelligent, witty, caring version of yourself. The benefits are obvious, Hunicke observed: Facebook "makes people feel like they matter, like they have friends and family across all kinds of distances," she said. "How many games make you feel loved?"[11]

Many kids play games to work through personal problems and frustrations, and many turn to them to vent or grieve. A surprising number of young men I met, many from families of divorce, play games to spend time with their fathers, both in the same room and across great distances. I met a young college student named Erik Martin who discovered *World of Warcraft,* or *WoW,* the massively multiplayer online role-playing game, or MMORPG (it's often shortened simply to MMO), while recovering from a case of anorexia nervosa so severe that it landed him in the hospital for a month and a half during his freshman year in high school. The game, he said, saved his life. He's not alone: a Tumblr page, "How Games Saved My Life," details the "life-changing power of video games."

Probably the best example of an MMO, *WoW* takes place in a vast fantasy world populated by trolls and elves and fire-breathing dragons, but Martin, fourteen years old at the time, found refuge, strength, and unconditional support in the human friendships he forged there. "I found it exhilarating to be in a space where I couldn't be judged on anything except how well I did in the game," he told me. "It's sort of a pure meritocracy. Nobody cares where you're from (he was from rural southern Maryland), nobody cares what you look like, nobody cares about anything except *how you play the game.*"[12] Martin began playing *WoW* at a friend's house— he knew his parents wouldn't approve, and actually, he thought the game was a waste of time at first. But it quickly grew on him and he eventually saved up enough cash to buy himself a laptop computer so he could play in bed, under the covers, at night. By seventeen, he was a guild co-leader, directing the strategy, tactics, and movements of forty players, but also remembering to send guildmates birthday presents and baby shower gifts in the real world. "It gave me this space that was actually very, very empowering," he said.

Video games were also growing so fearsomely realistic and sophisticated that they were giving rise to a strange phenomenon: players were using them to learn about and reflect on the world in ways their early developers had never intended. Games were recalibrating players' expectations of life itself, a development about as far removed from the hand-eye predations of *Pac-Man* as anyone could possibly have imagined. Visiting London once, video game critic Tom Bissell wrote that he found his way from Trafalgar Square to the British Museum simply from memories of having played the open-world driving game *The Getaway*.[13] Alex Hutchinson, creative director of the best-selling *Assassin's Creed* games, told me that he had gotten letters from players who had visited Venice because of *Assassin's Creed II*. He also heard from students saying they had aced exams based on what they'd learned in-game about the Borgia family. No one would confuse the Mature-rated series with educational games, but the response, he said, proved that history can be "alive and intense and fascinating, something that sticks with them and isn't just disposable."[14]

In his 2011 book *Video Games and Learning,* Kurt Squire, the University of Wisconsin researcher, remembers sitting in high-school history class as the teacher quizzed students on Spanish colonialization. In a Ferris Bueller moment, the teacher asked if someone—anyone!—knew what kinds of ships each European nation had. Squire raised his hand and, as if channeling the textbook, said the Spanish had galleons to carry gold. "The French mostly had *barques.* The Dutch, *fluyts.* The English, merchantmen. If you saw a *pinnace,* that was French, Dutch, maybe even a pirate." Squire explained that the Dutch "were mostly traders. They didn't have much territory, although Curacao was a great trading base." His classmates were stunned—Squire's on-the-spot dissertation delayed an inevitable test—and they wondered where he had consumed all this material. "It was, in fact, the result of my spending way too much time playing *Sid Meier's Pirates!* on my Commodore 64," he wrote.[15]

The stories kept coming. Tampa Bay Buccaneers coach Raheem Morris once told the producers of *Madden NFL* that playing their game had influenced the way he runs his team. In 2009, while scoring a game-winning touchdown, Denver Broncos receiver Brandon Stokley killed five crucial seconds from the clock by running parallel to the goal line, "an unconventional move familiar only to anyone who has ever picked up a control pad," wrote ESPN's Patrick

Hruby.[16] A few weeks later, in Super Bowl XLIV, New Orleans Saints coach Sean Payton told his players to go for a touchdown on fourth and goal at the end of the first half, bypassing an easy field goal. They opened the second half with an onside kick. Former NFL coach John Madden, the video game series' namesake, reportedly watched the game from his California studio, "incredulous and oddly transfixed" at the spectacle. "I was thinking, 'S—, this guy is playing a video game!'"[17]

In preparation for the 2010 World Cup soccer tournament, Gordon Durity, audio director for Electronic Arts Canada, which produces EA's sports titles, sent a crew to South Africa a few months in advance to capture the sounds of a typical game. He sat down with an engineer to listen to the audio they'd captured. "I kept hearing this *beehive* going on," he recalled. "What *is* this thing? This is driving me bonkers!" The engineer said the drone was coming from thousands of plastic *vuvuzelas* blown by fans. "You *have* to have it or it's not authentic," he told his boss. Durity decided he'd keep the *vuvuzelas* but give players the option to simply turn the drone off. When the actual World Cup began, he recalled, "People were saying, 'How come the TV channels can't just put a mute button like they do in the actual video game?'"[18]

In a way, British journalist Jim Rossignol offers the best explanation for games' appeal. They're a "voracious" medium, swallowing up most of the others—music, comics, fiction, television, sculpture, animation, architecture, and history. Games, he wrote, are "a kind of ultimate decadence. They are as expensive to produce as anything else on earth and utterly rooted in the pursuit of pleasure. These are sophisticated, arousing experiences that have few of the ugly side effects of drugs or debauchery. They are the indulgence of animal impulses without actual violence or brazen depravity."[19]

In other words, they're the perfect thing to bring to school.

As soon as I started poking around the world of games, I found teachers trying to sneak games into their classrooms, convinced that they would improve learning. To my delight, I found that most of those who had laid the groundwork for this movement were not only still alive and well, but also eager to talk. I initially thought I'd be able to track down everyone, count them on two hands, and interview them all. I not only found that there were more people than I could talk to—there were more people than I could *ever* talk to. Even now, almost every day I encounter game designers and educators whose work I can't believe I've overlooked. I found that most of them had gotten into this discipline not because they love games, but because they love children and want something better for them. After a while, I stopped counting the number of times that someone leaned in and told me, "I am *not* a big gamer."

As with most everything in the world of games, I soon discovered that all is not as it seems. When, after months of trying, I finally got access to Quest to Learn, the school in New York City that everyone calls "the video game school," I realized with a shock that most of the games being developed and tested there were paper based. Even as I visited classrooms there and elsewhere, where I *knew* that games were happening, I had to rethink my own prejudices. Once, as I walked around a noisy classroom at the PlayMaker School, a sixth-grade program that had recently become part of the private New Roads School in Los Angeles, I noticed two girls sitting together, staring idly in the corner. They seemed to be taking a break from an intense class-wide game that resembled a sort of Assyrian-era commodities trading floor. I came over to ask what they were doing, and one of the girls asked if I could keep a secret. I leaned in to hear it. They were, she said, checking out the looks on their classmates' faces, searching for a tell that would reveal who had the one commodity card they were searching for. What looked like slacking was strategizing.

These encounters were a tonic, a welcome break from covering school reform, which is almost entirely focused on proxies for learning, not actual learning. The fierce divides of our current education debate almost always seem important when you're weighing one side against the other, but they often boil down to two sides of the same coin. Which is better for low-income kids, a charter school or a district school? A charter school, except when it's not, and research shows that while many charter schools are great, most are not. Are teachers' unions bad for kids? Possibly, their opponents say, though many of our most awful schools have not one unionized member on staff, and many of our lowest-performing states don't even allow teachers to organize. High-stakes tests? Absolutely not, unless the results are good—but not too good, because that's a sure sign of cheating.

Even efforts that seem to focus specifically on learning don't actually focus on learning, but on markers for learning: phonics or whole language? Calculators or no calculators? Homework or no homework? The discussions go round and round, one big *lather-rinse-repeat* cycle with little to show. Plus it is depressingly expensive. In 2010, Facebook CEO Mark Zuckerberg pledged $100 million to help rebuild public schools in Newark, New Jersey, but within two years, more than $20 million of his gift and matching donations were spent on consulting firms, many of which charged $1,000 a day for *individual consultants*. At one point, Vivian Cox Fraser, president of the Urban League of Essex County, told a reporter, "Everybody's getting paid, but Raheem still can't read."[20]

As in Newark, much of the reform was top-down and technocratic, leaving little room for smart teachers to strike out on their own if they wanted to try something different. Games, it seemed, offered just that. Here was a bottom-up reform, often championed by individual teachers fed up with how little had improved in their own classrooms. Teachers could not only get behind games, but they could encourage others to try them, sharing them with colleagues across the hall or around the world. A few teachers were even discovering the power of creating their own games, not simply enacting someone else's vision.

Teachers, it turns out, have historically held new technology at arm's length, and probably for good reasons. For more than a century, they have looked on as progressive education reformers pushed to move classrooms away from teacher talk and toward more interactive ways of delivering information. Reformers' ideas have taken the form of a series of mostly ill-fated technical innovations, each of which they touted as the Next Big Thing. One hundred years ago, Thomas Edison himself tried to persuade teachers that silent movies would revolutionize school. An early investor in films for the classroom, he predicted they would soon make books obsolete. "Our school system will be completely changed in ten years," he told a New York newspaper in 1913.[21] Edison envisioned armed guards at schoolhouse doors, "a big army with swords and guns" to keep eager kids out. "You'll have to lick 'em to keep 'em away." Teachers weren't as eager—whatever virtues silent movies possessed, showing one required turning off the lights. As Harvard scholar David Dockterman said of the educational film, "Darkness proved to be one of its major weaknesses."[22]

In the 1930s and 1940s, thousands of classrooms tuned in each day to instructional radio programming, broadcast by state-sponsored "schools of the air" that were, in all likelihood, the most useful educational innovations of the first half of the twentieth century. Historian Randall Davidson told the story of one Wisconsin teacher who, while warming up her classroom radio one morning to prepare for the sing-along program *Journeys in Music Land,* found that the unit wasn't working. She ordered her students to put on their hats and coats and join her outside, where she flagged down a passing motorist. The willing driver pulled over and flung open his doors so the students could sing along to the program. Davidson recalled that "the driver joined in."[23]

In the 1950s and 1960s, the federal government and private foundations poured millions of dollars into instructional television, much of it produced locally on closed-circuit systems. "Studio teachers" taught classes of a hundred students or more. A decade before *Sesame Street,* the tiny Washington County, Maryland, school district, in the rural western part of the state, employed a TV production staff of more than seventy, twenty-five of whom were studio teachers.[24]

In the 1980s, schools began buying what were then called "microcomputers," a shopping spree that continues today with laptop and one-to-one tablet programs. As early as 1980, many advocates saw the personal computer as a kind of subversive device that would make school *less* central to children's lives. MIT computer scientist Seymour Papert called it "the children's machine" and predicted that it would "enable us to so modify the learning environment outside the classrooms that much if not all the knowledge schools presently try to teach with such pain and expense and such limited success will be learned, as the child learns to talk, painlessly, successfully and without organized instruction."[25]

Many early computer enthusiasts had hoped that teachers would create their own software, but historian Paul Saettler found that most teachers "lack the time, the energy, or the expertise to engage in such a task."[26] Stanford scholar Larry Cuban, perhaps our foremost expert on how teachers actually work, has said teachers are skeptical of technology because, at heart, they're deeply practical people who want tools that solve problems *they* see as important. They want tools that buttress their authority, not undermine it. He and others have noted, for instance, that even chalkboards initially got an icy reception from teachers in one-room schoolhouses, where large-group instruction was rarely emphasized. Reformers who want to use technology to make teaching more "planned, systematic and engineered" will always be disappointed, Cuban said.[27]

But what if technology took teaching in another direction, with risk-taking—and a touch of subversion—at its center?

In a small second-floor studio in New York's Flatiron District, David Langendoen searched a computer screen and found the tiny digital counter near the bottom. He pointed at the number: Watch it, he said. Every time it changes, another slave has escaped to freedom. Langendoen was sitting at a small conference table at Electric Funstuff, a tiny video game company that he and his partner, Spencer Grey, founded in 1998. Since then, they've produced a series of award-winning educational games using simple graphics but rich historical detail. When I met them in 2012, they were immersed in the minutiae of a free-to-play series, called *Mission US,* that invites kids to learn about American history by role-playing as young teenagers living through key historical periods. The duo had a standing monthly date with a group of historians to audit the accuracy of the games. Stacks of history books and biographies teetered on a worktable nearby.

The game's first chapter, *For Crown or Colony?* features a young boy in Revolutionary War–era Boston who must choose sides in the conflict. The second game and, at the time, the series' most popular, *Flight to Freedom,* features a young female slave named Lucy on a Kentucky plantation in 1848. In the course of the game, she must undertake an escape to Ohio. A computer screen showed real-time player data, and as Langendoen and Grey sat down to talk one afternoon, the digital counter read 22,850. This was the number of times that a student playing as Lucy had escaped. Because *Mission US* is web-based, the creators can track every escape attempt and see which ones are successful. About one in four ends well, Langendoen said, but the odds improve with each try. Three out of four times, Lucy is recaptured and must either try again or remain enslaved. About 80 percent of students succeed by their third attempt. The game counts how many times a player has endeavored to free Lucy; the more she tries, the greater the chances she'll succeed. "We wanted the player to experience failure, but in a controlled manner," said Grey. At the time, he and Langendoen were hip-deep in research for the next chapter, which drops students into a Northern Cheyenne settlement in 1866. The designers insisted that all the Native American roles be voiced by authentic Cheyenne voice actors—it seemed a good idea at the time, Langendoen said, but there are only a few thousand Cheyenne *left on earth* and it was a safe bet, he joked, that few of them are trained voice actors who live in New York City.

As we talked over the next few minutes, the counter slowly crept up: 22,851 . . . 22,852 . . . each click a player, likely a school kid, sitting in a classroom and playing as Lucy. Prior to their escape, the game gives players a choice: Do they interact with their simulated keepers in a more obedient or defiant fashion? What surprised the game's creators was how many kids, given the choice, chose to be, in Langendoen's words, "good slaves" while in school. "When they're playing games at home they'll screw up all over the place," he said. "Most kids, when they're in the environment of school, feel like they need to behave and do the right thing." Sitting in school, most kids understand that obedience, not defiance, is what's expected, he said. "It takes the teacher, actually, nudging them toward resistance. Like, 'Try it.' It surprised the hell out of us."[28]

TWO

TO THE MOON AND BACK IN FIVE MINUTES

*How Disdain for Centralized Authority
and an Impulse to Play Brought Us
"Supercomputers Everywhere"*

If a lab-coat-wearing MIT or Stanford researcher from the 1950s were to visit the typical home right now and sit in front of your family PC, poke at your daughter's rhinestone-studded iPhone, or take a spin on your son's PlayStation, he (they were mostly men) would be utterly amazed. There are supercomputers everywhere, and sharing is optional. This was not supposed to happen. Computers as they were first envisioned were decidedly *not* for people like you and me, and certainly not for our children. Many influences combined to force this change, but chief among them was a countercultural disdain for top-down, centralized authority, as well as an irresistible impulse to *play*.

The idea for the personal computer was actually born in the 1960s, nearly a decade before anyone ever saw one. Only later, when costs fell and technology improved, "would the box itself arrive," wrote journalist John Markoff.[1] Stewart Brand, the Stanford-educated founder of the influential *Whole Earth Catalog*, based in the heart of what would become California's Silicon Valley, has said that the counterculture's scorn for centralized authority provided the philosophical foundation for both the "leaderless Internet" and the personal computer.[2] Years before they developed the Macintosh computer, Steve Jobs and Steve Wozniak manufactured and peddled "Blue Boxes" that allowed users to make free long-distance phone calls. "If it hadn't been for the Blue Boxes, there wouldn't have been an Apple," Jobs later told biographer Walter Isaacson.[3]

Many early computer pioneers took part in early experiments with LSD, as did the writer Ken Kesey, who participated in a key series of trials at the Menlo Park Veterans' Administration hospital in the late 1950s and early 1960s. And the strain of computer research that eventually gave rise to the personal computer was guided less by a push to replace humans with "artificial intelligence" than by one to augment human intellect, to enlarge our memories and, quite literally, expand our minds. "Man's population and gross product are increasing at a considerable rate, but the complexity of his problems grows still faster, and the urgency with which solutions must be found becomes steadily greater in response to the increased rate of activity and the increasingly global nature of that activity," wrote computer pioneer Douglas Engelbart in 1962.[4] Play emerged repeatedly in this effort, as when Engelbart, under the influence of LSD, invented a "tinkle toy," a floating water wheel to train boys to pee in toilets.[5]

If the computer is, as Jobs once said, "a bicycle for our minds," the video game is a Vespa, pure stylish pleasure. The love child of a pinball machine and a mainframe computer, the first video games were a bit of open-source amusement among Cold War hackers fascinated with the hands-on idea of moving dots of light on a dark screen. In the process, the hackers helped democratize computing. Like the nineteenth-century tinkerers whose first impulse, upon gaining access to electricity, was to figure out better ways to make ice cream, young engineers at MIT, Stanford, and elsewhere who got their hands on computers with displays in the early 1960s soon started creating games. Today we look upon computer hackers as shady, often malevolent figures, but in the 1960s they were "free-thinking, future-obsessed, truth-seeking uber-tinkerers," wrote journalists Heather Chaplin and Aaron Ruby.[6] A hack as it was originally understood was "a project undertaken or a product built not solely to fulfill some constructive goal, but with some wild pleasure taken in mere involvement," wrote Steven Levy.[7] The first video games were hacks.

The precursor appeared in October 1958, at an open house for Long Island's Brookhaven National Laboratory. William Higinbotham, a Manhattan Project physicist whose team had designed the timing mechanism for the first atomic bomb, was by the late 1950s running Brookhaven's instrumentation team. He wanted to "liven up the place" with a game that would "convey the message that our scientific endeavors have relevance for society." He got the idea to attach two homemade mechanical switches to a five-inch oscilloscope and asked a colleague to engineer it. Together they created the green-tinged *Tennis for Two,* a kind of proto-*Pong* that was immensely popular for two consecutive open houses. But when the second event ended in 1959, Higinbotham recycled the parts.[8] Three years later, at MIT, a recent Dartmouth transfer named Steve Russell used the school's new PDP-1 computer to create a two-player rocket-ships-and-torpedoes game he called *Spacewar!* It earned the admiration of Russell's fellow hackers, who programmed a gravitational pull from the sun in the middle of the screen, an accurate solar system map, and a "hyperspace" button that made the player's spaceship disappear. Its code traded among computer networks spanning several campuses, *Spacewar!* was "inescapable," wrote J. C. Herz, "because the impulse to convert million-dollar calculators into intellectual jungle gyms was simply too great."[9] The game spread to other research facilities and eventually the PDP-1's manufacturer shipped later models with the game preloaded as a way to test whether the computer and display were in sync. By the early 1970s, computer pioneer Alan Kay, then a researcher at Xerox's Palo Alto Research Center, told *Rolling Stone* that *Spacewar!* "blossoms spontaneously wherever there is a graphics display connected to a computer."[10] Long before most of us knew about carpal tunnel syndrome, all-night players complained of "*Spacewar!* elbow."

One of those all-nighters was a young University of Utah engineering student named Nolan Bushnell, who, after losing his tuition money in a poker game, began managing a pinball arcade at a carnival midway. He'd found *Spacewar!* "mesmerizingly powerful" and would search for a decade for a way to create a midway version. Bushnell had fallen in love with the game's responsiveness, a novelty in computers in an era when punch cards ruled. "There was no question that when you pushed the 'rotate' button, the ship *would* rotate, and when you fired a missile it would *fire* and it would observe the laws of physics," he told me. "And when you thrust, the rocketship would speed up, and if you wanted to slow it down, you had to turn the rocketship around and reverse thrust. *Wow!* That was just magical."[11] And it gave Bushnell a borderline crazy idea. He wanted to build a coin-operated computer that would stand unguarded in a restaurant, bar, or student lounge and allow a single user or, more remarkably, two *simultaneous* users, to repeatedly perform just one function that had no research value or practical application and produced no tangible result.

He wasn't the only crazy one. By 1971, a pair of young competitors had developed *Galaxy Game,* another *Spacewar!* clone, by connecting an actual PDP-11 computer that sat in a Stanford University music room, via a 100-foot cable, to a gaming cabinet in a campus coffeehouse. It was a hit among the Vietnam-era student body, who crowded around the cabinet and lined dimes atop it to reserve the next session. Tech writer John Markoff has called *Galaxy Game* "a precursor that hinted at the hunger for computing as a new medium that would lead directly to the personal computer."[12]

Meanwhile, *Computer Space,* Bushnell's 1971 *Spacewar!* arcade game, flopped, mostly due to instructions that were too complex. He formed a new company and moved on to another project, telling his lead engineer that this time he wanted a game "so simple that any drunk in a bar could play."[13] The company was Atari and its first game was *Pong,* released in 1972 with a single instruction: "Avoid missing ball for high score."

A decade before Jobs reinvented the personal computer, he was Atari Employee Number Forty, a twenty-year-old college dropout toiling for Bushnell, who put him to work hacking the company's own arcade games to make them simpler and cheaper to produce. Jobs wasn't trained as an engineer, so he persuaded his friend Steve Wozniak, who *was* an engineer, to help him by moonlighting. They split Jobs's salary—unfairly in Jobs's favor, as it turned out—and in the process invented a little game called *Breakout*. Wozniak later said he first conceived of how to create a color computer monitor during the sleepless four-day frenzy in which the pair created the game.

Since then, of course, two generations of engineers have squeezed vastly more capability out of computers, getting them to operate more quickly, efficiently, and cheaply, and in astonishingly smaller enclosures, thanks in large part to a principle known as Moore's law. Named after Intel Corporation co-founder Gordon Moore, it is less a law than an observation: in 1965, Moore predicted that the number of transistors that could fit onto an integrated circuit would double every year. He later modified the prediction to say that the number would double every two years, and this is essentially what has happened. Moore's law has foreseen rapid advances in digital technology and helped guide how small, fast, efficient, and cheap—and thus how accessible—computers would become.

The change is hard to overstate—actually, it's key to our discussion, so an illustration is appropriate. Imagine if American cars had followed the same speed, efficiency, cost, and size curves as microprocessors since 1970. To be sure, cars have improved greatly, but if they'd done so even remotely along the lines of Moore's law, they'd be unrecognizable as cars, according to Ed Lazowska, a longtime computer scientist at the University of Washington. While researching this topic, I came upon his seminal writing, dating back nearly twenty years. I e-mailed him to ask if he had updated it, and Lazowska wrote back just a day later to tell me that after he'd read my query, he and a pair of colleagues had gotten together and crunched a few numbers to compare microchips from 1970 to today's versions. What they found is nothing short of breathtaking: if cars had matched microchips' improvements in speed, the typical car would now go 6 million miles per hour, getting you from New York to San Francisco in 1.7 seconds, or to the moon and back in five minutes. As for efficiency, it would now travel 100,000 miles on a gallon of fuel, or from New York to San Francisco on a half cup of gasoline. The price for such a magic car? Nine dollars, Lazowska and his colleagues calculated, which is probably just as well—given its miniaturization curve since 1970, you couldn't find the car in your driveway. It would be about as big as the head of a match.[14]

So the computers in your life these days are *not* the same ones you first encountered a few decades ago. Good teachers have figured this out, said researcher David Williamson Shaffer. "Computers give children access to new worlds," he wrote, "to parts of the real world that are too expensive, complicated or dangerous for them except through computer simulations, and to worlds of imagination where they can play with social and physical reality in new ways."[15]

But for all of their jaw-dropping improvements, computers have had a minimal impact on educational achievement overall. A few critics point out that schools have never really figured out what to *do* with all those computers, or how to train teachers to use them effectively. Imagine, said Alan Kay, the computer pioneer, that if instead of computers, reformers had rolled pianos into every classroom in America, then left teachers to fend for themselves. We'd be disappointed in the results. "If there is no other context," he said, "you will get a 'Chopsticks' culture."[16]

The current push to bring digital games into school is, strictly speaking, not the first, nor even the second time that educators have pushed for individualized instruction via machines. But it is decidedly the most nuanced, humanistic, and thoughtful. The first actually took place in the 1950s and early 1960s, when a small group of educational psychologists proposed doing away with teachers altogether and replacing them with self-paced, pre-programmed instruction on so-called "teaching machines." Operated mechanically by individual students as they sat at desks, the devices *ka-chunged* as students worked the levers, picking their way through multiple-choice and fill-in-the-blank problem sets on punched paper templates. Advocates said the machines would keep kids actively learning since "continuous active student response" was required to keep the lesson moving forward. The machines also offered immediate feedback and self-paced instruction, with "faster students romping through an instructional sequence very rapidly" while slower students were "tutored as slowly as necessary, with indefinite patience to meet their special needs."[17]

Many of the devices had actually been developed as early as the 1920s, but the Great Depression dampened interest in the field and putting teachers out of work. By the 1950s the devices were back, buoyed by a Harvard psychologist named Burrhus Frederic Skinner, who had long been interested in using machines to train rats and pigeons through reward and punishment. It was a 1953 visit to his daughter's math class that persuaded B. F. Skinner that children might benefit from "automated instruction." In 1954, he showed off a prototype machine for arithmetic training that offered, he said, "vastly improved conditions for effective study."[18] By 1958, he and a handful of colleagues had designed and programmed a machine used to teach an introduction to natural science course at Harvard and Radcliffe. The work was funded by the Ford Foundation.[19] The machines, many of which can still be seen in historic demonstrations on YouTube, were purely behavioral devices that rewarded correct answers but responded to incorrect answers either by forcing students to stare at the material again or simply try another answer. One device, originally developed in 1925, actually dispensed Life Savers when a student punched in a correct answer. In a 1964 demonstration, Sidney Pressey, an Ohio State University psychology professor, said that by the 1960s the candies had grown too large for the machine. It dispensed Tums instead.[20]

Teaching machines actually enjoyed a few years of popularity. In 1960, the National Education Association's Department of Audio-Visual Instruction published a 724-page "source book" on the devices, and in 1961, the U.S. Air Force purchased eighteen Autotutor Mark I teaching machines, at $5,000 to $7,000 apiece, for electronics training at Keesler Air Force Base in Biloxi, Mississippi. In 1962, the National Science Foundation offered funding to develop a programmed textbook for first-year college calculus. Unfortunately for the behaviorists, within a decade after Sputnik, the machines fell out of favor. In 1965, a widely circulated report found that the devices offered no real advantage over a good teacher with a textbook. A teaching machine couldn't teach careful, sustained reading or independent problem solving and wasn't, as advocates asserted, the equivalent of a private tutor. It wasn't even the only path to self-paced instruction. A teaching machine, said Smithsonian historian Peggy Kidwell, "might motivate pigeons but in the long run bored people."[21]

The current push to get video games into schools may be more nuanced, more aimed at helping teachers rather than replacing them, but it's also based on what's essentially a misunderstanding. Whether you're a proponent or an opponent of electronic games in school, you can thank Jim Gee for their presence there. Now in his mid-sixties, James Paul Gee is as responsible as anyone for the explosive growth of the field over the past decade. A theoretical linguist who began his career at Stanford studying the grammar of infinitives, his early work focused on research topics like naked infinitives, "a topic that sounds a lot sexier than it is," according to him.[22]

Gee discovered video games by accident more than a decade ago. He had bought a *Pajama Sam* computer game for his six-year-old son and thought, "I shouldn't just hand it to him, I should play it with him."[23] He sat down at the computer with his son and was impressed. The game, *Pajama Sam: No Need to Hide When It's Dark Outside,* was funny, absorbing, and smart, a great way to introduce children to problem solving. But most of all, it was *hard.* Like many adults, he had assumed that games were easy, mindless entertainment. *Pajama Sam* was anything but. He wondered, *If this is the kind of game they're making for children, what are they making for adults?*

At the store, Gee picked out "a random title," *New Adventures of the Time Machine,* took it home, and popped it in. It was even harder than *Pajama Sam* and he was terrible at it. "I do remember failing at the game massively and yet finding something really very energizing about it, very life-enhancing," he said. Gee realized that he was enjoying learning something *completely new,* and in a completely new way. It was the first time since his first semester of graduate school, he said, that he'd been confronted with something so maddeningly complex, for which he had no background. "What was interesting is that you confront yourself as a learner and it's pretty disappointing. You perseverate on the same solution—you've lost your learning muscles."

He began playing other games and realized, with his educator's brain, that game designers faced the same challenge as schools: how to get users to master challenging material that requires practice and persistence. He realized that the game designers were doing a better job than the schools.

Most teachers work very hard, of course, and all of them want kids to succeed. But when kids don't learn what's been laid out for them, schools typically look for answers in the things that are going wrong in children's lives: poverty, trauma, bad parenting, poor nutrition, disability, sleep deprivation, lousy study skills. All of these are real problems that can have a tangible effect on kids' ability to learn, research shows. But if players fail at commercial video games, game designers can't blame bad parenting, poor nutrition, or sleep deprivation—actually, these attributes are virtually *guaranteed* in many gamers. Designers must create experiences that anyone, even the sleep-deprived, can master and enjoy. Gee realized that the designers were also, without realizing it, modeling the "scaffolded" learning that cognitive scientists said worked best. Real learning, games showed, was always associated with pleasure and is ultimately a form of play, an idea "almost always dismissed by schools," he said.[24]

At the time, Gee taught in the Department of Curriculum and Instruction at the University of Wisconsin–Madison's School of Education. "It was, like, my fifth tenured job," he said. The department had been top-rated for most of the previous twenty-five years and that brought freedom to pursue topics that interested him. "Senior people could do anything they damn well pleased," he told me. "There were really no constraints for what I wrote." So in 2003, the theoretical linguist whose previous book was titled *An Introduction to Discourse Analysis* published *What Video Games Have to Teach Us about Learning and Literacy*. Written in a conversational tone and with a popular audience in mind, it was a minor sensation and has never gone out of print. Gee's was by no means the first book about games and learning—Marc Prensky, the business consultant, in 2001 had written a comprehensive take on the topic, but his focus was as much on corporate training as on K-12 education. One of Prensky's most memorable assertions was that games offered an attractive alternative to the "AFTRB" approach to workplace professional development. AFTRB, he explained, stands for "Another *%$#! Three-Ring Binder."[25]

What Prensky and Gee had realized early on was that game designers had lowered the cost of failure so players would take risks. They'd figured out that well-designed problem solving that gives players a second chance and a way to share their successes is almost irresistibly attractive. In just a few years, game designers had discovered the principles of deep and pleasurable learning that it had taken educators more than a century to apply in schools. Game studios had hit upon "profoundly good methods of getting people to learn and to enjoy learning," Gee would later write. "Here the creativity of capitalists has far outrun that of educators."[26]

At the time, he discovered, schools were actually moving backward. On January 8, 2002, President George W. Bush signed the sweeping federal education law that eventually became known as No Child Left Behind. The result of a bit of rare, post-9/11 comity between Democrats and Republicans in Congress, the law, like so many reforms before it, had a social justice component at its core. It sought to reduce the nation's yawning achievement gap by raising the basic skills levels of millions of low-income children. Its basic policy tool was simple: it required that about half of the nation's nearly 50 million public-school children sit for annual skills tests each spring and that schools report how well students performed. If a greater percentage of students didn't improve from year to year, schools would face a cascading series of sanctions that eventually included a requirement that they offer free after-school tutoring or a no-cost way for parents to transport their children to a neighboring public school. The result, within just a few years, was less a commitment to improved instruction in many schools than a rush to routine test prep, and, inevitably, a well-documented narrowing of schools' once-broad curricula, especially among schools with large numbers of low-income students. By late 2004, about one in four school districts reported that it had reduced instructional time in social studies to make more room for reading and math lessons. One in five said it was cutting back on science, art, or music.[27]

Meanwhile, Gee found, games of the early No Child Left Behind era were expanding, not narrowing, their scope. While educators debated whether children learn to read best through drill-and-practice phonics or "whole language" instruction, Nintendo was, quite informally, teaching a generation of children how to read. *Pokémon* also taught children how to analyze and classify more than 700 different types of creatures through trading cards that were dense with specialized, technical, cross-referenced text. Gee would later call *Pokémon* "perhaps the best literacy curriculum ever conceived."[28] He offered the observation that he knew of no "*Pokémon* gap" among poor or minority children. "Certainly the capitalists who made and sell Pokémon have more trust in non-white and poor children than that," he said. Gee predicted, a bit cynically, that if we were to turn *Pokémon* into a school subject, "certain children, many of them poor, would all of a sudden have trouble learning *Pokémon*."[29]

What Gee was discovering, as well, was that games make players think like scientists. Game play is built on a cycle of "hypothesize, probe the world, get a reaction, reflect on the results, reprobe to get better results," a cycle typical of experimental science.[30] But game studios had also created assessment systems that could tell players exactly how well they were doing on hundreds of variables without subjecting them to multiple-choice tests.

Even before the book appeared, Gee's "plea to build schooling on better principles of learning" was being interpreted by readers as permission to bring commercial video games into school as a kind of magic bullet—decidedly *not* his intent. He wanted the book and the appeal of games to act as a "virus" that used games to spread his views on literacy and learning, but much of the book's audience read it the other way around. His views on literacy and learning served as a way to legitimize the idea of commercial games in school. Many people who loved games were waiting for an academic "to say games were good," he said. Perhaps it's just as well, since the book has also helped gamers themselves understand that games "are worth taking seriously outside gamer communities," Gee said.[31] Though his name has become synonymous with the games-in-school movement, he'll be the first to tell you that it's not that simple. "Any good learning network has multiple tools," he said. "We don't get rid of pencils because we have a computer. We don't get rid of crayons because we have *KidPix*. We recruit the whole thing."[32]

Several titles followed up Gee's 2003 book, and perhaps more importantly, he established the first graduate program, at Madison, focused on researching games in education, which has spread, virus-like, to other universities. Among his first dozen students was Constance Steinkuehler, a University of Missouri graduate who had triple-majored in math, English literature, and religious studies and who had arrived in Madison ready to deconstruct what motivates people to learn. "I did not go to grad school to study games," she told me. "I would have laughed at you had you said I would ever be doing this. The problem is that I turned around and actually looked at what kids were doing. And once you look at what kids are doing when they're playing, it's very hard to keep laughing. It's very hard to consider it trivial, at least as a researcher." With any new medium, she said, we tend to underestimate its reach unless we've actually engaged with it—and it's usually the younger generation that engages with it first.[33]

"When I first started studying games, people said, 'It will tank your career. You are over,'" she said. "And I did it because I was really tired of studying people being forced to do stuff."[34] A few years later, she would become the first games researcher to work in the White House, serving as a science advisor to President Obama as part of the White House Office of Science and Technology Policy.

Even as he has reached and then passed retirement age, Gee is as big a celebrity as ever, and the games-in-school movement looks to him as its Gandalf, though these days he more often resembles its irascible uncle—imagine a slightly more laid-back version of the cantankerous comedian Lewis Black, with a PhD in linguistics. Now at Arizona State University, Gee seems to enjoy the notoriety, frequently appearing as a keynote speaker at "serious gaming" conferences, where he rails against the evils of standardized testing and dumbed-down curricula. He cuts an unusual figure. Nearly bald and with a quick smile and flash of white teeth, he storms around the stage, his shaggy white eyebrows sometimes looking like they'll swallow his eyes. Even as his ideas have entered the mainstream, he has gotten more, not less, cynical about schools' ability to shake off superficiality, both at the K-12 and higher-education levels. In his most recent book he concluded, "Our formal institutions of education have, by and large, given up the task of deep education for the short-term goals of test passing and tuition payments."[35]

Occasionally, though, he seems to be back at the beginning of his journey. Gee has said on many occasions that one of his favorite games is the Japanese Nintendo GameCube title *Chibi-Robo*, in which the main character is a four-inch-high house-cleaning robot who must keep a family happy both by cleaning the house and solving their problems—all with an improbably short power cord and a frequent need to recharge. Gee is not afraid to admit that the first time he played *Chibi-Robo* to the end, he was so moved he wept. "If they can make being a four-inch housecleaning robot who is running out of electricity motivating for hours and have you pay sixty bucks for it," he said, "they can certainly make algebra motivating."[36]

THREE

· ▶

"DON'T KISS THE ENGINE, DADDY, OR THE CARRIAGES WON'T THINK IT'S REAL"

How Games Work by Getting
Us a Little High

I should be at the beach. I'm in Santa Monica, after all, and it's a Saturday in May. Instead I'm lying nearly motionless on too many pillows, iPad in my lap, obsessed with getting a little virtual marble to fall, pachinko-style, through a colorful obstacle course so it hits a big red button. I've been doing this for three hours.

I'm hunkered down in a hotel room on level fifty of a game called *Newton's Gravity,* and nothing in my life right now could be simpler. The marble rolls out of a chute and onto a steel frame that has a gap in the middle. A tiny collection of virtual blocks of various shapes helps get the ball, its own momentum the only engine, over the gap and up a little ramp. Clear the ramp and the button waits at the bottom. That's it. Puzzle solved. Actually, the ball doesn't even have to hit the button—push one of the blocks over and that will do. Just get *something* to clear that ramp and hit that #*&!ing button. It is a primal urge that, quite frankly, I don't understand, but it's powerful, I think, a vein of gold that our schools could possibly tap.

Level fifty has haunted me, on and off, for weeks. I had actually abandoned the entire game after spending a few days on it. Now I'm back. This devilish game was made by a British outfit called Extra Mile Studios, and they've made it just hard enough that I'm interested, but not so hard that I give up. The iPad's touch screen only magnifies the magic, allowing me to move the pieces with an index finger as easily as if I were willing them into place with my mind.

OK, I should stop. Why don't I stop?

As it happens, the date is May 21, 2011. On this date, a fundamentalist radio preacher named Harold Camping has predicted that the world will come to an end around 6 p.m. Eastern Time. Back home in Baltimore, 6:19 p.m. is post time for the Preakness Stakes, the second leg of the Triple Crown, and the single most important day of the year in Charm City. I check the time: 5:15 p.m. Pacific, 8:15 Eastern. I've played *Newton's Gravity* through both the end of the world *and* the Preakness.

What is going on here? What is it about this game that sucks me in and erases my surroundings, that focuses me obsessively on a single task and won't let go? What makes me *try again,* over and over? The shortest possible answer: it's *fun.* But that three-letter word is as misunderstood as the $68 billion industry that rests atop it.

Conventional wisdom holds that video games are a mental dead end turning an entire generation's brains to mush, a digital anesthetic that makes television seem harmless. At best they're a waste of time. At worst, games are turning our kids into a mindless race of cop killers, night elves, and bird flingers. More than any other form of entertainment, video games "tend to divide rooms into Us and Them," wrote journalist Tom Bissell. "We are, in effect, admitting that we like to spend our time shooting monsters, and They are, not unreasonably, failing to find the value in that."[1]

When the British government in 2006 got the results of a study on the nation's universal "literacy hour" in elementary schools and found that more than one child in three didn't like to read, MP Boris Johnson blamed parents who let their kids play too many video games, "bleeping and zapping in speechless rapture, their passive faces washed in explosions and gore. They sit for so long that their souls seem to have been sucked down the cathode ray tube." Writing in *The Telegraph,* Johnson, who two years later would become London's mayor, called gamers "blinking lizards, motionless, absorbed, only the twitching of their hands showing they are still conscious. These machines teach them nothing."[2]

Leaving aside the implicit insult to lizards, Johnson's characterization would get a bit of pushback these days from researchers who have spent more than a decade teasing out just what "these machines" teach and how they teach it. For starters, a handful of studies long ago established a clear link between video games and improved visual acuity. Researchers are also starting to discover more unforeseen benefits, such as attentional control and emotional regulation. Brain science holds that these "core constructs" are important for well-being, but that standard cognitive "brain training" techniques, as well as home remedies such as crossword puzzles or Sudoku, often produce narrow or disappointing results. People who do these things typically show marked improvements on tests, but a 2012 review found that transfer to real-world applications, or even different standard tests of attention, "has proven more elusive."[3]

Your brain, in other words, may not consent to be trained. But it will improve a few of these key skills if you let it enjoy a few hours of the first-person shooter *BioShock*. Recent research, the 2012 review noted, has revealed action games' positive effects, not just on attentional control and emotional regulation, but also on decision making, "mental rotation" (the ability to create a mental image of an object and manipulate it in three dimensions), and the ability to switch rapidly between competing tasks. The effects develop after just a few hours of game play and can last for days, months, and even years. Researchers also noted that expert action gamers have something in common with, of all people, those who excel at meditation: both show a "lower recruitment of the fronto-parietal network," which helps people regulate their attention. Essentially, both gamers and gurus get better at paying attention and exert less effort to stay focused.[4] In another recent trial, Italian researchers found that just twelve hours of playing action video games "drastically improve" the reading abilities of children with dyslexia. Nine daily play sessions of eighty minutes apiece improved children's reading speed better than a year's worth of "highly demanding traditional reading treatments," the researchers found.[5] "You get better at a lot of things, not just the game," said neuroscientist Daphne Bavelier, who has pioneered the field.[6]

So much for blinking lizards. But how do video games do it? To figure it out, we must first understand how games work. To understand how games work, we must understand a little bit about the brain, which evolution has prepped for modern life in an unusual way. If you believe Darwin—and you should—the world is a dangerous place. Millions of years of natural selection have forced us to adapt again and again to drought, floods, and, on occasion, the unfortunate asteroid. Taken collectively, these disasters have killed off countless awesome species, including a few of our closest ancestors. So what business do we have wasting our time with *fun?* Why aren't we a more businesslike species, like ants?

Because play is how we learn. Ten thousand generations of natural selection have pruned our ranks to the point where we, the living, the lucky ones who survived, have evolved to be curious. We're "infovores," born with an innate hunger for information and connections, according to neuroscientist Irving Biederman.[7] We are paid to be curious. The banker is our brain and the payment is a curated selection of drugs with names like endorphins, dopamine, serotonin, and adrenaline.

We are not alone. Neuroscientist Jaak Panksepp wrote of animals' "seeking drive," an innate restlessness that makes them "intensely interested in exploring their world and leads them to become excited when they are about to get what they desire." It allows animals to find what they need for survival, including food, water, warmth, and, of course, sex. In humans, Panksepp wrote, this may be one of the main brain systems that generates and sustains curiosity, even for intellectual pursuits. We're constantly shaking down our environment for information, he wrote, for everything from "nuts to knowledge."[8]

Think of the human brain, then, not so much as a banker but as a three-pound, pattern-seeking drug dealer. When we learn something or make an association between what we see and what's already in our memory, our brain squirts a little shot of endogenous morphine, or endorphins, into our bloodstream. This acts as a neurotransmitter but also as a kind of mild painkiller. The more "richly interpretable" the scene, Biederman and co-researcher Edward Vessel have found, the more endorphins produced, since the brain is casting about for ways to understand what it's seeing and fit the new mystery into its experience. In their often-quoted 2006 study, participants viewing a dramatic photo of a lightning strike on a dark night, for instance, rated it "more pleasurable" than a photo of a drab parking lot. And the researchers found that the so-called "association area" of the brain, where new information gets tied back into our memories, lit up more. The association area has the greatest density of "mu-opioid receptors" activated by endorphins, they noted, providing "ample evidence that the brain is wired for pleasure."[9]

This is not a gratuitous little squirt, but an ancient act of self-preservation, since for hundreds of thousands of years the key to survival lay in our ability to recognize and remember patterns. Does that ice look safe or unsafe? When we figure it out—when we recall what safe ice looks like and compare it to what's in front of us—that feels good. When we don't, it feels bad, in several ways. One recent evolutionary hypothesis holds that the constant presence of venomous snakes, our "first predators" according to anthropologist Lynne A. Asbell, had a significant impact on our brain's expansion and development, as well as our visual skills. We evolved to be particularly sensitive to color and movement because the alternative was a snakebite. Put snakes and mammals in close proximity, Asbell wrote, and an "evolutionary arms race" emerges, forcing the mammals to evolve in one of two ways: develop a resistance to snake venom or enhance their ability to detect snakes visually before they strike.[10] She noted that in Madagascar, where isolated species of lemurs evolved without snakes, to this day they don't fear them. They also have poor eyesight for a mammal.

Anything that directly threatens our survival "automatically commands our full attention," wrote game designer Noah Falstein.[11] This focus also feeds us, he said, since the same pattern-seeking has long helped us separate edible mushrooms from poison, ripe berries from thorns, and one limping antelope from a giant herd. Every time we come out alive, every time we learn something new, our brain naturally wants to keep the party going, said game scholar and designer Raph Koster: "Mother Nature seems to have mastered this recipe pretty well. And the way that Mother Nature does this is by getting us high."[12]

In a sense, suggested Koster, we're being played. Our brain is fooling us into doing the hard work of learning how to survive. "I think there's a good case to be made that having fun is a key evolutionary advantage right next to opposable thumbs in terms of importance," he wrote.[13] When we successfully take risks or make predictions that turn out to be correct, we get a shot of another neurotransmitter: dopamine. The system only activates when the outcome isn't assured, said psychologist Michael Apter. The flip side, of course, is that the greater the risk, the greater the reward. "One buys excitement with fear," he said, "and the greater the cost, the better the product."[14]

We had to move to survive as well, chasing down prey and, on occasion, running from predators. So when we exert ourselves over a long period of time, our brain rewards our efforts with another shot of dopamine. This is what produces, among other conditions, "runner's high," the euphoric state resulting from long-distance running. Recent research suggests that humans and other "cursorial mammals" that evolved the ability to run over long distances are the only ones who experience runner's high,[15] though rats seem to experience a variation of it. A 2008 study found that rats trained to self-administer cocaine through a catheter ingested far less when their cages were outfitted with exercise wheels.[16]

Faced with adversity, our brain produces another neurotransmitter, serotonin, which helps us cope with stress. Chemically almost identical to LSD, it's known in some quarters as the "molecule of happiness." It's also the "Don't panic yet" neurotransmitter, according to Oxford University psychopharmacology professor Philip J. Cowen.[17] Figuring out exactly what role it plays in learning is difficult, but researchers say its absence can lead to anxiety, depression, and panic attacks, among other conditions. Drugs like Prozac and other "serotonin-specific reuptake inhibitors," or SSRIs, essentially preserve the brain's supply of the chemical for any "shovel-ready receptor that will have it," said science writer

Natalie Angier.[18] Panksepp said that reducing human strivings to a "welling up of ancient neurochemicals in primitive parts of the brain" may be difficult to swallow. In the end, however, he said, "the evidence now clearly indicates that certain intrinsic aspirations of all mammalian minds, those of mice as well as men, are driven by the same ancient neurochemistries."[19]

We came inside from the African veldt long ago, but our brain is still seeking, still attracted to richly interpretable scenarios, still convinced each morning that its survival is at stake. On a conscious level we know this isn't true, but biologists say our stubborn brain never got the memo. It thinks that man-eating tiger is still in the brush and that antelope is limping along, an easy kill just out of view. That cluster of ripe berries—the best one ever!—is around the next bend in the path. And even if we catch the antelope or gather the berries, our brain still tells us that we may have to fight our fellow human beings to keep our catch. We are, in a sense, overprepared for modern life, in which no one really wants our antelope or our berries, but after 200,000 years we're still hooked on "adrenaline-generating decision-making," according to Lennart Nacke, director of the Games and Media Entertainment Research Laboratory at the University of Ontario Institute of Technology. Most of us have office jobs and don't have to fight for our dinner, he said. "But it's still hardwired in humans. Our brain craves this kind of interaction, our brain wants to be stimulated."[20] So each morning, almost as soon as we get out of bed, we stretch, yawn, look around, and begin to hunt and gather and fight. Since the modern world mostly frowns upon actual hunting, gathering, and fighting, we settle for *simulations*.

First the hunting: When we run or bike or drive a bit too fast on the way to work, when we go bowling or shopping (especially for bargains), we're hunting. When we gaze at NASCAR, Olympic sprinting, America's Cup, or a children's swim meet, we're taking pleasure in watching a handful of skilled fellow hunters chase down their prey. The events may be completely abstracted from their roots—the prey has disappeared, replaced by a ball or clock or finish line—but it is hunting nonetheless. The thrill of going very fast to bring down that antelope or escape from that tiger has been replaced by the thrill of simply going very fast.[21] Actually, a handful of sports, such as skiing, horseback riding, mountain climbing, dancing, riding merry-go-rounds, and children's whirling in circles, go even further, said French philosopher Roger Caillois. They're attempts "to momentarily destroy the stability of perception and inflict a kind of voluptuous panic upon an otherwise lucid mind." He calls this *ilinx,* after the Greek term for vertigo.[22]

When we're not hunting, we're gathering. We collect coins and stamps and cookie jars. We're *Doctor Who* completists who labor each morning over the same nine-by-nine grid of a newspaper Sudoku puzzle and every night over the same square of needlepoint. We are suckers for patterns, said Koster, because "learning is the drug." Its opposite, boredom, is what happens when the brain is casting about for new information but can't find any. "It is the feeling you get when there are no new patterns to absorb."[23] (Koster is mute on whether any rage, spread thick or thin, is involved.)

As it turns out, this is one of the reasons we love music so much, according to Elizabeth Hellmuth Margulis, director of the music cognition lab at the University of Arkansas. Repetition in music "serves as a handprint of human intent," she wrote. A phrase that might have sounded arbitrary the first time "might come to sound purposefully shaped and communicative the second." Recurring patterns in music, as in rituals, "harness the power of repetition to concentrate the mind on immediate sensory details rather than broader practicalities," she wrote. Margulis recalled an experiment by the Swedish psychologist Alf Gabrielsson, who asked thousands of people to describe their most powerful experiences with music. Many reported that their peak musical experiences involved "a sense of transcendence, of dissolved boundaries where they seemed to escape the limitations of their bodies and become one with the sounds they were hearing." That can be partially explained, she said, by the shift in attention and the "heightened sense of involvement" brought about by repetition.[24]

The coin labeled "pattern" has a flip side: surprise. Humans have a "special affinity for novelty" that has helped us survive all these earthly disasters, wrote journalist Winifred Gallagher. We like new things so much she called us "neophiles."[25] We plunge our hands into cereal boxes fishing for a prize, and we shake wrapped packages, wondering what's inside. We watch *Storage Wars.* A few of us gamble away the mortgage payment playing slot machines, and many more of us buy $2 scratch-off lottery tickets. We check Facebook obsessively, hanging on that little number at the top of the screen that tells us how many times our friends have responded since the last time we checked. We love surprises because they both fulfill and undermine our expectations of neat patterns. We want the same old thing, but in a new way. We solve mystery novels, grimace at *Law & Order* corpses, and hang expectantly on Letterman punch lines, night after night. We love the new Wilco album, mostly because it sounds a lot like the old Wilco album, only *different*. The new movie version of *Hamlet* ends the same way that each *Hamlet* has ever ended for the past 400 years, yet we're still on the edge of our seats during that final, deadly duel with Laertes.

Then, finally, we fight, struggling for power, status, and recognition. We play chess and *Risk* and *Monopoly*, flag football and fantasy baseball. We watch *Hardball* and argue about politics, which itself is a highly ritualized fight for power. We spend years tracing the week-to-week performance of our favorite competitors as they strategize over the paths of balls. We do our best to follow hockey pucks, but mostly just enjoy the hubbub caused when they're near. We grant near-mystical significance to two nearly naked people who put on big, padded leather gloves and beat the crap out of each other.[26]

When we're not hunting, gathering, fighting, or watching others do these things, we can at least take a break with a good book, right? Wrong. Cognitively speaking, reading turns out to be nearly the same thing as *doing* the actual things. Recent research has found that when people read sentences such as "John grasped the object" or "Pablo kicked the ball," fMRI scans show activity in parts of the brain's motor cortex devoted to moving the arm or leg, respectively, wrote science journalist Annie Murphy Paul. Reading words such as "perfume" or "coffee" lights up the region that processes smells. Likewise, reading metaphors like "The singer had a velvet voice" or "He had leathery hands" stimulates readers' sensory cortices. "The brain, it seems, does not make much of a distinction between reading about an experience and encountering it in real life," wrote Paul. "In each case, the same neurological regions are stimulated."[27]

So the simple act of dragging our eyes across a page of print is a hack of our brain's struggle for survival. Reading, after all, is a fairly recent development in our long history—humans have only been able to perform the activity for about 4,000 years, a blink in evolutionary time. We've been baking bread, by contrast, for about 30,000 years, recent research suggests. Our brain hasn't had time to develop specialized "reading circuits," wrote French neuroscientist Stanislas Dehaene. "Nothing in our evolution could have prepared us to absorb language through vision," he said.[28] Yet even young children are adept at pulling meaning from words. Any reader easily retrieves meaning out of at least 50,000 candidate words in a few tenths of a second "based on nothing more than a few strokes of light on the retina."[29]

How did we do it? Over the past few millennia, we've co-opted brain circuits already in use to scan the world for food or danger, in a sense fooling ourselves into paying attention to the inert little symbols on the page. Brain scans have shown that areas once used exclusively for scanning the horizon—for recognizing animal tracks, ripe berries, and snakes in trees—became the region that allowed us to quickly recognize letters and words. We've trained our brain to read by modifying the structures we once used to sense danger and movement and odd shapes in the grass. Dehaene and other researchers have found that most of our letter shapes are actually transpositions of key shapes from nature to which we've learned pay attention: a "Y" resembles the crook of tree branches, a "T" (on its side) the shape formed whenever one object masks another—imagine a telephone pole breaking the line of the horizon. "T-detector" neurons help us determine which object is in front, Dehaene wrote. "We did not invent most of our letter shapes: they lay dormant in our brain for millions of years, and were merely rediscovered when our species invented writing and the alphabet."[30] So even reading, that most sedentary act of lean-back leisure, is a kind of hunting and gathering for meaning. Thanks to all that exhausting horizon searching, we've developed the nearly magical ability to extract thoughts from a sheet of type, or, as Dehaene put it, to "listen to the dead with our eyes."[31]

So to review: Freed to do whatever we want, our main leisure activity is participating in experiences that we know are not real. We retreat to the imagination, the pleasures of which "hijack mental systems that have evolved for real-world pleasure," wrote psychologist Paul Bloom. As with reading, our brain doesn't really distinguish simulations from the real thing, he said. "This is a strange way for an animal to spend its days."[32] Bloom noted research showing that children with imaginary friends turn out to be more socially adept than those without them, and that fantasy is more intense for children, recounting a 1991 experiment in which researchers showed a box to young children and asked them to *pretend* that there was a monster inside. Given the chance a while later to approach the box, the children often refused to put their fingers inside. "It's not that they really believed in the monster," he wrote, "it is that the imagined monster takes on such force in the child's mind that it is felt as if it were real."[33]

In a more recent experiment, Stanford University researchers Kathryn Y. Segovia and Jeremy N. Bailenson invited sixty preschoolers and young elementary school students to a lab and outfitted each with a set of high-tech virtual-reality goggles. For a few minutes, each child experienced an immersive simulation that offered the illusion that they were swimming with a pair of killer whales. Two weeks later, the researchers invited the kids back into the lab, sat them down, and asked: *Have you ever swum with killer whales?* Half said, *Yes, I have.*[34] Yale University philosopher Tamar Gendler has even coined a term for this phenomenon: *alief*. She calls it a cognitive state "more primitive" than either belief or imagination, one that plays "a far larger role in causing behavior than has typically been recognized by philosophers."[35]

This has everything to do with games. Our brain is enjoying the fantasy, but on some level it believes the killer whale is real. Just as a cat chases a ball because it's "chasable," like a mouse, our imagination turns the objects of our attention into antelopes or snakes or tigers. They become keys that fit into our psychological locks, "counterfeit coins which make the machine work when dropped into the slot," said British game designer Chris Bateman.[36]

Game theorists talk about "the magic circle," a concept first introduced in the late 1930s in Dutch historian Johan Huizinga's treatise on play, *Homo Ludens* (the title means "Man the Player," a riff on the term *Homo sapiens*—Huizinga considered it just as significant that we *play* as that we are wise). The magic circle, he said, is a kind of temporary sacred space that games share with religious rituals, plays, festivals, and even legal proceedings. The Olympic arena, the living room card table, the movie screen, and the courtroom all are "forbidden spots"[37] where special rules apply. The magic circle persists until the final whistle, until someone acts like a "spoilsport" or, as sometimes happens, until someone cheats.

Actually we should thank the cheaters—they help us clarify how immersive play is and how deeply we value it. Most games, after all, are meaningless, done strictly for their own sake. But when cheating happens in a game, we understand it immediately and have an almost primal reaction, one that's outsized even in comparison to dramatically worse offenses in the real world. Few of us remember the names Jerome Kerviel, Bruno Iksil, or Kweku Adoboli. This trio merely disrupted the world banking system, losing their employers and thousands of investors billions of dollars— Iksil, a rogue trader known to insiders as the "London Whale" or simply "Voldemort," singlehandedly lost his employer, JP Morgan Chase, as much as $9 billion in 2012. But their crimes barely register. On the other hand, millions of people—perhaps even you— secretly hope there's a special place in Hell for Lance Armstrong, Barry Bonds, and Tonya Harding, three people who messed with the magic circle and whose crimes most of us can easily recite—in Harding's case, we remember the details more than twenty years later.

Play, wrote theorists Katie Salen and Eric Zimmerman, is "free movement within a more rigid structure."[38] What's really at work is not just our brain enjoying rules, but improvising a path through them. That's what makes it a game, an endeavor that the philosopher Bernard Suits called "the voluntary attempt to overcome unnecessary obstacles."[39] Our brain is such a hopeless pattern seeker that, given the tiniest opportunity, it will even invent a game on the spot and hold the rest of the body hostage until it's done. How else to explain the popularity of the Urinal Fly, a waterproof sticker that restaurants and bars now install in men's bathrooms? The stickers are modeled on an effort to keep men's bathrooms cleaner at Amsterdam's airport. After workers began etching flies into urinals, "spillage" dropped by eighty percent.[40] The Colorado-based company that markets the fly stickers advertises them with a photo of a fetching blonde in a little black dress and red pumps who seems to be enjoying the cool black tile of a restaurant men's room floor— perhaps she's simply dozing, or she has had too much to drink and wandered into the wrong restroom. In any event, the ad reads, "Are your floors clean enough for her?" The company also markets tiny bulls-eye targets for preschool boys with the slogan, "Give the boys something to aim for!"[41]

Perhaps most importantly, wherever play happens, the magic circle spontaneously creates a kind of instant collective illusion. The very word *illusion,* Johan Huizinga noted, comes from the Latin *inludere,* meaning "in play." He recalled a story in which a child set up a row of chairs as make-believe train cars. As the boy sat in the front seat, pretending to be the locomotive, his father approached and gave him a hug. The boy scolded him: "Don't kiss the engine, Daddy, or the carriages won't think it's real."[42]

This is the world we need to think about when we're thinking about video games. Simply by clicking on a game icon or picking up a controller, the player has already done half the work. The magic circle appears, as if on command. The game begins. Now the *really* jaw-dropping stuff happens.

◖ · · · · · · · · · · · · · ·

"Games are designer food for infovores," said designer Daniel Cook.[43] Because they reside on computers, even the simplest video games respond immediately to any input, no matter how small. Press a button, get a reaction. Press it twice, get a different reaction. Your actions matter and you can feel their effects. This may seem a minor detail, but for most of us, video games are the most efficient feedback machines we'll ever encounter. At their core, they're built around a constant stream of "mastery feedback."[44] If video games have achieved anything, they've finally perfected the elusive reward schedule. In real life, we're rewarded at the end of a task, if at all. Often the reward feels arbitrary—it's the trophy handed out to every kid on the soccer team or the outsized compliment for something you barely remember doing. In games, by contrast, rewards are everywhere, but they're decidedly not arbitrary. Games reward effort at the moment of accomplishment and are "nuanced, specific and whimsical," according to Harvard's David Dockterman and game designer Alex Sarlin.[45] Rewards work best, they say, when they're markers of progress, not ends in themselves.

At their core, video games, like books or movies, are mass media, but they offer free movement within a more rigid structure honed to the smallest detail. Everything from the sounds, music, and button choices to how individual characters gesture, speak, and move is designed to elicit a response. In Nintendo's legendary *Super Mario Bros.* side-scrolling platformer games, it's no accident that Mario's jumps last about twice as long as any you or I could pull off—they give players the momentary sensation of flying.[46] Likewise, in *Angry Birds,* the popular birds-in-a-slingshot smartphone game, each member of the eponymous flock flies from the slingshot in a lazy arc that's much slower than real flying, giving players the opportunity to watch it unfold and try a different trajectory next time if they miss their target.

Game designers use terms like texture, mood, and "game feel" when describing their creations. "We say a lot of times, 'We really want the player to feel clever here,'" recalled designer Tim Schaefer.[47] Ken Levine, whose epic, atmospheric *BioShock* series has consistently earned top honors, said the first game was under development for two or three years before the idea of a doomed underwater utopia emerged as its setting. "We don't start with a story," he said. "We start by thinking, 'What are we trying to accomplish here? What *feeling* do we want the player to have?'"[48] When he was creating the sound for his iPad game *W.E.L.D.E.R.,* a mesmerizing, industrial-themed word-building game, designer Britt Myers combined eight sound effects loops—each one a combination of five or six original loops—simply to create the background sounds. "It's a lot of layering and different things to get the right tone," said Myers,[49] a recording engineer who worked out the ideas in his Manhattan studio.

Games, in other words, are designed experiences, much like school.

As far back as 1997, multimedia designer Janet Murray was writing about the pleasures of being transported "to an elaborately simulated place," a phenomenon she called *immersion,* as in water. "We seek the same feeling from a psychologically immersive experience that we do from a plunge in the ocean or swimming pool," she wrote, "the sensation of being surrounded by a completely other reality, as different from water is from air, that takes over all our attention, our whole perceptual apparatus."[50] Games create immersion any number of ways, but usually it's by offering rich, detailed, "cognitively demanding environments" full of threats, pathways, and items players can snap up, said psychologist Jamie Madigan. The more senses you recruit and the more those senses work in tandem, the better. "A bird flying overhead is good. Hearing it screech as it does so is better." If the environment works, players tend to forget the technology standing between them and the game world and begin to favor this new world as their "primary ego reference frame." It's simply where they "are."[51]

Many games theorists cite the work of Hungarian psychologist Mihaly Csikszentmihalyi (pronounced "chick-CENT-mee-hi") who in the 1980s developed the notion of "optimal experience" or "flow," a mental state in which a person's abilities match the task at hand so perfectly that the work becomes invisible. Situated midway between boredom and anxiety (skills without challenge equal boredom, while challenge without skills equals anxiety), flow emerged from Csikszentmihalyi's work studying, among others, painters who became so consumed with their work that they ignored the need for food, drink, or sleep. "The best moments usually occur when a person's body or mind is stretched to its limits in a voluntary effort to accomplish something difficult and worthwhile," he wrote. "Optimal experience is thus something that we *make* happen."[52] In fact, the symptoms of "runner's high" sound an awful lot like flow.[53] In one account, a long-distance runner remembered the one and only time she experienced it: "For a mile, maybe two, I slipped into another world, a timeless one where there was no effort, no clocks, no yesterday, no tomorrow. I floated along for fifteen minutes, aware of nothing, just drifting."[54]

Although most Americans enjoy a fair measure of free time and ample access to leisure activities, Csikszentmihalyi found, they don't often experience flow. Watching television, which Americans do for about thirty-four hours a week, rarely leads to flow. Csikszentmihalyi found that people actually achieve the flow state—"deep concentration, high and balanced challenges and skills, a sense of control and satisfaction"—about four times as often *on the job* as when they are watching television.[55]

Perhaps the best description of what it feels like to experience flow in a video game came at the dawn of the video-game era, from the most unlikely source: a middle-aged San Francisco sociologist and jazz pianist named David Sudnow. His 1984 memoir *Pilgrim in the Microworld* recounted his unexpected attachment to the Jobs-Wozniak game *Breakout.* A well-known piano teacher, Sudnow one night stumbled into a video arcade to pick up his son and became transfixed with a coin-operated *Defender* game. "Thirty seconds of play, and I'm on a whole new plane of being, all my synapses wailing," he wrote. Soon he'd purchased a home version of *Breakout* and found himself practicing nearly nonstop, marveling at "the full caressing potentials of the human hand realized in creative action on screen."[56]

Practicing sometimes for five hours per day, Sudnow wrote that when he wasn't at the console perfecting a certain *Breakout* sequence, "I was practicing the sequence in my imagination, walking down the street, sitting in a cafe twirling a salt shaker, looking up during dinner in a Japanese restaurant at a bamboo and rice paper trellis with *Breakout*-like rectangles on the ceiling."[57] He soon came to see the little Atari console in his living room as a "genetically predestined instrument," much like his beloved piano. "It was five years at the piano before I looked down and saw my hands appearing to make music all by themselves," he wrote. "But within two weeks at *Breakout,* I watch them handling fast slams, with no consciousness of guiding their movements."[58]

Before long, Sudnow realized that competence in video games arises out of "lucratively programmed caring" that keeps players coming back for more—that's how they hone their skills. Ten years before psychologist Anders Ericsson proposed the idea of "deliberate practice," Sudnow marveled at the cleverness of his little Atari console: "The way to be kept caring," he wrote, "is most delicately built right into the program."[59] Like many players, both before him and since, Sudnow began to understand video games as a breed of behavioral device designed to keep him engaged for hours on end, "hitting the reset switch again and again like a homebound Vegas gambler feeding slots at the airport beyond all hope of success." He eventually admitted that his habit had gone beyond pleasure—he simply wanted to feel "just the right final dab of remorse to round out the vacation. Take all my money but let me keep pulling the handle until it's time to go."[60]

Sudnow's experience with *Breakout* actually tracks closely with those of many Las Vegas gamblers, specifically those who can't stop playing modern electronic slot machines. Obsessive players seek the "machine zone," a mental state where nothing else matters but their ability to keep playing, said sociologist Natasha Dow Schüll. These gamblers don't actually play to win, she wrote; they're "time-on-device" players who "play to win to play" until they're out of money. Decades of research on feedback loops, reward schedules, and the flow state have resulted in a new breed of electronic machines so powerful, Schüll said, that they're no longer simply devices tucked in alcoves to help the wives of visiting blackjack players fill a few idle hours. Slots have "become the central nervous system of the casino." Since the mid-1990s, she found, most of the attendees at Gamblers Anonymous meetings in Las Vegas show up because of problems with machine gaming. One video poker player told Schüll, "I don't care if it takes coins or pays coins: the contract is that when I put a new coin in, get five new cards, and press those buttons, I am allowed to *continue*."[61]

Video game advocates would take exception to the slot machine comparison, and with good reason, since most video games require at least a modicum of skill, an active imagination, and, of course, a commitment to learning a thing or two. Flow, after all, emerges when a person's *abilities* match the task at hand. More to the point, games also invite a different kind of failure, embracing players in an open-hearted way that slots, for all their finely tuned reward schedules, never will. In fact, video games stand apart, not just from slot machines but from nearly every endeavor in our lives, in this way: we're disappointed if mastering one is *too easy*. Imagine being disappointed to find that operating a snowmobile, filing your taxes, or mastering calculus was easier than you'd thought. Now imagine a game in which you *couldn't fail*—games theorist Jesper Juul has suggested a single button reading "Press Button to Complete Game."[62]

That may actually be the key to their ability to get under our skin. Games allow us to fail again and again without risk, in a constant cycle of death and rebirth, until we succeed. In fact, we may secretly enjoy failing in a game as much as succeeding. When Finnish researcher Niklas Ravaja and his colleagues attached skin-conductivity and facial-expression sensors to undergraduates and had them play a video game, they found something they weren't expecting: failure was fun. Ravaja asked subjects to play *Super Monkey Ball 2,* a Japanese home-console title with awful upbeat music that features monkeys trapped inside translucent bowling balls. A successful roll wins a prize, but a gutter ball sends the monkey flying off the edge of the lane and into the endless abyss of outer space. The researchers found that for players, failing in the game was not just fun but actually borderline joyful. A bad roll elicited a negative emotional response, as measured by the sensors. But almost simultaneously, the sight of the monkey falling off the edge made people smile, eliciting "positively valenced high-arousal emotion (i.e., joy), rather than disappointment."[63] *Super Monkey Ball 2* lowered the cost of failure so dramatically that it reduced it to a joke. More recent research suggests that even if we fail at such tasks, our brain releases dopamine if it thinks we *nearly* won. Our seeking brain gets rewarded either way, so we may as well keep trying.

Game designer Chris Bateman has called this mechanism "grip," and most of the best games take advantage of it. In fact, many early video games, like *Pac-Man* and *Tetris,* relied heavily on it, since their underlying mechanic essentially didn't allow players to win or even come close. Why would you play a game that you couldn't win unless the reward lay outside of winning?

Learning theorists would say that players have simply developed a vision of themselves as people who are about to succeed and won't let go. In the end, we try again because games *let* us try again. It's the rare game that doesn't let us restart our efforts at a moment's notice. In fact, any game that doesn't is doing so to make a point. *We the Giants* by Dutch experimental game designer Peter Groeneweg is, more or less, a game about sacrifice. Players, in the shape of little blinking cartoon squares called "giants," try to reach the sun by climbing farther up the screen than any previous player. But just a few minutes into the game, they realize that this is a trick. They eventually reach a point where it's impossible to get any closer to the sun, given the restrictions on moving and jumping. So they're asked to voluntarily commit suicide in a spot that will allow future players to climb over their fossilized bodies and get one step further, all in a collective attempt to build a staircase to the sun. It is less depressing than it sounds—each giant most closely resembles a piece of Chiclets chewing gum, and they go painlessly. Along the way, players meet a computerized nonplayer character, or NPC, who says, "Your time is coming soon. Will you be ready to sacrifice yourself? Do you know what wisdom you will leave behind?" Before they make the ultimate sacrifice, players get the chance to leave behind a 140-character final bit of advice that will live on with their calcified body. The game uploads players' final messages automatically to its Twitter feed, @wethegiants, and players leave profound aphorisms, bits of poetry, one-word exclamations (the f-word seems most popular, though one recent player wrote "Waffles"). Inevitably, another NPC instructs the player to use the escape key to perform the sacrifice. "I hope we'll meet in another life," it says. Then you watch yourself slowly, quietly die.[64]

After about a year and several thousand digital suicides, Groeneweg created a YouTube video that traced players' collective attempts to reach the sun.[65] In the video, stacks of giants' bodies rise like digital Watts Towers in spindly shapes that inevitably find their target. With its mournful electric piano soundtrack and inescapable endgame, *We the Giants* is about as moving and unsettling an experience as you're likely to have with a three-minute Flash game, precisely because it asks you to contemplate a video-game world in which you *can't* try again. Once a player dies, she can't go back. In fact, she can *never* play the game to its conclusion again, at least on the same computer. She only dies once.

Anyone who has spent even a little time with games will see how "hardcore" this mechanic is, just a few steps removed from Juul's "Press Button to Complete Game" and much more bleak. So remember that button and those fossilized giants as you read this book. What follows in the remaining chapters is a series of narratives that explore the improbable magic that happens when people are given the opportunity to try and fail and try again. Contrary to our deepest fears, giving our kids ample opportunity to fail will turn them not into abject failures but into gritty, impassioned, self-reliant learners. The blooper reel of deliberate practice, of 10,000 failures, is a video labeled "Success."

As for me, after what seems like 10,000 hours at *Newton's Gravity*—but is merely three with bathroom and snack breaks—I admit to myself that I will never solve this level. I've had my fun, now I'm defeated. So I do what defeated people do: I go online to search for other players' solutions. The most promising comes in the form of a confessional blog written by a twentysomething brand ambassador for Microsoft Xbox Singapore named Sheylara, who has, for some reason, linked to solutions of the game provided by a friend named The Goonfather. He seems to have played through all 100 levels and created screenshots of his solutions for each level. Snapshots of victory! I follow his prescription for level fifty and it doesn't work. I tweak and try again, tweak some more and still nothing. Why did I trust someone named Goonfather?

I try a few more times and then, after moving one piece just a hair to the right . . . it works! My heart does a little dance and I'm breathless for a second, hardly able to transport myself to this new reality, this other side, this "level fifty is solved" half of my life. I'd gotten so used to the other half. With dopamine coursing through my bloodstream, I watch the "Level Complete" banner quietly unfurl and am dumbstruck with satisfaction. Other than the banner, the game gives back nothing—no cash prizes or flashing lights, no pats on the back. Only bragging rights and the next puzzle. My drug-dealing brain, as Koster promised, has done the rest.

Just as the game sat patiently waiting for me to try level fifty again and again, the game now waits, this time on level fifty-one. I dig in, but if there were an instant replay of my Goonfather-induced solution (and, note to Extra Mile Studios: you need an instant replay), I'd watch nothing else all night.

FOUR

. . . . ❯

THE GAME LAYER

*How Three Inventive Teachers Use
Game Principles to Engage Students*

The competition was to begin at 4 p.m., no exceptions, but at two minutes to four, none of the competitors has arrived. Jennifer Allard, the math club sponsor at Thomas Jefferson High School for Science and Technology in Alexandria, Virginia, glances up at the clock and assures me they'll be here. As if on cue, Joseph Park appears in the doorway in an oversized gray University of Rochester hoodie. Dark-haired, handsome, and tall, he finds a chair, throws off his enormous blue backpack and begins typing. Moments later, Robin Park (no relation) rushes in, finds a quiet spot across the room and does the same. On each boy's screen is a math problem the likes of which most of us spend our lives avoiding.

The next thirty minutes go by in total silence as the two stare into the face of a nine-question Math Test from Hell. But this is no ordinary hellish test. A closer look at each boy's screen reveals a digital scoreboard at the top. On one side is the combined average score of Joseph and Robin—a senior and freshman, respectively, at Thomas Jefferson, a renowned suburban Washington, D.C., high school affectionately known as "TJ." On the other side of the screen is the combined score of four students sitting at that moment in a similar room in a similar high school, 600 miles away in the Indianapolis suburb of Carmel, Indiana. The four opponents are solving the same nine problems simultaneously, and each time someone gets one correct, the counter moves on all six screens.

If math ever becomes a spectator sport—and stranger things have happened—we can look back on these problem sets and the massive tournament they eventually spawned and send a thank-you note to Tim Kelley. He is the one who dreamed up *Interstellar,* the curious piece of software that he hopes will change how students feel not just about math, but about academics of nearly every sort. Kelley has spent most of the past five years cold-calling school administrators, flying around the United States, and figuring out how to build NCAA-style bracket competitions in academic subjects. In Kelley's dream, *Interstellar* will pit class against class, school against school, and, someday, nation against nation.

Wait—this is not what we bargained for, was it? Interscholastic math competitions? Nation against nation? Isn't that a bit . . . old-fashioned? Well, yes—but it may also preview the future of school, or at least one possible future.

A Chicago native and perpetual graduate student—he holds degrees in law and business, among others—Kelley got the inspiration for *Interstellar* while volunteering to help the rowing team train at his old high school. He watched as rowers took a routine but grueling endurance test, and saw that the atmosphere was "electric." Though the numbers didn't really mean anything in the long run, the rowers were obsessed, pushing to achieve their personal best. Kelley began to wonder how to replicate that spirit in the classroom. He soon imagined a computer application that would use students' day-to-day results to match them on any given day with comparably skilled competitors in head-to-head academic competition—from classroom pickup games to bleacher-filling, live-broadcast amphitheater tournaments. He was working on a master's degree in public administration at Harvard's Kennedy School of Government when he mentioned the strange idea to one of his professors, Martin West. A one-time education advisor to Mitt Romney during the 2012 presidential campaign, West had studied, among other things, the public perceptions of schools. He urged Kelley to pursue the idea, and Kelley soon began contacting school districts to find teachers willing to let their students pilot the competition.

In September 2012, Kelley cold-called Steve Dunbar, director of the American Mathematics Competitions, or AMC, an elite program sponsored by the nonprofit Mathematical Association of America, with the idea of a competition based on AMC problems. The competition, founded in 1950, enrolls about 400,000 students, but it still uses pencil and paper and can take weeks to score. Dunbar had actually been searching for a way to bring it into the twenty-first century, and as soon as Kelley described his vision, Dunbar realized this was what he'd been searching for. In two months, Kelley had a prototype. In five months, he and Dunbar had selected sixteen high schools to field-test the software. By February 2013, the first trials began.

Allard, the math club sponsor at TJ, said her students love being recognized for their hard work as much as athletes do. "This is what they're good at," she said. To those who blanch at making academics a spectator sport, Kelley said the focus, as with the rowers' fitness test, is on helping students achieve "personal best" milestones, a strategy that most schools rarely use. "Once kids see they're getting better, it just perpetuates improvement," he said, noting that a kid shooting free throws by himself doesn't improve as quickly as a kid competing on a team.[1] When I met Kelley, he was working on a tool that would allow spectators to view *Interstellar* matches live online. He said he hoped that would "bring enough glory to the math department, or enough glory to the math students, that everybody else says, 'I'd like to try this too.'"

Kelley's vision is to recruit high schools for an annual 64-team bracket each December with a minimal cost attached—$5 to $10 per student per season. Schools like TJ would gladly pay the fee, he predicted, as they now must pack their entire math team onto a bus or airplane to compete nationally.

The platform, Dunbar said, could bring high-level math to a larger audience—at the moment, AMC is focused on a group of academic one-percenters, just the top 10 percent of students in the top 10 percent of schools. "One of the things that I do, one of the things that gets me up and here into the office every day, is that I want to get more good math in front of more kids, more often, in as many ways as I possibly can," he said. International competitions pitting our best students against the best in the world could be thrilling. "If you look at the top level of competition, the United States is as strong as any other country in the world," he said. "It would be good and it would be competitive. It would be exciting."[2]

In September 2013, after the first pilot testing, 468 schools showed up for the beginning of the *Interstellar* fall competition, and Kelley soon had 10,000 kids on the platform working weekly through math problems. By November, he had arranged the highest-scoring 384 teams into six 64-team brackets. Two weeks before Christmas, the Final Four teams in each of the six divisions fought for their division's title. In the highest division, TJ actually made it to the Final Four but was outscored by the Academy for the Advancement of Science and Technology in Hackensack, New Jersey. Hackensack lost in the finals to San Jose's Harker School. The Carmel, Indiana, team never made it out of the first round.

For Kelley, there were no feelings of exuberance when it all went off smoothly. "How can I say this? I'm a worrier. I take after my German mother." When it was over, he mostly felt relief. Kelley has wagered his life savings, his career, and, to some extent, his personal life on the game. So he was understandably relieved the following September when nearly 600 schools and 15,000 students showed up to play. And they were now paying a modest fee, between $120 and $195 per school, to give students access to the platform for the entire season. "We do have decent sales, so that's great for me mentally," Kelley said. "We're very much in the black. That's a total load off my mind."[3]

North Lakes Academy inhabits one of those big, brutalist, vertical concrete-block buildings that, from the outside, could be just about anything: an office building, a tire warehouse, a forlorn self-storage facility. The tiny windows give away nothing. North Lakes sits on a lonely back road in Forest Lake, one of those far-flung Minneapolis suburbs that boasts plenty of retail—it's sandwiched between a Target and a WalMart—but sits so impossibly far from the city, and so close to open wilderness, that calling it a suburb seems an overreach. It pulls students from nearly twenty-five surrounding towns.

In the fall of 2008, Eric Nelson found himself teaching there. He was miserable. A Minnesota native who grew up in a family of teachers—he jokes, "I couldn't escape it"—Nelson majored in history at the University of Wisconsin and returned to Minnesota to earn his master's degree in education. While he earned his degree, he was student-teaching, and like virtually every new teacher who ever lived, he'd begun his career with a hazy *Sound of Music* idea that everyone surely loved learning as much as he did, and that his students would hang on to his every word. "I was kind of shocked, when I started teaching, at how zombified ninth graders were," he said. "They just sort of looked *through* me."[4] But he knew that among his students were several dedicated gamers, and they had learned how to work hard and overcome obstacles in the games they loved. Kids love video games, he said, "because they can just hit the reset button. That's how a lot of life should work—you make new mistakes instead of repeating the same ones over and over again."

At the time, Nelson was trying to figure out how to engage his students in world affairs, foreign policy, and the role of the United States in the world. The students had come of age in the wake of the September 11, 2001, terrorist attacks, which shocked most Americans' geopolitical sensibilities awake. Yet to these heartland kids, the rest of the world still seemed remote.

Late one night in 2009, in the throes of a self-described "existential crisis" as he struggled to prepare for a morning class, Nelson took a break from fretting long enough to check his fantasy football team. He had been playing since 2004—his teams were back-to-back Super Bowl champions in 2005 and 2006—so he knew the game intimately. Both years he'd picked up a running back who had started the season slowly but "got hot" by the end and lifted his team to the playoffs. In just a few years, Nelson had begun to understand the NFL from the inside out, how a team worked and how the pieces fit together. "I was watching games differently," he said. As he researched whether to start Jay Cutler or Drew Brees at quarterback the following Sunday, Nelson's mood improved and his mindset shifted. Simply by thinking like a gamer, he realized, he was making a dull task into something enjoyable.

Digital technology made the task easy: rather than sifting through a week's worth of newspaper clippings for the players' standings and statistics, he could simply look online. At a glance, he saw where each player stood. Then it came to him: what if he wasn't swapping Cutler and Brees, but China and Brazil? Just as fantasy football team owners draft, cut, and trade players based on their performance, his students could do the same with countries. He'd replace passing yards and points per game with political crises and popular uprisings. Since he was struggling to get students interested in international developments, each country's ability to fight its way into the news of the day would make it more valuable. Students could draft teams of countries—it didn't matter if they were related—and compete for the newsiest cluster. Lackluster countries would quickly sink to the bottom and get traded, but if an earthquake or military coup struck, say, Indonesia, the student who was following the news most closely could snatch it up before anyone else found out. Nelson dubbed the game *Fantasy Geopolitics*.

Forget for a moment that his game was an adaptation of an abstraction. He brought it to a ninth-grade civics class in September 2009, and students immediately clung to countries with funny-sounding names. Djibouti was in great demand, but as soon as kids found it didn't make news, they traded it. On the other hand, Mali may have seemed like just another unremarkable West African country at first, but when revolution came, the student who was paying attention picked it up unnoticed and pulled ahead. Soon *everyone* was paying attention. In December 2010, students began to notice that the kids who held Tunisia, then Libya, Egypt, and Yemen all began scoring points. The Arab Spring had arrived, and suddenly it meant something.

"It's kind of like a way to nerd out without having to do it outside of school," said Alissa Gmyrek, a senior who first played the game as a freshman. "You definitely have to research a lot." During the World Cup last year, she picked Brazil and Argentina. "Latin America was really booming at that time," she said. She noticed that political protests were roiling Venezuela, so she picked it too.

As the game caught on, Nelson began automating it, moving from a simple Google spreadsheet to a full-blown news tracker keyed to mentions in the *New York Times*. He created a "hall of fame" for the highest-scoring players, and soon realized that it was populated almost entirely by girls. "They do quiet research, they pick up the countries quietly," he said. "They just kind of quietly paid attention, made those changes and crushed their competition." At the end of the semester, the winner got a T-shirt that read, "Kickin' Djibouti," and everyone got the joke, said Gmyrek. Ask most high school seniors to stick a pin in Djibouti on a map of the world and they'd be lost. Gmyrek not only knows where the tiny North African country is—in the Gulf of Aden, opposite Yemen— but that it is "kind of a strategic place for the U.S. to have a base in." Still, she said, "it never scores a lot of points, I guess. It's just a tiny, tiny country."

What happened outside of class was more surprising. Without Nelson's urging or even his knowledge, students created a Facebook page that synthesized the international news they were following. They created a daily "White House brief," a concise summary of what was happening worldwide. And they invited him to join a discussion group. "They were having these conversations on social media that I wanted to have in my classroom." Even kids who lost interest after the game ended still benefited. As part of the game, Nelson encouraged students to add international newsfeeds to their personal Facebook pages. When the season ended, they went back to their old habits of reading about "Miley Cyrus and all the other crap," Nelson said, but their pages were shot through with news from around the world. "This sort of made my students the teachers," he said. "Once we kicked off the game and they got into it, they were sort of coming into my classroom saying, 'Hey Nelson, have you heard about what's happening in Syria?' and telling their classmates about these things too. It became a different kind of experience, and I became a little obsolete by choice, which I loved."

❰·············

This is what's often called "the game layer," a carefully designed overlay of game mechanics added to everyday tasks to make them more compelling, more thrilling or, in a few cases, more consequential. Often called "gamification," at its best it's less a mindless escape from reality than "a mindful escape from so many poorly structured experiences," said business journalist Aaron Dignan.[5]

Businesses have spent the past few years gamifying work in imaginative and sometimes strange ways. In 2005, Cold Stone Creamery hired Georgia Tech researcher and game designer Ian Bogost to develop *Stone City,* a game that trains workers to create mix-your-own ice cream servings using "profitable portion sizes."[6] In 2011, the restaurant chain Average Joe's began encouraging its servers to complete "missions" that pushed them, for instance, to sell nine specials over the course of a Monday shift or twelve soups and salads on a Tuesday. As they arrived at work, servers could see a leaderboard with their ranking for the week, average tips, and how much cash they were bringing into the restaurant. The typical bill grew two to three percentage points, from $17 to $17.50—barely worth the effort, it would seem, but over 60,000 transactions a week that translated into $1.5 million more revenue annually. Average Joe's expanded the experiment across its chain.[7]

Does gamification work? It depends on what behaviors you're trying to squeeze out of people, and how you squeeze them. During a three-day experiment in 2010, a new sign on a busy Stockholm street encouraged drivers to slow down because they were passing a "speed camera lottery." Speed cameras are familiar enough, but the lottery got people's attention. It was based on an idea by Kevin Richardson, a San Francisco game designer who believes that traffic enforcement, which punishes just a few bad or distracted drivers, is a "mis-distribution of energy and attention." In his experiment, the sign announced that the camera was photographing all cars, the speeders and the law-abiders alike, and automatically levying fines against the speeders, as such cameras do. But it also said a computer would periodically pick a random winner from the ranks of the law-abiding drivers and award a portion of the speeders' proceeds to one of them. Simply by following the speed limit, drivers believed they were entering themselves into a free lottery. According to Volkswagen Sweden, which sponsored the experiment, drivers' average speed during the trial dropped from 32 kilometers per hour, or about 20 mph, to 25 kph, or 15.5 mph, even though the sign was part of an experiment—the system wasn't actually levying fines or paying out jackpots.[8]

Many critics write off gamification, turning the word itself into a term of derision that suggests a race to the bottom via "flawed pop behaviorism."[9] *Sim City* designer Will Wright once complained, "Game elements aren't the monosodium glutamate of fun that you can simply add to an activity to make it motivating and engaging."[10] But teachers, who must leverage productive behaviors again and again from sometimes unwilling students, might take a more broad view. Those who have tried such ideas tend to see the game layer as a set of lightweight behavioral training wheels that helps kids establish healthy attitudes while they come to understand the value of the material itself. It is a tricky distinction and even a few teachers say they're uncomfortable with the idea. Constrained play, they say, is no play at all. (We'll get to that in Chapter 8.)

But even when games find their way into a traditional school setting, they're hardly an automatic solution. When the stakes are too high, the game becomes a crushing competition that's fun for spectators but a chore for most students. Think of your typical spelling bee, with its public humiliation and permadeath "one-mistake-and-you're-out" rule. When the stakes are too low—well, actually the stakes can't get too low, and perhaps this is the point.

Schools have long relied on games—they call them sports, clubs, and band competitions—to get students excited about coming to school. In fact, these are often all that keep kids there long enough to graduate. But schools have rarely used academic competition to reach more than just a few top students, even though research suggests that kids who *aren't* at the top would benefit most from it. As far back as 1959, sociologist James Coleman was urging schools to use competition as a way to change students' attitudes about academics. At the time, he was head of Johns Hopkins University's Department of Social Relations (later renamed the Department of Sociology). He'd just spent two years studying nine Midwestern high schools and found that more than 40 percent of boys wanted to be remembered in school as a "star athlete," but fewer than 30 percent favored the epithet "brilliant student." This despite the fact, Coleman observed, that school is "an institution explicitly designed to train students, not athletes."[11]

In schools from the inner city to the most privileged suburbs, Coleman discovered one key similarity: kids were intensely social, spending most of their free time playing sports and hanging out. "Adults often forget how 'person-oriented' children are," he wrote. "They have not yet moved into the world of cold impersonality in which many adults live." The paradox of modern schooling after World War II, he said, was that just as our complex industrial society made formal education more important, adolescent culture was shifting teens' attention away from education, prompting adolescents to squeeze "maximum rewards for minimal effort." Like factory workers or prison inmates, to which Coleman directly compared them, high school students in the 1950s had responded to school's demands by "holding down effort to a level which can be maintained by all."[12] They were protecting themselves from extra work by ostracizing high achievers.

It was, Coleman suggested, a rational response to a system whose rewards sat on a bell curve. Schools had created a kind of free market in which every student was competing against every other student for relative rank. Grades, he found, were almost completely relative—when one student achieved more, it "not only raises his position, but in effect lowers the position of others."[13] The result, even in the best suburban schools, was intense social pressure to minimize, not maximize, studying.

But these same students didn't think twice about honoring athletes. Coleman theorized that because most athletic events pit school against school, star athletes' achievements bring prestige to the entire school, which benefits everyone. A student spending her lunch hour studying "is regarded as someone a little odd, or different," he wrote. But the basketball player who shoots baskets at lunch "is watched with interest and admiration, not with derision."[14] So Coleman proposed that schools replace the competition for grades with interscholastic academic games, "systematically organized competitions, tournaments and meets in all activities,"[15] from math and English to home economics and industrial arts. These competitions, he predicted, would get both students and the general public more focused on academics and ensure all students a better education.

Coleman would later go on to lead the team charged by Congress with looking at school conditions and achievement data across the United States. It produced the 1966 study *Equality of Educational Opportunity*. Popularly known as the Coleman Report, it concluded that black-white segregation was pervasive in many areas, especially in the South, where it was "nearly complete," noted author Sarah Garland.[16] It popularized the idea that a student's at-home life mattered more than what happened at school. Most significantly, Coleman asserted that disadvantaged black students would do better academically if they attended schools in which the majority of their classmates were white. The report, required under the Civil Rights Act of 1964, gave President Lyndon Johnson a mandate to push harder on segregation, Garland wrote, codifying "what a desegregated school district should look like."[17] The Coleman Report would change American schooling forever, providing the theoretical basis for court-ordered busing plans and widespread "white flight" to suburbs in the 1960s and 1970s. It's largely considered the most important educational research document of the twentieth century, but in a follow-up study nearly a decade later, Coleman concluded that busing had become an empty exercise. As political support for busing waned, many civil rights leaders, policy makers, and educators who had supported Coleman's recommendations "blasted him for abandoning his earlier commitment to desegregation," wrote journalist Barbara J. Kiviat. A few members of the American Sociological Association even moved to have Coleman expelled from the group. In the end the campaign sputtered, and in 1991 Coleman was elected ASA's president.[18]

Even as schools redrew their boundaries, fired African American teachers and principals,[19] and tore up foundational structures to comply with desegregation orders, they largely ignored Coleman's earlier research on motivation and academic achievement, which found that competition "has a magic ability to create a strong group goal."

Every so often at Walker Mill Middle School in Capitol Heights, Maryland, a working-class suburb on the eastern edge of Washington,

D.C., Principal Nicole Clifton spends the four minutes between classes peering into monitors that display the school's security camera feeds. She switches on the public address system microphone and calmly describes to everyone what she sees: a sea of students, virtually all of them African American, all wearing maroon or Navy blue golf shirts, making their way to class. "Second floor, looking good," she said one recent morning, her approval reverberating throughout the hallways. "Looking at the camera, thank you for your co-oper-*a*-tion."

School administrators like Clifton long ago perfected that every-thought-in-a-single-sentence cadence, and as the clock ran down she warned, in one breath, "Still a few stragglers, still a few stragglers, we have five seconds left to get out of the hallway, students, you have five seconds to get into your classrooms and seated, three, two, and one." She finally took a breath and then, as if emceeing a quiz show, instructed adult monitors to sweep the hallways and corral the strays down to the front lobby for detention.

In Room 106, Timonious Downing was doing his best to ignore the cacophony. His students had made it to class and sat down long ago, and now they were just enduring the ceremony playing out on the PA system. What they were really looking forward to, what they looked forward to every day, was the computer-generated Random Event. For a few students, it was the highlight of their day. If Downing somehow forgets to produce a Random Event in each class period, his students will insist—they won't leave the classroom until he keeps his promise.

Like many teachers these days, Downing had affixed a copy of his college diploma (in his case, from Morehouse College) in a prominent place—he slapped it onto the front of his desk. Powerfully built with his head shaved, Downing was dressed in a crisp brown shirt and standard-teacher-issue Geoffrey Beene wool striped tie, his gray leather shoes casual enough to pass for fancy sneakers. He peered out from behind thick black-framed eyeglasses, his thin Vandyke beard and moustache clipped into submission. He stepped up to his Macintosh laptop and asked if students were ready for the Random Event. Yes, they said, they were.

Downing was field-testing what may be the strangest, most sophisticated game layer ever applied to the day-to-day routine of school. It all but replaced the typical student-teacher relationship with a point-based behavioral program that coaxes students into carrying their weight in class and working together. They gain "experience points" (XP) and "health points" (HP) by doing what's required in class each day: Answer a question correctly and you earn sixty. Help a friend with his classwork, you earn seventy-five.

But the system cuts both ways. Arrive late to class or argue with the teacher and you lose ten HP. Hand in incomplete homework, lose thirty. Lose enough points and you'll "fall in battle," which could possibly hand you over to school-based authorities for a typical punishment, such as Saturday detention. On the other hand, if you earn enough XP, life in class becomes very, very sweet. Depending on what kind of character you've chosen to play as, you're eventually given very real, very coveted powers: You're allowed to arrive late to class, eat a snack, listen to music, hand in assignments late or even get extra time on tests, all rewards that can be customized by teachers. You can also help out struggling classmates by "taking damage" when they misbehave or otherwise mess up. Such powers only come after students have spent months earning XP and leveling up.

A twenty-eight-year-old Canadian physics teacher named Shawn Young dreamed up the scheme, quite by accident one day in early 2012, when one of his students answered a question correctly during class. Young knew the boy was an ardent video-gamer, so he joked, "You know, if this was a game, you would get XP."

"Well," the boy replied, "it would be fun if it *were* a game."

Young thought, *Hmmm.*

The class discussion soon shifted to what "powers" students would like to earn for all that XP, less an attempt at problem solving than a thought experiment about how to make school *more fun*. Over the next few weeks, Young began to draw up rules for an "augmented reality" laid over the top of the typical classroom. He talked to students about what powers they'd like to earn in class, and, inspired by *World of Warcraft,* he created what were essentially mini-guilds in each class. Every team member would play as one of three archetypal roles—warrior, healer, or mage. Each role held different powers and vulnerabilities, but every team needed at least one of each. He built a bare-bones game that was more Excel spreadsheet than anything else. He also renamed the teacher "the game master." Young called his invention *Classcraft* and put out a call to colleagues to see if any were interested in piloting it.

Like many teachers, Young had long believed that school resembles nothing so much as a badly designed game. The behavioral incentives are all wrong and the feedback mechanism is so delayed it's essentially broken. The typical classroom—even the typical Canadian classroom—hasn't been modernized in a hundred years. "It was well designed in the 1900s, the turn of the century, but school hasn't evolved," he said.[20] Could a game redesign the baseline experience of school?

The roots of the modern school system lay in late-nineteenth-century management ideas developed for factories, huge halls of efficiency born in a "highly practical age" and designed to turn out standardized products as quickly and cheaply as possible. Progressives of the era loved the transparency and efficiency of corporations, which at the time held the same place in the public imagination that high-tech startups do now. Quite naturally, reformers of the day pushed to make schools operate more like factories. They brought in professional "superintendents" meant to run floor operations more efficiently, independently of politically connected school boards. Never mind the fact that underlying much efficiency thinking of the time was a kind of creeping anti-intellectualism that saw book learning as nearly irrelevant. Andrew Carnegie once famously said that for most college students, learning Greek and Latin was "of no more practical use to them than Choctaw."[21] But the efficiency idea scratched an itch of American business interests, who saw taxpayer-supported public schools as "a colossal and needless waste of human energy."[22] Educators, eager to shake off such labels, gladly complied. Frank Spaulding, superintendent of schools in Newton, Massachusetts, soon extracted the price of each of his schools' "important products or results," calculating, for instance, that he was buying 5.9 pupil recitations of Greek for a dollar. He complained, "The price must go down, or we shall invest in something else."[23]

The efficiency model actually worked pretty well through much of the first half of the twentieth century, when schools' missions were to produce a better factory worker. But now, more than 100 years later, Young and many other educators say the model is broken. Students today need to know why they're doing what they're doing, how well they're doing it, and what it all means. They need to learn how to experiment with ideas. "Learning is about getting feedback and then acting on that feedback," Young said. "The more feedback they have, the more they're likely to learn."

A "pretty big gamer all of my life," Young had experimented with different schemes to encourage collaboration, but hadn't quite hit on the right one. One time he paired up all of his math students, strong ones with weaker ones, and told the pairs that on every test they'd be graded using the lower-scoring student's score. "I was pretty hardcore," he said, but the idea was clear: to motivate stronger students to help weaker ones, and to motivate weaker students to work harder. He ended the experiment after a semester, but the idea lingered: how could he push his students to work *together*?

Like Coleman, Young said most adults don't understand how strongly kids feel the need to be part of a group, fighting together for a common cause. In that sense, letter or percentage grades "are horrible as general motivators," especially for struggling students. Going from a D to a B in a class is such a long-term endeavor, he said, that most feel it's a lost cause. "If you've had D's for five years, you're convinced you're a D student and you'll always have D's, because even if you do more work it's not going to have an immediate repercussion." *Classcraft,* he hoped, would help break the cycle. As kids level up, they actually pay less attention to grades and more attention to keeping their team alive. Part of what makes it successful is that the game's rewards and penalties have real meaning for students. "That process was there since the beginning," Young said, his Canadian accent peeking through—he pronounces it "*pro*-cess."

After a brief pilot, Young officially launched Classcraft in August 2014 and soon boasted 75,000 users in 50 countries, with the platform translated into 7 languages. When I spoke with him in late 2014, he was signing up 150 teachers a day, mostly through word of mouth. Virtually all of the teachers using it said it increased student engagement and fostered constructive, collaborative behavior in class.

Along the way, his students came up with the idea of the Random Event. Simply put, they wanted another layer to the game that made stuff happen each day in class, something weird and wonderful and totally non-negotiable, something *not* controlled by the teacher. "I said, 'OK, let's have stuff happen." He had them draw up a list, which soon grew to around 300 ideas. His only guideline was that each one had to be able to take place *that day*. For each pleasing event there had to be a corresponding displeasing one. He especially remembers one cold Canadian February morning when the game randomly ordered him to throw open the classroom windows. "There's kind of this feeling of surprise and delight," Young said. It also added another layer of tension that got kids to sit up straight. If the teacher respects it, the kids will get behind it. "They feel like it's a fair system."

As a science teacher, he said, "Whenever I tell the kids, 'This is the first time I've done this, I don't know what's going to happen,' they get really excited because they feel like it's not a controlled, prepared experience. It's something completely new. And I think the events distill that in a little way, that idea that we're all here living an experience and it's not just something we could watch on TV."

Standing at his laptop back in Maryland, Timonious Downing was enjoying the moment. "What's . . . today's . . . event?" he said. His hand hovered above the keyboard, drawing out the suspense. A fifteen-year classroom veteran, Downing had recently begun experimenting with "flipping" his English classes, recording his lessons on digital video and uploading them to a website so his students, all seventh graders, could watch them at home, then come to school and do their homework under his gaze. His laptop was connected to a projector, and the class watched intently as he said, "Hopefully I don't have to sing today." A few days earlier, the program had instructed him to sing a song of a student's choice and the student chose a Katy Perry song. He didn't remember which one.

By the time I met him, Downing had been testing out *Classcraft* for more than three months and had come to rely on it so heavily that he didn't even call on students to raise their hands in class anymore—he let the "Wheel of Destiny" (previously known as the "Celestial Selector") pick someone, which is probably a good idea—classroom management research suggests that randomly calling on students, rather than simply calling those whose hands are up, is an effective way to keep them on their toes. Waiting to see that all eyes were on him, Downing clicked the Random Event button and the screen read, "Glory to Warriors: A group of warriors is seduced by ladies—all warriors get a hundred XP." The class erupted in pandemonium. A hundred XP! Downing had to take a few moments to quiet them down. "Three, two, one," he said, echoing the principal's warning for order.

Earlier that morning, in first period, the computer randomly picked one of Downing's students and declared that she had "accidentally drunk poison" and wouldn't earn XP that day. It also ordered the entire class to call the student "Butterfly" for the rest of the period. The chosen student, a compact girl named Kaila, sat quietly, her hair pulled back with a little purple tie, her school ID held on a Howard University lanyard. Pink earbuds in her ears, she worked on an assignment in her school-issued Chromebook. "It's OK," she said, "I like butterflies." But it was clear that losing all that XP carried a little sting. Or maybe it was the silly nickname, or the fervor with which her classmates yelled, *"Butterfly!"* each time they called her name. She admitted that she'd been upset a few minutes ago, but "not anymore." She just hoped the name wouldn't stick.

............................➤

FIVE

MATH WITHOUT WORDS

How Euclid Would Have Taught
Math If He'd Had an iPad

Luis Zepeda is relentless. Nine years old and finally losing his chubby cheeks, he has been sitting in front of a computer screen, poking at the same math problem, for close to five minutes now. He's surrounded by his fourth-grade classmates in a large prefab building dubbed the "Learning Lab" at Rocketship *Sí Se Puede* Academy, a charter elementary school in San Jose, California. "*Sí se puede*," a longtime rallying cry for Hispanic farm workers in the Southwest, is Spanish for "Yes we can," but the way Luis is working, the place might as well be called *Trata Otra Vez*. "Try again."

As we're seeing, the games-in-school movement is built on several principles, but perhaps most essential among them is this: we must lower the cost of failure. This was distilled beautifully by Irish playwright Samuel Beckett, a man who knew a thing about trying again. "Ever tried. Ever failed," he wrote. "No matter. Try again. Fail again. Fail better."

The devilish little puzzle that Luis is trying to solve is built around rectangles' axes of symmetry, and as he tries solution after solution, his friend Brian Aguilera appears behind his chair. As kids do, he begins offering unsolicited advice. Brian, who says the software helps him beat his brother at math, pokes the screen with an index finger and suggests a multistep solution. Luis tries it, but it doesn't work. Their teacher, who could offer help, is nowhere in sight. Luis keeps trying. A glance in every direction reveals the same thing: kids working independently, tiny headphones over their ears and the reflections of computer screens in their eyes.

I've pulled a chair up behind Luis and Brian to watch and I blink at the problem, thinking, *Surely fourth-grade math can't be this hard*. I offer an obvious suggestion and Luis glances over at me, wondering who exactly I am. He tries it, but my solution doesn't work any better than Brian's or any of the others he has already attempted. I apologize, but I sense he's had plenty of experience with meddling adults. The school gets hundreds of visitors a year, and many of them come after hearing tales of what happens in the Learning Lab. Eventually Brian loses interest and wanders away. I sit by for a while, but I can't solve the problem and my mind drifts. Luis keeps at it, quietly restarting the puzzle each time a solution fails. Finally, after another ten minutes of work, he cracks the code and it all seems so simple, so elegant, as if the solution had been hiding there, in plain sight, all along. He restarts the level and shows me how he did it. Of course!

Onscreen, Luis's reward appears almost immediately: another, harder puzzle.

Actually, before that happens, a certain cross-eyed penguin appears. It's JiJi, who thrilled the students in Washington, D.C. She passes wordlessly from left to right, then disappears. All around the room, each time someone solves a puzzle, from the simplest to the most stunningly difficult, the same thing happens again and again in an endless cycle. "It's almost Zen-like in its simplicity," said *Sí Se Puede* principal Andrew Elliot-Chandler. "You just want to move that penguin across the screen, fundamentally, and the kids love it."[1] A week after parent Juan Carlos Martinez enrolled his children in a neighboring Rocketship school, his daughter Vivian came home and said she'd experienced a breakthrough in math. "I asked, 'How did your teacher show you?'" Martinez said. "She said it wasn't the teacher. It was the penguin."[2]

The school sits on an impossibly thin sliver of city-owned property in the shadow of an on-ramp to I-680, the highway that cuts through the east side of the San Jose. Built in 2009 using a carefully placed series of prefab buildings, some of which had to be lowered into place piece by piece from the highway, *Sí Se Puede* serves more than 650 students, with an overwhelmingly low-income population. Nine in ten students qualify for free or reduced-price lunches via the federal government, and for nearly two-thirds, English is a second language. *Sí Se Puede* is the second of eight original Rocketship schools, a chain that has carved out a striking niche in the charter school world. As a group they've set themselves the task of eliminating the United States' achievement gap by 2030. They share an unquenchable thirst for young, inexperienced teachers—the chain has become one of the main consumers of both current and former "corps members" of the teacher-training program Teach For America, known widely by its acronym, TFA. Journalist Richard Whitmire, who spent an entire school year in Rocketship classrooms, called TFA the chain's "de facto personnel department."[3] Elliot Chandler was thirty when I met him, and he'd opened the school three years earlier.

Starting from eight schools in Silicon Valley, the first of which opened in 2007, Rocketship plans 60 nationwide by 2018, serving 25,000 students—that's actually a heavily scaled-back version of its original, nearly metastatic growth plan, which called for 2,000 schools, 50 cities and 1 million students by 2020. That would have made it as big as the New York City school system, the largest in the nation. Even with the scaled-back plans, Rocketship has grown so quickly that it created its own real estate development corporation.

Perhaps most significantly, Rocketship has pioneered an approach to instruction that has become key to the schools' success. Because kids like Luis spend time with games and simulations to learn and practice their basic skills, classroom teachers have more time to teach big ideas. Charlie Bufalino, Rocketship's national development associate, called it "buying back those minutes for teachers," and it shows in obvious fashion: In a nearby kindergarten classroom, a teacher holds out an illustrated book and asks her class, "How did the characters in the story seem *empathetic?*" In another class, a visiting scientist stands at a whiteboard and admits that his hypothesis, about a hammer and feather falling at different rates on the moon, is wrong. "But that's OK," he says. "It's OK if your hypothesis is wrong. You're guessing. That's why we do experiments, because we want to know how things work."

As I watch Luis and his classmates work, Andrea Chrisman, a fourth-grade math and literacy teacher, strides into the lab with a paperback copy of the children's novel *Island of the Blue Dolphins* under her arm. I ask her how she feels about all the screen time—a game at that moment is teaching a few of her students about basic grammar and punctuation, as well as math. "I don't have to spend my time teaching homophones," she said. "If a computer can do that, I can talk about themes in books."

The chain may even be pushing the field forward. In March 2010, after Netflix CEO Reed Hastings, one of Rocketship's early supporters, stopped by and saw students working through math problems with an adaptive game called *DreamBox Learning,* he e-mailed his old friend, software engineer Dan Kerns, who was DreamBox's chief architect, to tell him how much he liked the software. The two had worked together years earlier, and Kerns wrote back saying that, actually, the four-year-old startup was in trouble. It couldn't compete with huge textbook publishers and was facing an almost certain shutdown. They hadn't paid employees in months. Hastings bought the company, then gave it to the nonprofit Charter School Growth Fund, a gift worth about $11 million. The purchase helped turn DreamBox around, but Hastings, a former president of the California State Board of Education, said he didn't want to own the company. "I'm still active in California education politics," he said. "I didn't want people to think I was doing this to make more money."[4] DreamBox is now one of the most talked-about educational games studios and Hastings now sits on its board, as does Rocketship co-founder John Danner.

Since 2011, Rocketship has experimented with variations on the Learning Lab, in some cases scrapping it altogether and moving sets of computers into classrooms. But on this day, about 130 students—nearly one-fifth of the entire student body—sit quietly, working through exercises on desktop computers, each student separated from his or her neighbor by a brightly hand-painted plywood partition. Classes move in and out constantly, but once students settle in and stretch pint-sized headphones over their ears, the room takes on the hushed charm of a prep-school study hall during final exams. At first glance it seems that everyone is doing exactly the same thing, but watch a row of students for a few minutes and you quickly realize that even if they start out on the same exercise, each student works at a different pace. Soon each one is working on different skills.

That's more significant than it seems, said Principal Elliot-Chandler. A student's skill level should be a private matter, between him and the teacher, and students who are behind should be able to work comfortably, without embarrassment. "They know they should know more. They know they should not be working on tens and ones when their friends are doing division and fractions and all that, and there's no shame in working on it with the computer." Actually, the same principle applies to kids who are off-the-charts advanced: if they just want to relax and do high-level work without the stigma of being a brainiac, he said, "Nobody needs to know."

That particular morning, Luis was moving through exercises thrown at him by *ST Math*, one of a small but well-regarded group of software tools that challenge students with a gradually escalating series of thousands of animated math puzzles. Part of a new breed of math games built around long-standing motivational research, *ST Math* and others like it may be the most pure expression of what computers can do for education. About half a million students in twenty-six states learn math through the games, supported by JiJi.

Matthew Peterson, the games' developer, said JiJi's little walk is less a reward than simply a clear indicator that the problem has been solved. "Your reward is that you solved the puzzle," he said. "That builds this joy of learning, the joy of problem-solving." He originally used a kangaroo named KiKi, but kids wondered why she didn't just jump over the obstacles. A penguin, he said, clearly needs your help. "It's kind of obvious to them that this little penguin is not going to try to make its way across anything that is remotely dangerous."[5] That builds engagement, which helps kids stick with problems longer and learn skills more fully. Though its scores on state reading, math, and science tests have dipped in recent years as it has experimented with different ways to teach basic skills, the school still outpaces other California elementary schools in all three areas. In math, 81 percent of students were proficient or higher in 2013, compared to 63 percent statewide.[6]

Kids naturally want to learn, Peterson said. "All kids have that drive to do something that's hard." Where schools go wrong is in demanding that they perform—on exams, in recitations, in groups—before they've mastered the material. Instead, he said, why not find a way to immerse them in the material, teaching and re-teaching key concepts in simple but enjoyable ways? "There are so many things wrong with math education, but if you picked one thing, it's persistence," he said. Peterson set out to encourage persistence with one simple fix: The only way to play his game is to do the math. Game play, he said, is not a reward for the drudgery of doing math. "The game *is* the math."[7]

The concept closely follows the most basic ideas of self-determination theory, which above all cautions against rewarding people for things they're already doing. "If you're doing something that you like to do and then someone starts giving you special prizes, you end up doing it for the prizes," Peterson said. "When prizes go away, you no longer like it."

As far back as 1999, Georgia Tech researcher Amy Bruckman pointed out that most attempts at making software both educational and fun "end up being neither." Most educational software, she wrote, was "all pretty much the same old junk: drill and practice." Fun is often treated like a sugar coating to the educational core, which "makes as much sense as chocolate-dipped broccoli."[8] Her sentiment, which has morphed into the ubiquitous and derisive phrase "chocolate-covered broccoli," has become a kind of rallying cry for people who don't like games that separate drill and practice from game play. Most educational titles rely on this approach, presenting little more than digital flash cards followed by an opportunity to shoot aliens or other assorted bad guys. British researchers in 2011 found that it doesn't work that well. They designed two versions of a math game called *Zombie Division*, one in which mastering math drove the game forward and another with play followed by a math quiz.[9] Both contained the same content, but students playing the first version learned more math. Given a choice between versions, those who played the first ended up spending seven times longer doing math.[10]

Peterson's games also set themselves apart in another way: they are almost entirely wordless. That's intentional. "In school, the way of conveying ideas is through *words*," he said. "A teacher walks up to the board, writes words, says words. Students receive books with words and are expected to respond to questions with words. The vast majority of teaching is done through words."[11] Peterson, who grew up dyslexic and didn't learn to read until he was in fifth grade, found that many students who are struggling to master math are also struggling to master English. Either it's not their native language, as with many students at *Sí Se Puede* and throughout California, or they have difficulties reading and processing language.

So he built his games around visual cues and animations, with conceptual understanding coming "before you even know how to talk about it." The ideas come first. This actually strengthens students' abilities to discuss the topics later on in the classroom, when their teacher puts words to the ideas. He called it "Math without Words," and it turns out he was not the only one thinking in this way.

❰ ··············

When he was in high school, Keith Devlin had a revelation: Math is not a spectator sport. It's not body of knowledge, it's not symbols on a page. It's something you play with, something you *do*.[12] He remembered reading Martin Gardner's legendary "Mathematical Games" column in *Scientific American*, which ran for twenty-five years, from 1956 to 1981. "Pretty much anyone in my generation who became a mathematician will say that one of the influences that made them do it was reading that column . . . because it was an incredible antidote to the drudgery of school mathematics that we had been subjected to."[13]

Devlin, who would go on to teach math at Stanford University, realized that, like Gardner, all great mathematicians spend much of their time *playing* with ideas. Actually, he realized, it's very similar to what musicians do. In both music and mathematics, the symbols on a page are merely static representations of mental processes, laid out on a flat surface for easy reference. Representing math symbolically makes it easy to record and pass on to others, but it's not the actual math.[14]

Because so many of us have intimate experiences listening to and even playing music, we know this instinctively. Twentieth-century technology, from the gramophone to the cassette tape to the MP3 player, has taken music off the page. But most of us believe that math is flat, that doing it involves nothing more than manipulation of symbols. Partly this is due to the lousy math education we received in school and partly to the image of mathematicians in popular culture. When most movies or TV shows want to show that a character is a mathematician, Devlin realized, they show him or her writing symbols on a piece of paper, on a blackboard, "or, quite likely, on a window or a bathroom mirror." Never mind that real mathematicians never write on glass. People identify doing math with writing symbols, often obscure ones. This "symbol barrier," as he dubbed it, being unable to get beyond the symbols to the math behind them, prevents most of us from going further than we could.

But just as no self-respecting pianist would have you believe that his musical education ended with the ability to read the notes in a score, no self-respecting mathematician would say the symbols on that the page are the actual math. Devlin remembered research from the early 1990s that looked at the math skills of young street vendors in the markets of Recife, Brazil. Faced with complex arithmetic, the children in the study, aged eight to fourteen, mastered it, in their heads, to 98 percent accuracy. But when researchers asked them to solve the same problems with paper and pencil, their accuracy dropped to less than 40 percent.[15] They were experiencing the math in their heads, free from symbols, almost perfectly. Subsequent experiments found that Americans in a southern California supermarket did much the same. Asked to perform similarly complex math in the aisles, they did fine. But their performance suffered if they were asked to sit at a table and take a "test" with exactly the same math. Devlin, the British-born author of thirty-two books and National Public Radio's longtime "Math Guy," wondered if there was some way to break free from the symbols. It was, he realized, an interface problem, one that music didn't have. He began to consider perhaps the most perfect musical interface of all: the piano.

Though it has become a naturalized part of music-making since the first one was built in 1710, the *pianoforte* (its name means "soft-loud") was a technical marvel for its time, a machine that changed music in ways that are hard to imagine. Computer pioneer Alan Kay once observed that any technological advance is "technology only for people who are born before it was invented," and in the case of the piano, this applies to no one alive today. Seymour Papert, the MIT researcher, concluded, "That's why we don't argue about whether the piano is corrupting music with technology."[16] Four hundred years later, few can play the piano well, but just about anybody can sit down at a piano, pluck out a simple tune and perhaps even sing along. Devlin realized that foremost among the piano's virtues was its ability to enable just about anyone to play *real music* from day one, on the same instrument that professionals use. You could go from absolute beginner to Carnegie Hall soloist on exactly the same instrument, sitting in the same room, over the course of a decade or two. The piano delivers instant feedback on your performance, allowing you to easily gauge your progress.[17] You must touch the piano to play music, but the more you do, the more you'll learn, naturally, about melody, harmony, consonance, and dissonance. It is, in a word, immersive.

If you're hoping to someday play Chopin *polonaises,* you should probably learn a few notes, scales, sharps, and flats, but none of these obstacles by necessity stands in the way of you playing real music. But let's say you learn the symbols and decide to tackle a Chopin *polonaise.* Faced with a section you can't play, you'd break it down into smaller bits and master each one at a slower tempo. No teacher on earth would suggest you practice on a simpler piano or, heaven forbid, just work it out with paper and pencil. If anything, a good teacher would double down on the *real* music. She'd play the passage for you, suggest you listen to a few recordings and urge you to practice the tricky parts over and over again. You'd live in the world of the music, your hands on the keys of the machine to give you access to the music and reproduce what's in your head.

Devlin realized that a good digital game could do the same thing, helping kids "play" mathematics in much the same way. At their heart, video games are "activity simulators with a dopamine reward system"[18] that could help kids strip problems down, analyze their underlying patterns, try out solutions and practice these skills repeatedly. "Video game worlds are not paper-and-pencil symbolic representations," he wrote, "they are imaginary worlds. They are meant to be lived in and experienced."[19] Because they bypass symbols, he realized, they could give kids direct access to the math.

They weren't just a good medium for math education—they were probably the *ideal* medium. What the printing press was to reading and mass literacy in the fifteenth century, he decided, video games are to math literacy in the twenty-first century. For a math teacher to not know how to use them, he decided, would someday be akin to teaching English without being able to read.[20]

"If video games had been around in 350 BC, Euclid would have made a video game," Devlin told me. The thirteen books of Euclid's *Elements* would have been the supplemental material, a PDF file that you could read if you wanted to. "People think I'm joking—I absolutely mean that. Euclid would not have written a textbook, he would have designed a video game." Peek at any of his proofs, Devlin said, and you'll quickly find that the great Greek mathematician, often called the father of geometry, is asking the reader to *do* things. "He says, 'Draw this arc,' 'Drop this perpendicular.' 'Bisect that line.' These are *actions,* and actions are what you get in video games."[21]

But when he looked at the popular math video games on the market, he found the same thing Peterson did: most were "forced marriages of video games with traditional instruction of basic skills,"[22] rat-race wheels built around repetitive practice, or digital flash cards that delivered traditional pedagogy onscreen, "a new canvas on which to pour symbols."[23] They were, he realized, no better than the textbooks they sought to replace. "If you look at the vast majority of the games—and there are hundreds and hundreds and hundreds of them—you don't learn much, but you practice what you've already learned." They reminded him of the first early motion pictures. When people first started making movies, they essentially just filmed stage plays because that's what they knew how to do. "But then they realized that making a movie meant something very different from doing a play on the stage."[24] Actually, a better model might be those disastrous turn-of-the-century flying machines that tried to recreate the flapping of birds' wings. The early aviators, he thought, confused the larger, more complex phenomenon of flying with the simpler act of flapping, the one activity they'd observed.[25] He realized that to create a good math game, you had to separate the activity from its familiar representations.

In 2010, a mutual friend got Devlin in touch with John Romero, one of the legendary group of video game designers who had essentially created the first-person shooter genre in the early 1990s with the groundbreaking *Doom* and *Quake* games. Romero and his former id Software partner John Carmack were once called "the Lennon and McCartney of video games,"[26] but a decade after he left the company, Romero was interested in finding out if it would be possible to embed high-quality mathematics instruction into a genuinely engaging game. He took on Devlin as a kind of informal math advisor, and for four years the two talked regularly, the Stanford math professor and the rock-star father of *Wolfenstein 3D*. The "stealth project" generated no new products, but Devlin cut his teeth throwing out ideas for games he thought would be fun, only to have them "destroyed within two minutes" by Romero. "There were good reasons why these things wouldn't work," he said with a laugh. "The simple one was that kids aren't going to play it unless you stand over them with a whip."[27]

Devlin wasn't sure if Romero ever got anything out of the conversations, but they must have lit a fire, because when Devlin formed a small startup to create math games, Romero volunteered to help. The company's first game, which debuted for iPhone and iPad in August 2013, invites players to pick a series of locks by spinning little number dials that add, subtract, or multiply increasingly complex number combinations, all without any of the calculation symbols present in math exercises. *Wuzzit Trouble* presents players with a dial that looks much like a sixty-minute clock face, only it goes up to sixty-five (remember that number!). Each level asks you to figure out the most efficient way to hit a series of target numbers etched into the dial face using little cogs tuned to multiples of smaller numbers. You spin the dial forward or backward by generating multiples of these smaller numbers, in the process using one, two, and sometimes all three mathematical operations. For instance, one early level asks you to pick the lock by hitting three targets—six, eighteen, and fifty-four—using multiples of six. Easy enough. But the following level presents three new targets—thirty-five, forty-seven, and fifty-nine—none of which is a multiple of six. You soon realize that the only way to hit these is to dial *backward* from sixty-five (sixty-five minus six is fifty-nine . . . fifty-nine minus eighteen is forty-seven, and so on). As the game gets increasingly harder, the carefree playing around with numbers turns more purposeful. What for many levels had been a kind of practiced plucking of low-hanging mental fruit starts to demand a ladder. Pretty soon you've got five targets to hit and three different cogs with which to hit them, all in six moves or less. Where to begin?

Inevitably, if you have any hope of beating these levels, you must start thinking strategically, looking at the big dial and little cogs as a *system*. You may even ask yourself, "How did the level designer decide that I could do this in six moves or less?" Then, as the levels get progressively harder—at some point, the game adds a fourth cog, opening up the possibility of millions of sequences— something remarkable happens. Trial and error, while they were fun for a while, are no longer good enough. Getting the dial to turn *just so* takes on a strange urgency that can only be satisfied by a precise, clever solution. But you can't be precise and clever unless you're immersed in the numbers, intimately familiar with them and the intervals between them. They're like notes on a scale and you're playing a chord.

As the intervals become more complex and the need to keep track of them becomes more urgent, arithmetic turns to algebra. You may even pull out a sheet of paper and a pencil and start scribbling figures down (please, no writing on glass). But in the end, you must translate the paper-and-pencil figures into action to make the dials turn. You're living in the world of the numbers, your hands on the keys of the machine to give you access to the math and reproduce what's in your head. To succeed in *Wuzzit Trouble,* you have to practice. But when it works it is elegant. When you come up with a complex solution, all you really want to do is see it again and show to your friends. *Watch this,* you say. It is a performance.

Forty-year-old Jean-Baptiste Huynh, the Vietnamese Frenchman living in Oslo who persuaded the entire country of Norway to spend a week solving algebra problems, looks quite a bit younger than he really is. He has a shock of dark hair, white teeth, a big smile, an athletic frame, and nearly boundless energy, and when I met him at a tiny café near Dupont Circle in Washington, D.C., during one of his visits to the United States, he could have passed for someone just a few years out of college. I wanted to ask him about his popular iPad algebra application *DragonBox*. It had been in Apple's App Store for several months by then, and everyone I knew was asking me if I'd played it. One friend had breathlessly told me I *had* to get it. *It teaches algebra to preschoolers,* he said. *It's amazing!* But as soon as I sat down, Huynh pulled a travel-worn iPad from his bag and he said he wanted to get one thing straight about *DragonBox*. "It's not an algebra app," he said, swiping the glass touchscreen to bring up the game. "It's not about algebra."[28]

By the time we met in the spring of 2013, *DragonBox* had already been downloaded about 85,000 times, mostly by parents, and Huynh had become convinced that the iPad's ability to let children access the material directly, as well as the app's straightforward pedagogy, made them "the single best resource I can use" to teach children. I soon learned that Huynh had that trifecta of a great teacher's personality: a passion for his students and his subject, a bit of a foul mouth, and a dry, balancing wit. During our conversation, I made the mistake of asking what he thought of the school system he'd attended in France as a young man. It had gotten him pretty far, I thought. "You know what? This is a fucking *prison*," he said. "Your brain is *dead* when you're in prison. You don't want to *be* there." He may have sensed my shock, so he smiled and said, "I come with very strong words because I am French. I can do that."[29]

Huynh explained that he and his colleagues at We Want To Know, the Norwegian game company he'd co-founded with French cognitive scientist Patrick Marchal, had been trying to decide whether to sell the game to schools, which were beginning to buy iPads at a steady clip. "That's the natural place to play this game," he said. "And we decided, 'No, we don't do that,' because teachers are going to say, 'You do *that,* you do *that.*'" In other words, he said, teachers would find a way to take the fun out of his fun little game.

So if *DragonBox* wasn't about algebra, I asked, what was it about?

Speed and imagination, he said.

"Mathematics is creativity. It's play. You take an object and you ask, 'What if?'" But that's not how it's taught in schools. "We teach it as a dead subject—like Latin. A dead language. You have fantastic texts, but it's a dead thing."

He remembered a conversation he had had recently with his four-year-old son, Paul. They'd gone out for the day and Huynh was carrying him on his shoulders as they arrived back at their Oslo apartment building. Paul said he wanted to push the buttons for the building's security code, so Huynh told him: "It's 'ten-ten'—'one-zero-one-zero.'"

His son leaned in and pressed "two-three-two-three."

"I have a lot of time," Huynh told me. "As a parent, I think it's important to have a lot of time. I say, 'Paul, why did you enter this code? The code is "one-zero-one-zero."' And then I realized: the way you learn is by experiencing all the possibilities. And it's quite natural and sensible to [press] 'two-three-two-three.' Why shouldn't it work?"

He thought about it and smiled. "This is extraordinary!"[30]

Huynh is as responsible as anyone for the recent surge in interest, here and abroad, in high-quality, imaginative math games for children. For a while, before several equally offbeat competitors began appearing in the App Store, *DragonBox* was the go-to app that smart parents with iPads were recommending to their friends. After it was released in mid-2012, *Wired* magazine's "Geek Dad" blogger Jonathan Liu played the game with his daughters and said he was impressed that it "doesn't give you the answers, but it enforces the rules." *DragonBox,* he wrote, "is making me reconsider all the times I've called an educational app 'innovative.'"[31] Which is all very surprising when you consider that Huynh, growing up, wasn't a gamer. He remembers playing a PC version of Romero's early first-person shooter game *Doom* and thinking, *What a waste of time!* "I don't know anything about games still," he said. "I don't play."

Huynh has already had at least three careers: he'd started out as a stock portfolio manager, but then he and his wife, a child psychiatrist, began having kids—when I met him, their children were four, nine, and twelve. "I guess I got this crisis that any people working in finance hit at some point," he said. "You want really to use your energy on something really useful. So I decided that I would do something for children." He quit his job and started a children's magazine, but after a few years decided he should really be teaching. He sold the magazine and took a job teaching high school math and economics in Spain.

He was a miserable failure.

Huynh remembers spending twenty-eight hours one time preparing for a two-hour lesson. The results showed that his students afterward were performing only "marginally better." He decided, much like Devlin, that the tools were holding him back. He needed something interactive that would give students control of the experience, that could help them access the math quickly and without fuss. "My own children, I want them to learn as fast as possible," he said. Years earlier, he'd read two books that had a profound effect on his thinking: tennis coach Tim Gallwey's 1974 book *The Inner Game of Tennis* and Betty Edwards's 1979 book *Drawing on the Right Side of the Brain*. Both focused on what it takes to improve at a craft, separating the analytic parts of our brain from those that get the work done. Both suggested a new approach to teaching, Huynh said: "The more words you use, the less impactful you are."

He began to investigate games, but at a kind of arms-length distance. "I'm not a fanatic, you know, 'Games, gamers, game-based learning.' I hate this. I consider it more like Montessori of the twenty-first century." All he really cared about, he said, was putting the child at the center of the learning process. "It's about experiences and *not* games."

Huynh basically had to get his wife's permission to develop the app. "I'm married to a child psychiatrist," he said. "No screens at home! No TV. No Nintendo, PlayStation, name it—nothing. *Nothing*. When I say to my wife, 'Well, I think I'm going to design some games because that's the best way to teach,' she says, '*No!*' I have to argue. I say, 'You *know* I'm doing that because that's the best way—you have the prison which is school. *Please,* let me do that!' She says, 'Well, OK, show me what you have.'"

Huynh made her a promise: Whatever he created, he told her, it would get the job done quickly, with a minimum of screen time. When the game finally appeared, many users said the same thing, both in praise and complaint: *DragonBox* was strange, lovely, and engaging. It got their kids thinking algebraically in six minutes, five minutes, four minutes! And it was over way too fast. In a way, Huynh was the victim of his own success.

Shortly after the game appeared, Huynh met University of Washington researcher Zoran Popović, director of the university's

Center for Game Science. Popović had made headlines around the world in 2011, after he and a colleague helped two graduate students design *Foldit,* an online, crowd-sourced game that challenged players, most of whom had little to no biomedical knowledge and most of whom played the online game across great distances, to learn about the shapes of proteins and compete to fold them into the most efficient shapes. Dubbed *"Tetris* on steroids" by one player, *Foldit* took advantage of humans' puzzle-solving skills, in the process helping researchers make advances in treating cancer, AIDS, and Alzheimer's disease, among others. In a 2011 paper published in the journal *Nature Structural and Molecular Biology,* Popović shared authorship with eleven other researchers and two *Foldit* players' groups, one calling itself the "*Foldit* Void Crushers Group." In one of the game's more recent challenges, players analyzed a monkey HIV protein whose structure had eluded scientists for fifteen years. One far-flung team of *Foldit* players figured it out in ten days.[32]

Popović got the idea to use *DragonBox* to challenge large groups of children to work through thousands of online algebra problems, on deadline. He adapted the game to offer more help to students who needed it while allowing those who understood a concept to move on. In an early trial, 93 percent of students mastered the basic ideas after only ninety minutes of play.[33] In June 2013, he and Huynh persuaded more than 4,000 students in Washington State to spend a five-day work week solving algebra problems. The students continued after Friday rolled around, spending the equivalent of more than seven months doing math. In the end, they solved nearly 391,000 problems. A few months later, students in Wisconsin solved nearly 645,000 problems.[34] In January 2014, in Norway, students solved nearly 8 million equations. Nearly 40 percent of the work, Popović's team found, was done at home. "To us this is very exciting because it shows the engagement way beyond the brick-and-mortar school day," he said.[35]

DragonBox has undergone several modifications and expansions since it first appeared—a new version, which tackles geometry, came out in the spring of 2014—but it is still lovely, mysterious and a bit off center. One critic, *Forbes* games writer Jordan Shapiro, praised its "avatars that were simultaneously sweet and a little twisted."[36] And despite what Huynh insists, families are buying it to get their kids—in many cases their preschoolers—thinking algebraically. The game presents players with an odd little scenario: a mysterious box arrives, for no apparent reason, with a wide-eyed, omnivorous baby dragon inside, packed in straw. Also for no apparent reason, the dragon wants to be alone. He must be alone before he'll eat. Don't ask, just play.

The game board is divided into two sides, with your little dragon-in-a-box on one side. On both sides are "cards"—random images of lizards, horned beetles, deep-sea fish, and angry tomatoes. Again, don't ask. To win each level, you must touch and tap and drag the cards to get rid of all of those on the dragon's side. Once you do, he noisily eats everything that remains on the other side and the level is done. "The box is alone!" the game declares. The game is strange, but you keep playing. Soon you're encountering "night-cards" with darkened versions of the creatures that, you learn, will soon stand in for negative numbers. Pretty soon you're strategizing which cards to get rid of first—order of operations, anyone? On level twelve, one of the animal cards has mysteriously been replaced by a little black "a." Five levels later, there's a "c." Finally, on level eighteen, the little wooden dragon box is momentarily replaced by a floating letter "x." You're doing proto-algebra. It's been about three minutes since you downloaded the game.

This strange procession continues through 100 levels, with no explanation or elaboration. Addition, multiplication, division, fractions—all of them appear, without fanfare or explanation. You play sixty levels before an "equals" sign appears between the two sides of the board. By game's end, at level 100, you've moved seamlessly, baby step by baby step, from a cute baby dragon eating a spiky two-headed lizard, to this: "2 over x plus d over e equals b over x," which you solve, fearlessly and perhaps even a bit impatiently, in exactly fourteen steps. You are four years old.

····························>

SIX

RUBE GOLDBERG BROUGHT US TOGETHER

How a Group of New York City Teachers and Game Designers Are Redefining School

The rules of Triple Turbo Ball, or TTB, are simple. The game is played on a real wooden indoor basketball court with two teams of seven players apiece, and the object is to score fifty points before the opposing team does, though the winning score can be negotiated beforehand. TTB is untimed and is played with a small foam ball. Points can be scored either by throwing the ball through the opponent's hoop, kicking or throwing it into the opponent's guarded soccer goal, or throwing a touchdown pass to any team member standing in the small square end zone located to the left of each hoop. Any player in possession of the ball may dribble it three times, with hands or feet, before passing or attempting to score. Players may bounce the ball off of any wall at any time, including during touchdown attempts.

Seventh graders at New York City's Quest to Learn middle school, dissatisfied with their low-scoring pickup basketball games and inspired by a no-dribble, two-ball basketball variation they were already playing, created TTB during a five-day frenzy of invention in June 2014. "One kid who's interested in football, he might want to be a receiver," said Tyler Spielberg, the twenty-five-year-old wellness teacher who presided over the experiment. "Some kid who wants to play basketball, he might try to score on the basketball hoop. It's pretty cool." In end, Spielberg said, "We made up the game that we wanted."[1]

Triple Turbo Ball was born during final-exam week—to be precise, the game *was* the final exam, or to be more precise, the final project. Over the course of the week, fourteen students—all of them boys—designed, play-tested, and refined Triple Turbo Ball. On the sixth day, they showed it off repeatedly as classmates, teachers, and parents filed through the overheated seventh-story gym that the school shares with a handful of other small, specialized schools, all of them high schools.

Housed on two floors of the eighty-five-year-old Straubenmuller Textile High School building in Manhattan's Chelsea neighborhood, Quest to Learn, or simply "Quest," as it's often called, is the most closely watched games-in-education experiment in the United States and probably the world. The entire time I was reporting this book, whenever I told people I was writing about games and education they would ask if I'd heard of "that video-game school in New York City." I had, thanks. What I didn't realize until I'd spent some time there was that "video-game school" was an entirely inaccurate description, and probably wishful thinking on the part of a lot of people. For a video-game school, it had surprisingly few video games—actually, I never once saw a child operating a game console, though I did see the occasional kid on a laptop, bending the open-world game *Minecraft* to his will, or poking at *Motion Math* on an iPad. Mostly, I saw kids *doing* things: making movies, designing clothes, writing research proposals, building contraptions, arguing over the rules of board games, and, on occasion, testing out their friends' homemade obstacle courses. Like most places dispensing big ideas, Quest's vision and its reality were more complicated than people realized. Like most public schools, Quest is not perfect, and on some days it can feel quite ordinary. But like the best games its creators admire, it exerts a kind of quiet pull that is hard to describe. There's a purposefulness that captures the imagination and won't let go. Quite simply, it feels alive.

When kids step through the doors—or, more likely, when they step out of one of the big, dodgy elevators—they are confronted with a world that feels somehow separate and apart from the real world. One laminated sign reads, "Failure is reframed as iteration." Another, hand-lettered, reads, "There is always another way." This begins to make sense when you consider that one of Quest's co-founders, the game designer and theorist Katie Salen, is the same person who helped popularize the idea of the "magic circle" among game designers a decade ago. "We wanted kids to feel that when they stepped into school they were stepping into a space that was not the ordinary world," she told me. "Not that it was like magic or fantasy, but this place has a set of rules that organize how it works, and part of your job is to understand that."[2]

Names, it turns out, are important. Students call teachers by their first names, and teachers teach courses with odd-sounding names like *Codeworlds, Sports for the Mind,* and *Being, Space, and Place.* The weird names can seem precious at first—Codeworlds, it turns out, is simply an integrated math and English class—but Salen insists that she and the school's other designers "didn't name the classes weird things just to do it. We're trying to signal that there is something quite specific about the way we're thinking about disciplines in this school."[3] The subjects are, of course, interrelated and equally required when solving big problems or working on big projects. But because kids may be the only ones in their family who understand the significance of each course name, they must explain it to their parents when report cards come home or when dad asks for the fifth time this semester what's happening in English class. In a small but key way, the students act as experts who end up interpreting the school's mission. One student told a visitor in 2012 that school was fun, but that the biggest difference between Quest and his previous school was simple: "In this class, everybody's mainly awake."[4]

What most clearly separates Quest from your typical public school, and what first interested me in it, is an innovation that is at once both brilliant and a little nuts: an experimental endeavor, housed in a dingy fourth-floor office, called Mission Lab. A seven-person staff, including three full-time game designers and three learning designers (two of them full-time) originally worked there five days a week—and often 24/7 by text and cell phone—to help teachers build lessons around games and to help students create their own games. The group now works mostly part-time at Quest, spending the balance of their workweek training teachers in other schools. But in essence they're teaching the "habits of mind" of game designers within the walls of a public school, often through paper prototypes. The positions are privately funded by the Institute of Play and the designers, as one of them once told me, tend to take on the persona of "the cool uncle version of a teacher," interacting with kids on a more informal level. The result is a school that's steeped in invention, where teachers have the luxury of asking their students not to memorize the Pythagorean Theorem but to discover it.

Borrowing from the tradition of video games that get harder and harder and, finally, a bit too hard, Salen and the other cofounders crafted the framework for the end-of-semester projects—Triple Turbo Ball was one—as a summation of skills that kids develop throughout the year. In many video games, the difficulty ratchets up until the last level, when the player encounters the "Boss." You've likely encountered it without even knowing. It's Hitler in a robotic suit at the end of *Wolfenstein 3-D* or any big, bad, nearly indestructible monster, the one who repeatedly kicks your butt at the climax of your favorite iPad tower defense game. The Boss is the ultimate obstacle, the biggest bad guy, the villain who won't let you pass without one last, all-consuming, punishing fight. While you're in the thick of it, fighting the Boss usually feels insane, but beating the boss always feels transcendent. Salen and her colleagues dubbed the final projects "Boss Level."

In real life, this was middle school and it was springtime, so many of the projects were short of transcendent. But like the basketball variation, each one had students' peculiar interests and fingerprints all over it. Before I got to the gym that morning, I watched another group of seventh graders, each with a laptop, show off computer models of sewage systems they'd built, block by block, entirely in *Minecraft*. They had, it seems, spent the entire week voluntarily exploring and recreating, in painstaking detail, how sewers work. Outside, in the student commons area, a group of girls showed off clothing they'd designed using recycled materials, and in a room down the hall, another group showed off a self-produced "mockumentary" that poked fun at tourists' misconceptions about New York City. They created the characters, dressed them up, and filmed throughout midtown Manhattan—the routines were almost entirely improvised—then edited them down to a trim twenty-two minutes and forty-six seconds. One character assured his interviewer, "All of Times Square is destroyed on New Year's Eve, and they just *rebuild* it." Another, offering advice for future tourists, said, "If you see any squirrels, they're *not* to eat."[5]

As it was originally envisioned, Boss Level was a three-times-a-year, two-week intensive in which students and teachers integrated the work of the previous ten weeks. In Salen's eyes, it resembled a kind of graduate-level research project, complete with a public defense of the results. But pressures from both inside and outside the school have trimmed it to a one-week project just twice a year, and though the exhibitions are public, every time I ever observed, the school had the atmosphere of a carnival, not a dissertation defense. At the Triple Turbo Ball exhibition, I fell into a brief conversation in the gym with Evan Klein, the school's assistant principal. Like me, he had wandered in and found a space to stand behind one of the soccer goals. We watched as students played hard and spectators, lining the wall nearest to the door, followed the game as intently as they could without a scoreboard. I told him I was impressed that there was so much interest in the game and, for that matter, in all of the exhibits. The carnival atmosphere, I said, seemed somehow contagious.

"You know," Klein said, "this is the last day of school."

Like much at Quest, all of the projects, from the basketball to the sewage system, seemed intent on exploring one key question: what happens if we take apart a system and put it back together? This deconstruction/reconstruction process, it turns out, is what games do best.

Ever since Minneapolis middle schoolers in December 1971 stared at a teletype printout and pecked out their answer to the question, "Do you want to eat (1) poorly (2) moderately or (3) well?" games have been tempting students to engage in what's known as systems thinking. Forsaking the rote memorization that passes for learning in most schools, *The Oregon Trail* demanded that students

consider how the parts of a system work together, how one decision affects another and how everything affects the whole. Developed originally as a board game by a twenty-one-year-old history
teacher named Don Rawitsch, *The Oregon Trail* became a primitive electronic game in the fall of 1971, when Rawitsch was assigned to teach a unit on westward expansion. He didn't want his
students simply to read about it in a textbook, but decided that if
he showed them a John Wayne movie, "they'll get all the wrong
stereotypes."[6] So he traced out a sprawling board game with "flip
cards and rolling dice—a kind of '*Dungeons and Dragons* in a
Covered Wagon.'" It became a computer game only after his two
roommates, math teachers who were learning programming, convinced him that they could translate the map, cards, and dice rolls
into computer code. They wrote the program in a week, sitting at
a teletype crammed into a one-time janitor's closet off Rawitsch's
classroom. Played via telephone link to a statewide computer network, the game must have seemed to its young players—now in
their mid-fifties—like an amazing parlor trick. More text adventure than animated game, it was a revelation and something of a
technical miracle: an educational computer game before there were
any actual computers in classrooms.

Lines formed outside Rawitsch's classroom door every morning before school as students vied for a few minutes at the teletype.
The game soon developed a loyal following due to its verisimilitude
and its ruthlessness. Buy too few supplies and you could starve to
death. Buy too many and you might break an axle. Even the best-
laid plans often met a quick, unceremonious end as when players,
upon beginning a turn, learned from the printout, "You have died
of dysentery." *Game over.*

Like many early games, the first few versions were crude affairs—to hunt, players typed BANG as quickly as they could—
but students loved it. Though it would go on to a long life after
a statewide computing consortium acquired it, Rawitsch wiped
the game from the district computer system just before Christmas
break 1971, thinking no one would be interested. Before he left,
he printed out the code on a three-foot length of paper that he
rolled up, took home and tossed in a drawer. Eventually, he went
to work for the Minnesota Educational Computing Consortium, or

MECC, a state agency that provided computer services to schools. When his bosses put out a call for innovative software, Rawitsch volunteered to find the paper roll and type out the code.

The game soon became the agency's most popular title, and as computers began to sprout in classrooms nationwide in the 1980s, MECC sold millions of copies. Eventually, the state spun off MECC as a for-profit company—one estimate put receipts from *The Oregon Trail* at a third of its revenue. Eventually MECC and its intellectual property became part of a disastrous merger involving Mattel that, had it been successful, could have put Barbie on the Oregon Trail. In the end, Rawitsch and his partners never made a dime—as Paul Dillenberger, one of the two roommates, once told a reporter, "I got a jean jacket and a copy of the game instead of owning an island somewhere."[7]

The Oregon Trail was hardly the first or last game to leverage systems thinking. Actually, most play requires it. When systems thinking works, it is powerful, as a group of ninth graders found recently while play-testing *Reach for the Sun,* a plant-growing science game developed by the Wisconsin-based studio Filament Games. In the game, players take on the task of growing a sunflower from seed to bloom. Autumn inevitably arrives, and soon the game informs players, "Your plant has succumbed to winter's embrace." Dan White, Filament's executive producer, told a group of game designers in 2013 that the students "got super-attached to their plants, and they were really upset with us when we killed their plants, over and over and over."[8]

◖·············

Katie Salen, Quest's main co-founder, seems an unlikely candidate to have started a public school. A professor at Parsons The New School for Design and an MFA-powered game designer with a knack for getting people interested in what she's interested in, she has long kept her feet planted in both the games and art worlds. Only recently did she start thinking about education reform. Salen worked on the animation for Richard Linklater's 2001 film *Waking Life,* and in 2004 she co-authored *Rules of Play,* the seminal textbook on game design, with New York University's Eric Zimmerman. In 2006, she co-created the mobile art installation "Karaoke

Ice," a neon-trimmed ice cream truck that haunted the streets of Los Angeles and San Jose, California. At each stop, a performer in a squirrel suit handed out free plastic-wrapped freezer pops through a little hole labeled, "For Free." Once a crowd had formed around the ice pops, the squirrel opened the back of the truck to reveal a karaoke stage, lit by pulsing disco lights and ready for singers. Participants chose from a database of songs, played not by a cover band but by digital ice cream truck bells. At the end, participants took home T-shirts and bar-coded business cards that allowed them to scan a database and download a digital recording of their performance. The endeavor, its creators said, turned three familiar expressions of "network culture"—ice cream trucks, datasets, and karaoke bars—into a "vibrant participatory art experience."[9] It lasted two summers.

In 2007, Salen and a handful of game-designer friends at the New York–based firm Gamelab created the Institute of Play, a nonprofit that she hoped would "explode the notion of games and play" in ways that commercial studios weren't doing. "We wanted to help start to elevate people's opinion of game design as a kind of literacy."[10] Like James Paul Gee, the linguist-turned-video games scholar, she was trying to figure out how to help educators take the habits of mind of a game designer and apply them to something that wasn't a game. Salen, like many in her business, grew up with parents who were educators, and the idea of starting a school appealed to her. "It was just very concrete," she said. "I get tired of all the theory."

At the time, the novelist Dave Eggers and his writer friends were busy creating a small chain of hip and whimsical nonprofit afterschool tutoring and writing centers for kids in major U.S. cities. The first, which opened in 2002 at 826 Valencia Street in San Francisco, was supported, in part, by a retail "Pirate Supply Store" in front—students walked through the store to get to the classrooms hidden in back. Since then, the Echo Park Time Travel Mart in Los Angeles, the Greenwood Space Travel Supply Company in Seattle, and the Greater Boston Bigfoot Research Institute have popped up, among others. In 2004 in New York City, the organization's local branch, 826NYC, threw open the doors of the Brooklyn Superhero Supply Co. in Park Slope. One sign hanging on the wall tells customers, "Inside the store, butlers and wards are officially on their own time." The endeavors resonated with Salen's MFA sensibility—she remembered thinking that if she opened a school, she could learn everything she needed to know to run a superhero store. "I mean, *very* naïve thinking," she said.

But her timing was perfect. New York City was throwing open doors of its own, with an effort to create more than eighty new "Innovation Zone" or "iZone" schools that would leverage technology to individualize instruction. So city leaders were hungry for ideas. They turned to the reform group New Visions for Public Schools, a nonprofit that had been working in New York City since 1989 and had created more than 100 new, small schools. The group's president, Robert Hughes, paid Salen and Zimmerman a visit at the Institute of Play offices downtown to ask if they'd be interested in starting a school.

Hughes told them he'd read their book, the nearly 700-page *Rules of Play,* which struck Salen as amazing. "Any time someone says that they've read *Rules of Play,* what I know they mean is that they've looked at it, that they've kind of skimmed a couple of chapters," she said. "It's not a book you sit down and read." But she was impressed that Hughes was even aware of it, and that he and his staff were taking the subject seriously. "It felt very risky from their perspective to take a bet on games," she said. This was 2007, when it was still "a very tough sell to get people to think that games were anything other than about violence, addiction, or a waste of time."[11]

Salen's friends urged her to open the school, but she wasn't so sure. "I just kept saying, 'We really have to think about this. This is *school.* These are *children.* This is a *big deal.*'" She had just finished up work on *Gamestar Mechanic,* a multiplayer online game that helps players build their own games, and its reputation as a brilliant piece of software was spreading—the game would eventually spawn not one but two PhD dissertations, one of them by Robert Torres, a former school principal who had gotten into the business of designing schools. Salen sought him out for advice. "The first thing I told her was, 'You're crazy. It's the hardest thing you'll ever do in your life.'"[12] What she was actually asking him, it turned out, was if he'd help her design the school.

He wasn't so sure he could make her ideas work. "Creating shitty schools is in our blood," Torres told me. "I think we have a concept of what a school should be, and it's very nineteenth century." The son of Puerto Rican immigrants who had brought him to Brooklyn when he was still a baby, Torres had escaped the drugs and crime that had managed to swallow most of the rest of his family, a story he'd told in the documentary *Nuyorican Dream,* which screened at Sundance in 2000. He began his career teaching fifth grade as a Teach for America corps member, then earned a master's degree in policy and school administration from Bank Street College of Education, the enclave of child-centered, progressive education on Manhattan's Upper West Side. By the time he met Salen, he had worked in education reform for fifteen years, and in some of its most significant efforts. Torres eventually became president of TFA's national faculty. But by 2007, he was beginning to wonder whether all the effort had been worth it. "The impact was minimal," he said. "I just felt like, 'We're doing *nothing* here,' and it was depressing. So working with game designers for me just felt like"—he thought for a moment, then said: "I just wanted to pay attention to what our *kids* were doing for once. And also I wanted to be with really creative people."

Salen eventually came around to the idea of opening a school. "There was something about the scale of it and the complexity of it that felt like the right kind of problem," she said. A two-year development window and a $1.1 million research grant from MacArthur made the offer irresistible. Torres joked, "I was usually given $5,000 and nine months to design a school."

Salen had met Arana Shapiro, then a first- and second-grade teacher, at one of the private schools piloting *Gamestar Mechanic.* She persuaded Shapiro to help write the school's application and eventually made her co-director. Rebecca Rufo-Tepper, a member of Torres's PhD study group, also joined the team and became Mission Lab's director. One of their first moves was to open the school to all eligible students.

The city's school system, the largest in the country with nearly 1 million students, had essentially been perpetuating racial and class disparities for decades. In 2007, African American and Latino students together comprised nearly three-fourths of all students citywide—they were, for all purposes, the system's main clientele.[13] Yet statistics showed that fewer than half graduated from high school in four years.[14] Even those on a path to graduation encountered a school system almost entirely disconnected from the one that many white and Asian students did. In the most recent school year, for instance, African American students accounted for nearly 30 percent of students citywide. But when Stuyvesant High School, perhaps New York's most selective, announced the demographics of its freshman class of 830 students, it said it had offered slots to exactly nine African American students. Not 9 percent—nine *students*. Asian students, who are outnumbered more than two-to-one by their African American peers, claimed 620 slots.[15] Quest, which would eventually grow to become a high school as well, would be open to everyone in the city's District 2, which comprises much of lower Manhattan and most of the island east of Central Park. There would be no entrance exams or other hurdles, and a purposely diverse student body—racially, geographically, economically, and academically. It remains one of the city's most diverse schools. Stand outside as students arrive and you'll see some climb out of Yellow cabs, SUVs, and black Lincoln Town Cars, while others walk up the block, just off the subway from Hell's Kitchen.

❮··············

Recent research, Salen realized, had also found that most kids, of all races and ethnic groups, were simply bored in school. One 2006 survey found that of those who dropped out, only about one in three claimed to have done so because he or she was failing. Nearly half said classes weren't interesting and more than two-thirds said they were "not inspired to work hard." Eighty-one percent said that opportunities for "real-world learning" would have improved their chances of staying in school.[16] Just as more and more kids were becoming disengaged in school, Salen and her colleagues saw, they were becoming more engaged in digital media. Young people ages eight to eighteen were exposed to eight hours and thirty-three minutes of media—music, games, TV, movies, and Internet—per day. Among Latino youth it was higher: eight hours and fifty-two minutes. African American youths consumed the most media: ten hours and ten minutes *daily*.[17]

At the time, Gee and others, including a small group at MIT, were questioning many of our basic assumptions about learning. Students, they said, may be checking out at school, but they were learning deeply at home, spending hours and hours immersed in MySpace, Facebook, *World of Warcraft,* and *SimCity,* pastimes that at first glance might seem a colossal waste of time but "deserve a second, deeper, look at what's actually going on," according to Salen and two MIT researchers, Eric Klopfer and Scot Osterweil[18]—the latter had co-created the cult-favorite *Logical Journey of the Zoombinis* in 1996. The trio suggested that the "stance of playfulness" required of game players offered a new way to look at learning. "Gamers not only follow rules, but push against them, testing the limits of the system in often unique and powerful ways," they wrote. When "pushing against" becomes "questioning about," they said, that's when learning takes place.[19]

Salen and her colleagues would create the school around an approach to learning that "draws from what we know games do best: drop players into inquiry-based, complex problem spaces that are scaffolded to deliver just-in-time learning and to use data to help players understand how they are doing, what they need to work on, and where to go next."[20] The city signed off and in late 2008, Salen, Torres and the others began looking for teachers.

Al Doyle had actually heard Salen speak at a conference in midtown more than a year earlier, when she was trying to get people interested in *Gamestar Mechanic.* Doyle was teaching art and computer graphics at The Town School on Manhattan's East Side, and as he listened to Salen describe the game, he was "blown away." She told the audience she was looking for teachers to pilot it. Doyle approached her afterward, one of just a few teachers who went up to the podium and asked to get his name on the list. "The idea that you could be playful in a school, coming from my background as an art teacher and a theater teacher, it made perfect sense," he said.[21]

Doyle began piloting *Gamestar Mechanic* at lunch with a group of sixth graders, then at a summer camp in Maine where he'd been hired to create a digital art studio. "Kids were engaged to a certain level, but once I got to game design, their interest level exploded," he said. "All of a sudden we had to open the doors earlier so the kids could get into the computer lab. Then we were worried they were skipping breakfast and they didn't want to go to lunch. They didn't want to go swimming in the afternoon."

By December 2008, when Doyle answered a Craigslist ad for a teacher at a new startup school built on game principles, he'd been beta-testing *Gamestar Mechanic* for nine months—and he said so in his e-mail. The school was Quest, and Salen herself e-mailed him back to suggest he come in for an interview. A few weeks later, he showed up at a "job fair" that looked more like a lab experiment. "There were sixty people in the room," he said. "Half of them were looking for a job, half of them were evaluating candidates." Quest had job openings for six teachers.

The school opened in the fall of 2009 with Doyle and five others on staff—and seventy-six sixth graders. Rocco Rinaldi-Rose, one of the sixth graders, had already applied to several middle schools, but when he heard about Quest, he knew immediately that he wanted to go. Rocco actually wasn't that interested in games, but by fifth grade he was already thinking about the world in terms of systems. "A school that bases things on systems thinking seemed very interesting," he said. I asked him how, as a fifth grader, he even knew what systems thinking was, and his father, Joel Rose, overheard the question. "Welcome to Rocco's world," he said.[22]

Eventually, both Rocco and his little brother, Gio, would end up at Quest, and, in a way, under its spell. After teachers there championed the world-building game *LittleBigPlanet*, the family bought their first PlayStation so the brothers could play it at home. "It made a big impact on us because you could make whatever you wanted," Rocco said. When *Minecraft* overtook the school in 2011, it overtook them. Rocco "spent a very long time making things that were completely pointless—which is the point."[23] At one point, he spent about sixty hours digging the deepest hole possible—he simply dug until the game would let him go no further. Then he built an enormous ladder out of the hole and invited all of his friends to fling their avatars into the abyss. He charged them each five *Mine-craft* dollars for the privilege.

As with Gee's 2003 book *What Video Games Have to Teach Us about Learning and Literacy*, people who heard about Quest wanted it to be the "video-game school," even if they weren't quite sure what that meant. Requests for visits poured in, but few were granted. Five years later, Salen told me, about two-thirds of visitors still arrive thinking they're going to see kids playing video games. A few are excited, but most are "horrified that that's what they're going to see—and they have a very clear vision that this is a terrible school." They're relieved to find that most of the games are on paper, on square cardboard slabs, on homemade playing cards or, as with Triple Turbo Ball, in kids' heads. For those who had *hoped* that kids would be sitting around grasping controllers, Salen said, "we kind of take them on a journey of moving their mental model from kids sitting in front of a screen playing *Halo* to kids collaborating around a card game learning something around narrative and point of view."[24]

Part of the problem is messaging. Quest's first major funder was, and remains, MacArthur, which has poured an estimated $80 million into experiments in digital media in schools, museums, and libraries. In their haste to be a part of the experiment in 2009, Salen and her colleagues dubbed Quest "the School for Digital Kids." It seemed a logical step at the time. Talk of "digital natives" was on everyone's lips and many activists in the games-and-learning field were itching for a way to blow up the entire traditional school system. Quest's first major media exposure, a lengthy cover story in the *New York Times Magazine* in September 2010, featured a large photo of three rapt sixth-grade girls clutching video game controllers. The piece suggested that "the slipstream of broadband and always-on technology that fuels our world" could become schools' organizing principle. "What if, instead of seeing school the way we've known it, we saw it for what our children dreamed it might be: a big, delicious video game?"[25] Quest has since ditched the "digital kids" tagline in favor of the more anodyne assertion: "We challenge students to invent their future."

What's most amazing to a casual observer is simply how many ideas the school's teachers and game designers seem to be able to get across through simple board games, card games, and the like—many of them unabashed rip-offs of existing titles or modifications of games they've created for other lessons. Dice and foam core, it seems, are everywhere, and much of the school's energy seems directed toward hammering home the idea that the world is a *built* place, made of systems that work together, and that it will need people to continue building future versions of itself. Each year, Quest challenges sixth graders to build a Rube Goldberg–type machine, a complex system that performs a simple task. The project is part systems thinking, part team-building. Guidance counselor Rachelle Vallon once said that in her advisory group, known as home base, one student talked "all the time about how he feels that Rube Goldberg was what really brought us together as a home base."[26]

Specific games, it soon becomes clear, are actually less important than they might seem at first. The best games, said designer Shula Ehrlich, are those that are flexible so that teachers can adapt them to whatever lesson they're teaching. "And it has to be simple so that teachers can quickly jump in and play—they don't have to spend a whole class period explaining how to play the game," she said.[27] *Block Talk,* for instance, started out as a two-person game that challenged one player to describe to another how to stack a series of colored blocks so that they resemble the configuration in a picture. The second player must follow the directions silently, upping the pressure on the first player to describe the picture accurately. Teachers adapted the idea to teach points on a grid, geometry, drawing, and the names of foods in Spanish, among others.

What's perhaps more amazing is how many people running the place—teachers, designers, administrators—have no formal training in game design and hadn't even really thought much about the topic before they showed up for their Quest job interview. Alicia Iannucci saw the big orange Quest logo—also recently abandoned—at a hiring fair in 2009. She'd just earned her master's degree from Adelphi University on Long Island and mostly knew that she didn't want to go back to rural western New York, where she'd grown up. Iannucci had never heard of game-based learning, but Salen's assertion that children absorb information best on a "need-to-know" basis made sense to her, both for students and adults, she remembered. "If I have the *why,* I can do the rest of it," she said.[28] A math major and "huge nerd" who loved school as a kid, she was Quest's first Codeworlds teacher and as of this writing remains on staff.

But Doyle, who also earned a place in that first group of teachers, left after the first year, sick of kids who misbehaved in class. "At that point in my career, it just wasn't well-suited to my temperament," he said. He quickly found a job at a private school with no regrets. "My teaching is completely, irrevocably changed as a result of Quest to Learn," he said. "In most places, what passes for innovation or ground-breaking pedagogy is a pale, pale version of some retread that's basic nonsense. It's a rare thing to see real innovation and, you know, you take risks. That's part of it. You learn from failure. Not everything's going to work if you're trying something new. But if you build it into the model, then you're prepared for some hiccups." Failure reframed, in other words, as iteration.

In its first few years, Quest experienced the kind of turnover and turmoil that plagues most startups. Its founding principal, who had helped persuade dozens of families to take a chance on the place, left the school two weeks into the first school year. A handful of parents, nervous about student misbehavior, test scores, and their middle schoolers' chances of earning a slot in a competitive public high school, abandoned Quest after just a year or two. "There were a lot of people who were stunned at what they got, rather than what they thought they'd signed up for," said Rose, Rocco and Gio's father. "There were really emotional meetings and really high anxiety."[29] Rose, a novelist and comic book writer, said both of his sons have flourished at Quest. He surprised everyone—himself especially—by becoming one of the school's first PTA presidents. But even as other parents fretted, a few indicators showed that Quest was doing something right: In 2011, students there took home the first of three consecutive first prizes in the city's Math Olympiad. Three years after it opened its doors, in September 2012, an assessment by researchers at New York University found that 90 percent of parents believed the school "has high expectations for their children." Eighty-seven percent said their child was "learning what he or she needs to know to succeed in later school grades or after graduating high school."[30]

Quest has never shone brightly on the typical educational indicators by which most urban schools live and die. Though its staff brims with master's degrees and PhDs, and private funding supports an in-house research-and-development lab, its standardized test scores are merely respectable. "We knew kids needed to do OK on the test scores," Salen said. "It's never been a group that's said the kids have got to do the best. And in fact we'd think we were failing in our vision if our school had the top test scores."

Shapiro, the school's co-director, said testing "is a *huge* deal and it's a constant struggle. It's a constant struggle for us with parents, it's a constant struggle for us with teachers. It's hard to get teachers to believe that if you are teaching a standards-based unit and you are preparing kids for a test, you're not going to do three months of test prep—and we're not going to *let* you do three months of test prep. Just trust us—they'll do OK." Iannucci, for her part, said she spends about one day a year on test-taking strategies, since her students, until the day they arrive at Quest, have spent their entire school lives worrying about tests. "Really, I just ask them, 'What do you know about taking a test?'" They usually know all they need to know.

Though it remains one of New York City's "iZone" schools, in a way the school operates in an odd twilight zone between its own dreams and the harsh waking life of the city school system. One recent June morning during the first day of Boss Level demonstrations, signs taped to the windows of a few classrooms assured visitors that state testing was indeed taking place, at Quest as elsewhere in the building. The school that embeds assessment into everything it does must still sacrifice its students to outside assessments every spring.

For all of the school's frustrations, Rose said, it has helped his sons' minds develop "in the most unusual, fruitful ways," in spite of the turmoil. He still worries from time to time that the boys could use a more traditional education, he said, but "my wife usually talks me down from the ledge." The best indicator he could muster that the school is getting the job done actually shows itself in the late afternoon and early evening, he said. When his sons get together with their classmates, "They're talking about school."[31]

NYU's Richard Arum, who has spent nearly two years studying the school and whose team of researchers produced the parent satisfaction findings, told me he'd seen "robust evidence of a successful school." Quest has actually done a better job holding on to teachers than other city middle schools and has even turned in healthy improvements in test scores.

Among Arum's NYU Education School colleagues who are District 2 parents, he said, many "are now actively considering and talking about putting their kids there." When I asked him if they would have considered it just two or three years ago, he said, diplomatically, "I think it's fair to say professional educators are generally very cautious about putting their own kids in schools in their initial startup phase."[32] Rebecca Rufo-Tepper, who directs Mission Lab, said one of the key changes, after nearly five years, was how much the game designers and teachers had learned from one another. "They sort of blend together after a while," she said, with teachers creating their own games and designers expressing an urge to teach classes. "That's when you know that things have really settled in."[33]

During the Triple Turbo Ball exhibition in the gym, my chat with Evan Klein, the assistant principal, had been one of those casual, eyes-on-the-game conversations that is irresistible during children's sporting events. The text usually boils down to some variation of "Why isn't my kid in the game?" But since neither of us had a kid in the game, we fell almost immediately to critiquing Triple Turbo Ball. I chuckled at its complexity but admired its ambition—it seemed exactly the kind of overheated game a thirteen-year-old boy would design. Klein, with his mind perpetually on timetables, said he liked the idea that Triple Turbo Ball was untimed and that the winning score was negotiable. It could turn the game into a quick pick-up sport or a longer endeavor.

As the game progressed, I noticed that new players, picked out of the crowd as volunteers, had finally figured out that they could keep opponents from costly seven-point touchdowns simply by prowling the end zone and blocking passes. Watching the goalie stand a few feet away in front of the net, where he waited idly for a kick or throw, I decided that a team could get an advantage by pretending this was hockey and pulling him, since at most an unguarded goal gave up just two points. I was struck with a sudden, primal urge to yell, "Forget this loser job, kid! Get into the *action!*"

Watching the game made me think about Herbert R. Kohl, the progressive educator and theorist who helped popularize the use of pre–digital-age games in classrooms. In 1974, he wrote of observing a student teacher scold a group of children who were playing a modified version of chess, one with slightly different rules. "He pointed out that there was only one way to play the game, that they would never be 'real' chess players if they didn't play by the rules," Kohl wrote. One of the children cannily told the student teacher that she didn't want to be a real chess player—she was simply curious about what happened when you changed the rules.[34]

After I wandered out of the Triple Turbo Ball exhibition that day, I found myself unexpectedly lost in thought. I left the school and walked up Eighth Avenue, thinking about rules. Fourteen players, I decided, were too many—they crowded the court. Why not make it ten? Why not eight? What if, instead of free throws, as in basketball, there were penalty boxes and power plays, as in hockey? Why not a bigger ball? Why not *two* balls?

It occurred to me that, despite my addled, middle-aged brain, I was engaging in systems thinking. And I was preparing my mental soil, however improbably, for the teamwork required to make my Triple Turbo Ball version a reality. My mind easily alighted on an imaginary midcourt conversation—if I wanted to try out my crazy modifications, I'd have to persuade fourteen sweaty seventh graders to listen as I made my case. Would they cooperate? Would they even listen? What if they didn't? What if someone suggested *three* balls? Would I give in or stick to my plan? How would we know if the two-ball or the three-ball version was better? *Who would decide?*

Suddenly I realized: in the most ordinary way, Quest had made its central point. What had looked like a simple basketball demo was, in fact, a sly commentary on familiarity and strangeness, a student-generated piece of public art. It was another one of Salen's karaoke ice cream trucks.* "Game designers traffic in the space of possibility," Salen once wrote by way of explaining Quest's central philosophy,[35] and this overheated seventh-floor gym was, for all practical purposes, the space. How many hundreds of basketball games have we watched or played in our lives without *ever* thinking about the rules? Unlike a regular game of basketball, you can't

---

*In 2013, Salen got married and stepped down from the executive director's job at the Institute of Play. She's now known as Katie Salen Tekinbaş.

just *watch* Triple Turbo Ball. You naturally, almost instinctively, have to get your hands in it and try to *break* it. Simply by messing with the rules and inviting everybody to observe the tangled result, Quest was doing something truly subversive. It was cracking the whip on our feeble imaginations and exercising our involuntary *what-if* muscles. It was, for a fleeting moment, turning us all into game designers.

....................➤

SEVEN

"I'M NOT GOOD AT MATH, BUT MY AVATAR IS"

*How a Subversive Suburban
Teacher Is Using* World of
Warcraft *to Teach Humanities*

In August 2005, during a visit to her mother's and stepfather's New Jersey home, Meghan Deana "played the guilt card" to get her mother, Peggy Newburgh Sheehy, to create an account in *Second Life*. The virtual world had just opened a "teen grid" and Deana, who went by the "inworld" name coreina.grace, had just gotten a job at Linden Lab, *Second Life*'s San Francisco–based developer. Sheehy, at the time a fifty-one-year-old, two-time divorcée and library information specialist at Suffern Middle School—just across the New York border in suburban Rockland County—was at first baffled by *Second Life*'s interface, but Deana helped her create an online persona, or avatar, that she named Maggie Marat. Like Sheehy, Maggie was a slim redhead with a platinum-blonde streak and black-frame eyeglasses. Deana left for the three-hour drive back home to SUNY-Cortland, in upstate New York, where she was getting a master's degree in education, and Sheehy logged off, a bit confused, to be honest. Three hours later, Deana called and told her mother to get back online. Deana found Maggie, teleported her over to where she was hanging out with a few friends and began introducing her around. Sheehy was amazed. Who *were* all these people, and what were they doing in this strange place? They all had odd names and everyone was beautiful, welcoming, and anonymous.

"The teacher lens kicked in," she said.[1]

That day, Deana introduced her to "this adorable pixie-like female," a diminutive blonde named Jade Lily. Sheehy loved Jade's clothes, her braided hair, her style, and she said so via the program's on-screen instant-messaging app. Sheehy confided that she felt a bit lost and Jade replied, "I'll take you shopping. Come on, let's go." The two stole off together. Jade deposited fifty "Linden dollars," the inworld currency, into Maggie's account and showed her how to buy a different hairdo. More importantly, she showed the newcomer how to affix it to the top of her head, a complex process not immediately obvious to new users back in the summer of 2005. They instantly became close, chatting about clothes, work, hair, relationships. "I remember being very open, the way I would with a new girlfriend," Sheehy said. "We had girl talk."

That November, mother and daughter decided to attend the first *Second Life* members' convention in New York City. Actually, it was little more than a party, held in a crowded Manhattan bar. Sheehy, by now convinced that *Second Life* could revolutionize the classroom, cornered Philip Rosedale, the site's founder, and vowed that she would someday build an inworld school. Rosedale, who had come from a family of teachers, was enthusiastic, she remembered. Later that evening, as Sheehy and her daughter sat at a table chatting, Deana looked up and announced, "Jade is here."

Where? Sheehy looked around and couldn't find anyone who resembled the blonde pixie in the online world. But standing directly behind her was a strapping young man in blue jeans, with kind eyes and short blonde hair. Deana had already gotten up and was talking to him, and in a moment the two of them were laughing. Deana turned to Sheehy. Mom, she said, this is Keith Morris. Keith is Jade. Jade is Keith.

Morris was twenty-three years old, a graduate student living in North Carolina, volunteering in *Second Life* for the American Cancer Society, which at the time was actively fund-raising in the virtual world. "He sits down and I'm trying to rehash all of the conversations," Sheehy said, "like, 'What have I *said* to this guy?'"

It turns out that the Keith/Jade dyad wasn't unusual. When Stanford University researcher Nick Yee surveyed thousands of gamers in 2005, he found that "gender-bending" in online worlds is common, especially among males. Yee calculated that on a typical day in *World of Warcraft,* the chances of encountering a female character played by a male are a little better than fifty-fifty.[2] Sheehy asked him why he represented himself in *Second Life* as a woman. Morris told her, "Because I can."

Before long, Deana announced to her mother that she and Morris were dating. Three years later they got engaged, then married, in real life, in North Carolina. So Sheehy got to know Morris—she calls him "a lovely, sweet, gentle man"—and now jokes about "my son-in-law Jade. We were friends—we were friends before he became my son in law. We were peers."

The experience got Sheehy thinking about the power of avatars, or player-generated, customized characters, in online worlds. If Keith Morris could be Jade Lily, she wondered, who—or what?—could her students be? She remembered psychologist Erik Erickson's exhortation about teenagers: they need a "psychosocial moratorium," he wrote, an environment and a stretch of time in which they can explore different aspects of their personality and try on a series of identities without fear of consequence. In a way, that was what school was supposed to offer, but it didn't always do so with much success. She realized that this was exactly what virtual worlds offered all the time, to anyone with a computer and an Internet connection. Maybe, she thought, every student should have an avatar.

The term "avatar" is an old one, from the Sanskrit word for "incarnation." It's got religious roots—painters have long represented the Hindu god Vishnu by his ten avatars. In video games, the term was first used in 1985, in the game *Ultima IV,*[3] though the basic idea is as old as games themselves. Players have used physical placeholders to represent themselves as long as they've played games—think of the little pewter *Monopoly* tokens chosen at the outset of each game. Early video games used simple shapes, usually just a variation of a blinking cursor. The first American version of the *Pac-Man* arcade game was called *Puck-Man,* but the game's

Japanese manufacturers, fearing that vandals would deface the game cabinets by turning the "P" into an "F," changed it.[4]

As video games migrated to home consoles and desktop computers, they became more complex. Developers soon realized that players were spending long stretches of time interacting with games, and thus with their avatars. Why not make the relationship more personal? They began offering the opportunity to customize and upgrade avatars, a phenomenon that reached its apotheosis with online role-playing games and virtual worlds. Most recently, social networking sites like Facebook have offered users the ability to curate their profile with photos, videos, music, games, likes, jokes, and exhortations, all carefully selected to project a perfectly wrought yet offhand image of the person, with what researcher Sherry Turkle once described as "deliberated nonchalance."[5] An online avatar, one sixteen-year-old told Turkle, is like "a performance of you," a sort of ideal person or "little twin on the Internet" that you choose to send out to the world.[6] Sheehy realized that, as with Keith, a student working as an avatar could enjoy a semblance of anonymity and be anyone he wanted to be.

James Paul Gee's first popular book, *What Video Games Have to Teach Us about Learning and Literacy,* had just appeared in 2003, so a few teachers were talking about his adaptation of Erickson's psychosocial moratorium in game worlds. School, Gee wrote, was basically a place where students are asked, whether they like it or not, to create an identity—in first period, teachers may ask them to behave like scientists, while later in the day others ask them to behave like historians or journalists or musicians. It doesn't always work, he wrote, but if done well, it can be powerful: "If learners in classrooms carry learning so far as to take on a projective identity, something magical happens. The learner comes to know that he or she has the *capacity,* at some level, to take on the virtual identity as a real-world identity."[7] One of the reasons that school works so much more smoothly and efficiently in communities with a lot of well-off, well-educated families is that these kids have already been brought up from an early age to effortlessly imagine themselves as scientists or historians or musicians. It's a much greater leap for kids whose families don't have that expectation.

Well-educated parents talk and interact with their children differently than other parents, employing what sociologist Annette Lareau has called "concerted cultivation." In these families, Lareau wrote, organized activities, arranged by parents, dominate children's lives and give them a "robust sense of entitlement" that leads them to question adults "and address them as relative equals." In many working-class families, by contrast, parents tell their children what to do, but don't arrange many activities. Since concerted cultivation is basically the *de facto* mission of school, Lareau wrote, children who aren't comfortable with it "appear to gain an emerging sense of distance, distrust and constraint" in school and elsewhere.[8]

That spring, Sheehy met with Robert MacNaughton, her district superintendent, armed with a PowerPoint presentation that outlined her proposal to create a school in *Second Life*. She'd created an avatar for MacNaughton and quickly took him through the virtual world. He listened patiently, she remembered. "I finished and he looked at me and said, 'I haven't been this confused since calculus, but I believe in you. Go ahead and tell me what you learn.'"[9] Sheehy immediately rented three islands in *Second Life*'s teen grid and the school was born. She created accounts for 400 eighth graders, giving every one of them the surname "Hillburn," after the Rockland County hamlet where the superintendent's office was located. The following year, through a special arrangement with Linden Lab, she essentially smuggled in sixth and seventh graders with Linden Lab's consent, since the children were too young to meet the site's thirteen-year-old age cutoff. Actually she consented to a kind of verbal nondisclosure agreement, telling Linden that if anyone ever asked how old her students were she'd ignore the question or simply lie.

Word about the strange school spread quickly among teachers, and soon colleagues from across the country were wondering how they could join. For the next five years, 4,500 students and hundreds of teachers spent chunks of their school day guiding avatars and doing project-based work in *Second Life*. Three "teen grid" islands grew to six. An English teacher at Sheehy's school who was teaching *Of Mice and Men* staged a mock trial for Lennie. A health teacher, leveraging *Second Life*'s gender-bending powers, created a unit on body image that asked students to generate their ideal body as a member of the opposite sex—the site allowed instant gender switching at the touch of a button. With Sheehy's help, a social studies teacher recreated Ellis Island and assigned one half of the class to be immigrants, the other half immigration officers. On the first day, he found, students asked tough questions and turned away about one in three immigrants. On the second day, when the roles were reversed, the students who had played as immigrants let in 95 percent of their classmates. "Empathy kicked in," Sheehy said. "There's no other explanation."[10]

When a math teacher wanted students to learn about balancing a checkbook, they built a flea market and scheduled a beach party on one of the islands. At the end of the shopping spree, only students with enough money left to buy a ticket were admitted. Afterward, a teacher came to Sheehy with tears in her eyes and said one of her students, a selectively mute sixth grader who hadn't spoken in class since second grade, had just led a discussion on the lesson. Another time, Sheehy got a note from a student who confessed, "I'm not good at math, but my avatar is."

Giving kids the freedom to interact in a virtual world led, improbably, to greater engagement in real-life school. "I kept having teachers report back to me, 'Every one of my kids is participating,'" Sheehy said. It made sense. Yee, the Stanford researcher, has spent years investigating virtual worlds. He has found that the power of an avatar's physical appearance has the potential to influence people, including the owner. More attractive avatars, for instance, tend to walk more closely to others and taller avatars bargain harder than shorter ones.[11] In another study, New York University researcher Hal Hershfeld, along with Stanford virtual-reality researcher Jeremy Bailenson, of virtual-killer-whale fame, outfitted participants with electronic goggles that allowed them to explore a virtual environment that included a mirror. When they peered into the mirror, half of the subjects saw their normal reflection, but the other half saw a digitally aged representation of themselves, with "jowls, bags under the eyes, and gray hair." Asked afterward what they'd do with an imaginary $1,000, subjects exposed to the aged avatar said they would put away nearly twice as much for retirement as the others.[12] Yee and Bailenson have dubbed this "the Proteus Effect" after the shape-shifting Greek god.[13]

Though *Second Life* didn't, in reality, grant students anonymity—kids are curious and they all basically knew each other's screen names—the simple act of working together online somehow triggered a kind of suspension of real-life prejudices. It was a digital clean slate. "They're able to go in there without the social mores and cliques of middle school—'Who's got the Hollister clothing, who came to school on the little bus, who's on the football team?' None of that exists." Actually, Sheehy found, the kids who were most admired online were the ones who were most helpful, the best mentors. "They kind of develop a reputation: 'Oh, ask so-and-so, they're really good at that.'"

Then, in 2010, Linden Lab abruptly closed the teen grid and did away with its 50 percent educator discount. Rent for the six islands rose overnight from $1,500 per month to $3,000. Sheehy and her group reluctantly began looking elsewhere for virtual spaces. That summer, she met a North Carolina teacher named Lucas Gillispie, who had developed a language arts curriculum built on Joseph Campbell's "Hero's Journey," the "monomyth" that's the basis of many epics and, increasingly, of modern fiction and movie screenplays. Gillispie set his curriculum in *World of Warcraft*. Sheehy had been a *WoW* player since 2007 and had even helped form an educators' guild, with more than 500 members, named "Cognitive Dissonance." The name was a bit of a joke, since it is a psychological term describing how people can keep two contradictory ideas in their head at once. Psychologist Leon Festinger first proposed it in 1957, after infiltrating a doomsday cult whose prophecy failed to come true during an overnight vigil. In the immediate aftermath, the cult's leader maintained that God had spared the world *because* the group had sat up all night, waiting for the end. "It was an adequate, even an elegant, explanation of the disconfirmation," Festinger wrote. "The cataclysm had been called off. The little group, sitting all night long, had spread so much light that God had saved the world from destruction."[14]

That September, Sheehy started an afterschool *WoW* club with a handful of students. When the district cut most after-school activities, she told her boss she had no plans to stop. If the union, which frowns upon unpaid after-school work, were to ask, she told him, tell them she was simply offering "extra help" to students in the library. No one bothered to check what they were doing in there with the lights dimmed after school every day, two hours a day, four days a week, all year long.

In the spring of 2011, after hearing about her *Second Life* and *WoW* experiments, I began visiting Sheehy. I expected a front-row seat to the day-to-day workings of a teacher with an obvious love for her students and an unwavering belief in their potential. What I didn't quite expect was her almost total disregard for how school was expected to look and work. Like many educators caught in the pinch of standards-based mandates like No Child Left Behind and Race to the Top, Sheehy was, by then, fed up with the basic-skills tests and the inevitable test prep that her kids had to endure. "We've lost our way," she told me one day after school had let out. "We've totally lost our way. The cart is so far in front of the horse now. We need to get the focus back on the child, the unique, individual human being. What are their interests? What are their passions?" To her, public schools had long been running a kind of Race to the Bottom, narrowing the curriculum in the name of a dry compliance that served no one's purposes, least of all the kids'. "If we're looking to build a foundation of knowledge in each child, the system that seems to have worked, because it was based on an industrial-age America, was 'Line 'em up, feed 'em the facts, open up their heads, pour it in, close their heads, and then have them regurgitate it.' We're not trying to produce children to go work in factories anymore. We're trying to produce thinkers. We're trying to produce happy, creative individuals who are going to lead successful lives, be contributing members of society. To me, part of being a success in life is being happy, and to me you're only going to be happy if you're involved in doing something you love. But we're not giving kids that foothold."

Nearly as frustrating, from Sheehy's perch in the library, was that she had limited time with students. She was trying to figure out a way to help them reach their potential in spite of the pour-it-in approach. "I don't like being one of those whiners," she said. "My thing is, if you see that there's a problem, get into the solution." I pointed out that she seemed a sort of outlier among her colleagues, many of whom were simply focused on giving kids solid basic skills. After all, a lot of people, especially in the suburbs, seemed comfortable with how things were going.

She shot me a fierce look. "Not the kids!"

❮··············

As far back as she could remember, Sheehy was bored in school. She grew up in Levittown, New York, the original postwar prefab community, but recalled it less for the cookie-cutter houses than for the nature that surrounded them—this was the 1950s, and much of the rest of suburbia had yet to make it that far into Long Island. In kindergarten, the teacher told a misbehaving Peggy Newburgh to go sit under the piano. "It was downhill from there."

Her report card regularly featured the helpful observation "Does not perform to her ability."[15] She acted out. She was the class clown, the one calling the teacher out on stupid mistakes. By high school, she found she'd rather climb a fence, walk out onto the shoulder of the Wantagh State Parkway, and hitchhike to the beach "with my surfboard and sometimes my guitar, and sometimes a dog." Then as now, Sheehy had a big voice, so she taught herself to sing and play the guitar, though no one encouraged her to take lessons. "I fell through the cracks," she said. "I *know* where the cracks are." By January of her senior year she decided she didn't need a diploma to be a musician, so she dropped out and began what would become a thirty-year career as a singer/songwriter, first as a solo act, then in a folk-blues trio named Stryder, which opened for hundreds of top acts in the 1970s. Eventually it morphed into a twelve-piece band that found steady if predictable work in the Greater New York Bar Mitzvah and Wedding circuit.

By her late-thirties, though, Sheehy was beginning to get a little uneasy. With neither health insurance nor a retirement plan, she resolved to go back to school and get a white-collar job. In an interview room at Empire State College, the SUNY campus built around independent study for working adults, a professor assigned to be Sheehy's mentor asked her what kind of work she wanted. "I don't know," she said. "All I know is I'm not out to get rich if I can't put my head down on the pillow at night." She didn't want to sell real estate or work in an office. She couldn't stand "rote work" or being bored. She said, "I need to feel like I'm making a difference."

"You're a teacher," the professor responded. "Don't you *know* you're a teacher?"

◖···············

One afternoon in May 2011, I found myself standing at the edge of Sheehy's domain, a library with all the shades drawn, watching a table fill up with backpacks as a culturally diverse group of both current and former Suffern Middle School students filed in, took their seats, and got ready to play. Several, Sheehy informed me, began playing in middle school and continued to find their way to the club after high school classes let out. From the moment I set foot in *WoW* club, it was clear that something rich and strange was happening. Amid the fireballs and axes and broadswords, kids were solving logistical problems, thinking and talking about the Hero's Journey and quietly forging friendships. Two students who had arrived the previous fall speaking no English had improved their language skills quickly after playing the game for just a few weeks. A student named Austin later told me that the club, like most gaming, brings people together. "You get tight with the people you play with," he said. "It's good for social skills, and that's why I always laugh when people say gamers are antisocial. They're just not social with *you*."

University of Wisconsin researcher Constance Steinkuehler, the White House games scholar, in 2008 analyzed *WoW* players' discussion forums and found that 86 percent of the talk consisted of interactions that could be considered "social knowledge construction," built around a collective development of understanding, often through joint problem solving and argumentation. "In the overwhelming majority of forum talk," she found, "participants were solving problems through discussion, knowledge sharing, and debate." *WoW* users, in other words, were acting like scientists—in their free time, and with their virtual, presumably nonscientist friends. Only 8 percent of discussion posts were "mere social banter." Steinkuehler also found that a player's experience level didn't necessarily correspond to the sophistication of his or her arguments. Add it all up, she said, and the findings suggested that in schools pressured by testing and a narrowing of the curriculum, virtual worlds like *WoW* "might be a nice complement to classrooms, augmenting classroom instruction by situating informal science literacy in popular culture context."[16]

Games theorist Jane McGonigal has written that *World of Warcraft* is "without a doubt one of the most satisfying work systems ever engineered."[17] Created in 2004 and played, at the height of its popularity, by an estimated 12 million people, *WoW* presents players with a world that has zero unemployment. Players' primary objective, McGonigal said, is self-improvement, in the form of a perpetual bid at "leveling up." The real payoff for work in *WoW*, she wrote, "is to be rewarded with more opportunities for work." *WoW* constantly challenges players to try something "just a little bit more difficult than what you've just accomplished." She called *WoW* "the single most powerful IV drip of productivity ever created."[18]

Her IV metaphor was on my mind as I watched Sheehy's after-school club, where the productivity level seemed through the roof—which was all the more remarkable when Sheehy later described the challenges many of her kids face. Of the eighteen club members, seven had been diagnosed with learning disabilities. Four had an aide who followed them to class. Most qualified for free lunch, several were on medication, and just as many had "very good relationships with the school psychologist." I wandered around the library during several visits, often shooting videos with my phone, and I found it next to impossible, either then or later, to pick out the learning-disabled or the troubled kids from the rest of the group.

As I peeked over students' shoulders, I was dazzled and confused in equal measure by what was happening onscreen. Minute to minute, players' *WoW* dashboards often resemble less a fantasy world than a commodity trader's screen, with vast stores of resources that need managing. One boy named Jonathan told me, "It takes a huge brain to figure out everything." Sitting next to him, a boy named Eddie joked, "I figured out everything and I have a small brain." It took Eddie more than a year of showing up every afternoon to get his avatar, Wolfox, to Level 62. It took him a year just to be allowed to fly. "You work for it so long, when you finally achieve that goal, it feels so good."

Eddie wore his black hair shorn close, the beginnings of a moustache sprouting on his upper lip, his sneakers untied. Onscreen, Wolfox gripped the reins of a magnificent blue gryphon that transported him over a pink and purple wasteland. He was dropping off a parcel, his companion eagle following—once Eddie reached level 60, he bought the exotic pet at Weller's Arsenal, a sort of *WoW* swap meet. "I also have a robotic squirrel," he volunteered. Then he was on the ground and hunting for his lunch. Eddie's left foot popped up and down nervously as he hacked away with keyboard combinations. He explained that the game actually helps him manage his money in real life. "You do these quests, it's like having a job and getting money for it. It's like having a life but more exciting. A regular old life."

Perhaps the adults in the school district could use a little *WoW*-inspired money management. Though the club was thriving—Sheehy eventually persuaded her principal to join her guild—in 2013, a new superintendent, facing a $10.6 million budget deficit, cut about sixty jobs, including librarians' positions at each of the district's five elementary schools.[19] Seniority rules dictated that one of the displaced librarians be offered Sheehy's middle school job. A bit of horse trading followed and Sheehy's principal eventually came to her with an offer: She could stay in the building if she agreed to hand over the keys to the library and take a classroom position, teaching either sixth-grade math or humanities. Or she could find a job elsewhere. Sheehy chose humanities.

The morning I showed up for a visit to her new classroom, it was a gray Tuesday in November. I slipped into the room and noticed that the lights were out. Sheehy rose from her desk and gave me a powerful hug. Though she is a trim sixty, everything else about her is big. She wears oversized round tortoiseshell glasses and four big gold hoops in each ear, two big diamond studs in her left ear. Even when you can't see her, you can hear her coming from the jangle of a hundred bracelets. That morning, she was wearing a pink cashmere sweater and flowered dancer's flats, a silk scarf wrapped around her waist decorated with little illustrations of mixed drinks. Her hair, by then bleach-blonde, had wisps of pink and blue. She used to cut it short, but by then had begun letting it grow out, pulling it back with a plastic clip. A hank of blue hair hung in her eyes all morning. I hadn't seen her in months, but within seconds she was shaking a big plastic binder at me and telling me that she was fed up with the language arts program the state had adopted. "I'm trying to find the balance between this scripted, horrible curriculum that they gave me and what I believe in," she said. "Why did you become a teacher if you just want a script handed to you? We could hand this to a cafeteria lady." She announced that she was adapting Gillispie's *WoW* curriculum, making sure his quests stand up "under anybody's light, under anybody's rigor" without, as she said, "smelling like school."

As Sheehy's first class of sixth graders filed in, she took attendance and let them wander the classroom, getting out books and supplies. At the front of the room was a large, wall-mounted flat-screen TV connected to a PlayStation3. That morning it was loaded with the 2012 video game *Journey,* whose title animation ran on a loop, waiting for someone to play. After a few minutes, a brave student tentatively pulled down a controller and pressed START. Before long, seven classmates were surrounding him, watching the game unfold and making suggestions about where he should send his avatar next. Sheehy, looking for some lost item in her desk, noted the development from a few feet away and said, "I decided to go a little Sugata Mitra." She was referring to the Indian educator who in 1999 carved a hole in the wall of a private university building that faced a New Delhi slum. Mitra inserted a desktop computer and watched as children in the neighborhood taught themselves not only how to use the computer, but how to use search engines, chat programs, and e-mail. The hole-in-the-wall kids taught themselves enough English to navigate the Web and had better math and science scores in school than kids who didn't play with the computer. They were also more skilled at forming independent opinions and could "detect indoctrination," according to Mitra.[20] (In Sheehy's class, the impromptu gaming session led, eventually, to a writing prompt: Who is the avatar in the game? Why is she on a journey? Where is she headed?)

After ten minutes, Sheehy finally greeted her class: "Good morning, heroes!" She asked a student to throw open a window. It was 8 a.m. and thirty-nine degrees outside. A few weak cries of "No . . ." came from the students, but by then they knew not to protest too firmly.

Much of Sheehy's appeal, aside from her obvious regard for her students, lies in her performer's ability to bring the crowd inside, to invite them into her little uprising. Her classroom sits at the end of the hall and it is covered in strange, sometimes inexplicable signs. One, taped to her desk, reads, "REMEMBER! If a future you tries to warn you about this class, DON'T LISTEN." That morning, she made sure the classroom door was closed before telling students, with mock seriousness, "The door is closed and what are we do-ing? We're doing something *very revolutionary.*" Inevitably, the morning announcements interrupted the proceedings and Sheehy groaned, then listened as a student on the PA declared, "The caf-eteria serves delicious cold and hot food!" Unprovoked, she replied, "Mmm . . . what a *lie!*"

Then she began an impromptu talk about choices. Before long, she was counseling them to consider taking time off after high school. The students listened as they sorted through their papers and pried apart metal binder hoops to get at last night's homework. "I'm not an advocate of promoting my students to blindly step onto the treadmill," she said, then stopped herself. "What do I mean by that? What's 'the treadmill'?"

No one knew.

"You know she's getting on a soapbox here, guys. What's the treadmill?"

One student offered, "Life?"

"*What's the treadmill?*"

"You don't want to get trapped?"

"Ooh, I love that word, 'trapped.' Trapped in what?" As Sheehy went in for the kill, I had to remind myself that these were twelve-year-olds, most of whom knew no other reality than school, few of whom had ever considered a treadmill as a metaphor. And here was Sheehy, warning them not to mindlessly believe that getting good grades is the One True Path to Happiness. Then, speaking quickly, she spun a scenario that a lot of them had likely rehearsed: "I need to get *really high grades* in sixth grade on the ELA tests so I can get into the Advanced Placement classes in high school, so that I can get into Dartmouth, Yale or Harvard or Cornell, so that I can get *a really good job* so that I can have a really nice car and a really big house and have a *really happy life*." She paused. "*It's a lie*. And I've said the same thing to your parents."

I looked at my watch. It was 9:04 a.m.

As the bell rang, she said, "Go forth and be epic!"

A student shouted, "We still love you!"

"I love you too!" Sheehy replied.

I asked what the story was behind that strange little exchange. She smiled and said, "I told them the first day 'I love you, each and every one of you. Don't do anything to make me stop loving you.'"

That afternoon in *WoW* club, one of the students announced to Sheehy that a classmate had quit. Sheehy told him to deliver a message: if she's going to quit, she needs to come in person and say why. "That's what heroes do." As if on cue, another student volunteered, "Only villains delegate!"

Over the past decade, Sheehy has made a name for herself among teachers worldwide. She is in demand at teachers' conferences, having laid out her vision before adoring crowds in Mumbai, San Francisco, and Sydney, among many others. But at an open house that evening in her own third-floor classroom, few parents had any idea who she was or what she was doing. "Are games the be-all, end-all, magic elixir, silver bullet? No," she said. "But game-like thinking and a game-like approach to things—taking good, solid game mechanics that come out of a well-designed video game and applying them to education? That's important."

Then she informed the parents that they were not simply going to sit and listen to her talk. They would create a character in *WoW* and get comfortable with it. "The world is being reintroduced to being playful," she said. The adults shifted uneasily in their chairs, unsure of what exactly that meant. One of the parents wanted to talk about how uncomfortable he was with games like *WoW*. He worried that it will socially isolate his kid. "Gaming *is* social," Sheehy said. "Very social. Even when they're playing a first-person shooter, they have four friends around them. What is the key? Balance. Too much of anything is not going to be a good thing."

Sheehy had spent weeks getting the students excited about their avatars, reminding them that a good *WoW* name should sound like it is straight out of *The Lord of the Rings*. The task has sent her students scrambling to reference materials—"The Art of Fantasy Names" website is popular, as are baby name websites. Sheehy has a litmus test that she can recite on demand. Fill in the blank with your proposed name: "Gandalf, Bilbo, Frodo, Thorin, Oin, Gloin, Aragorn, and ____."

A mother in blue sweatpants, a gray pullover sweatshirt, and furry Ugg boots sat down at a terminal and listened as Sheehy announced that the parents were all about to take a spin in *WoW*. The mother was uneasy, likely feeling the same confusion that Sheehy felt nine years earlier as she stared down *Second Life*. The game's welcome screen is thick with instructions and she read them like the fine print on a credit card agreement. Finally her daughter, sitting by her side, told her she just needed to decide what kind of character she wanted to be: a mage, a rogue, or a hunter.

"I don't want to fight," the mother said.

"Mom, they *all* fight," the daughter said, suggesting they just choose a name. She let her mother know that it had to fit in with Tolkein: Gandalf, Bilbo, all that.

"Laurie?" the mother suggested.

"*Mom!*"

They decided on a mage named Styx and quickly got her walking around the ingame world. But the mother was having difficulties with the arrow keys—Styx got trapped in the basement labyrinth of an old stone library and couldn't seem to find an exit door. Sheehy was telling the group that students will be in a guild with peers from eleven other schools, "negotiating, communicating, having opportunities to be a leader, having opportunities to participate in teamwork," but the mother just wanted to know whether a child who doesn't have decent hand-eye coordination would ever be good at moving her character around the screen.

"You'll *get* good," Sheehy said. "It's constructivist, scaffolded learning. They start out with one thing and they give you opportunities to use that one thing so you understand it. Then, and only then, do they give you the second thing." It is, she said, "experiential learning at its finest." Sheehy wasn't getting much of a reaction, so she mentioned that much of the *WoW* text is written at a tenth-grade level.

"Oh!" That was meaningful.

Sheehy noticed that Styx was trapped in the library and offered to help. Her bracelets dragging across the desk, Sheehy took control of the keyboard and mouse and easily found a stairwell and exit door. Then, since Styx's display showed she needed food, Sheehy began dispatching a few wild beasts. The mother looked on in awe as Sheehy clicked away, collecting treasure for each kill. "The game will teach her, and what the game doesn't teach her, she'll get it from her guildmates. Fear not—she will not be left behind. We do not leave anyone behind."

The mother asked, "What's a guildmate?"

Sheehy patiently answered her questions and said that further on in the game there would be a chance for her daughter to select a profession for her character. She could choose to be an herbalist who picks flowers, finds recipes, and mixes potions to sell in the auction house. Or perhaps she'd be an alchemist, or mine metals and make armor. Or she'd be a tailor, working with linen, wool, and silk. Actually, it was all starting to sound a little . . . blue collar. Wasn't this class supposed to be preparing our kids for the critical-thinking jobs of the twenty-first century? But then Sheehy explained that the auction house is a "complete mini-economy" that students can impact directly. "You can go into the auction house and decide, 'I'm going to buy up all of this and put a few back on at a really high price.'"

Sheehy wanted to show the mother that players teach each other, so she opened up a browser window, got on the *WoW* wiki and clicked on a picture of a ring. "Each one of these is a hyperlink that takes you to something else!" she said, marveling at the collective body of knowledge. "You get two rings on your person. It's got agility—plus-201 agility and plus-301 stamina, plus-121 hit, 1.18 percent at Level 85 and 142 crit. OK, so, you have to go, 'Well, I'm a hunter, I really need that agility, but I have plenty of hit, and that's a waste, I have to figure out if I want to balance this out with maybe finding something else that has expertise on it. So they're doing math like you wouldn't *believe*. They're doing percentages and ratios and. . . .'"

The mother interrupted her. "I have to tell you, I didn't really understand anything you just said in that sentence."

"Good! That's what I mean—they learn that! I didn't understand what any of that was before I played, and I certainly didn't understand it the first week I played, the first *year* I played. I understood it once it became important." The mother was still uneasy, so Sheehy laid it all out. "Anything you name, I could teach it in here," she said, waving at the screen. "I could teach math, I could teach science, I could teach psychology, I could teach geography, social studies, history, you name it."

The mom seemed impressed, but still mystified. Finally she admitted that her daughter will probably be just fine. "It's me," she said, as if coming clean to a tenacious therapist. Sheehy leaned in, put her hand on the woman's shoulder, and, in a hushed, just-between-us tone, said, "You need to get a free trial account and start playing. You're going to get such gratification out of it when you start figuring things out." She walked away, leaving the mother to fail on her own.

Unlike in the movies, there was no revelation here, no a-ha moment or breakthrough. "I don't know," the mother said once Sheehy was gone. It was clear that, like many adults, deep down she was afraid of breaking something, of making a mistake that would erase the world, a fear that her daughter likely didn't have. "It's just that I'm not a computer person, so for me . . . but I mean, I could see how it would really help kids." She put her hand on the mouse and tried to move her avatar around the screen a bit. Thanks to Sheehy, who intervened, Styx was now free to wander around the game world. She did so, but a bit aimlessly. "It's just a different way of learning. There's nothing wrong with that."

◖··············

In New York as elsewhere, a battery of skills tests looms large over students, and thus over their teachers. But Sheehy, back in the classroom for the first time in years, stood defiant. "I've had a long philosophical discussion with a bunch of people about this, and I'm basically not teaching to the test," she told me. "I just will *not* teach to the test. I'm not teaching test prep, I'm not teaching, 'This will be on the test.' I'm teaching what the curriculum is and I'm teaching beyond that."

As the year progressed, she struggled to squeeze the *WoW* lessons to fit the state requirements, rewriting it to align with new Common Core standards that New York took the lead in piloting. She created a massive series of "quests," each built around key skills and ideas. At her students' suggestion, she began using the popular game *Sid Meier's Civilization V* to teach about ancient civilizations. Custodians began throwing her out of the building at 11 p.m. each night. She later said she suspected that they were just jealous they couldn't play video games in her classroom, which they dubbed "The Man Cave."

Sheehy swapped out one of her personal favorite Hero's Journey books, *The Hobbit,* for the required young adult novel *The Lightning Thief.* A few of her students had read it on their own and "totally lost interest" after she succumbed to a requirement that they annotate and dissect the story. "I will never do that to them again," she said that spring. She admitted that she fretted a bit too much about how her kids would do on the state exams and regretted doubting herself. By the time the tests came and went, three other humanities teachers said they'd like to try the *WoW* curriculum in the fall. "I could have just exhaled and realized that if I had had more faith in my program, I could have relieved myself of a lot of stress. My kids did really, really well on the tests. And I know why."

EIGHT

. . . .➤

PROJECT UNICORN

*How a Heartless Media Conglomerate
Could Spark a New Golden Age
of Educational Gaming*

The bare storefront banquet hall looks like the kind of place you'd rent for a massive poker game, if people rented halls for poker games anymore. Set back from a century-old cobblestoned side street in Dumbo, that bustling, almost wholly manufactured Brooklyn neighborhood at the base of the Manhattan and Brooklyn bridges, the hall has white-painted brick walls, exposed plumbing, an open kitchen, and well-worn wooden floors. A Craigslist ad might read "Hipster Bar Mitzvahs."

On a hazy July morning, eleven young people, each one exactly the right age for a Bar Mitzvah, sit at the back of the room, taking up all the spaces around a pair of eight-foot banquet tables. Someone has thrown a green-and-white-checked plastic tablecloth over the surface and it puckers as each kid pokes intently at a brand-new tablet computer. At first the scene resembles a kind of hyper-focused computer camp. But supervisors insist—several times, actually—that it's not a camp. They're not licensed child-care providers, for one thing, and more to the point, they're actually paying the kids to be here. Show up faithfully from 10 a.m. to 4 p.m., three days a week in the summer and play a bunch of unfinished video games, and you'll earn a $100 Amazon gift card. One more thing: as you play, you must be willing to let the adults in the room point one of several tiny digital video cameras at you. Propped on tripods, the cameras are scattered across the tables, aimed at kids' faces and recording their facial expressions as they play.

With the gift card comes the unofficial and decidedly un-hip title "junior game designer." At a smaller table nearby, an actual game designer named Joe Mauriello shakes hands with a boy whose *Hello, My Name Is . . .* sticker displays the handwritten word *Julian*. Each morning for the past few weeks, Julian and his best friend John have showed up from Pelham, in Westchester County. Julian's mother works in an office nearby. John sits nearby, playing another game, and this morning the boys are dressed identically, as best friends sometimes are: blue T-shirts, blue shorts, white sneakers. About the only difference is their hair: John's, blond and delicate, is shorn close in a clean summer cut. Julian's is dark, thick, and a bit messy, the beginnings of a little tail showing down his back.

Before Julian can get himself into a chair, Mauriello hands him a tablet. "So this is *Food Web,*" Mauriello says. Julian sits, scans the screen and presses *PLAY.* No instructions, no introductions, no explanations. He's in the game immediately, and Mauriello sits back and watches as the boy slides his finger around the screen to move an animated *agouti,* a kind of unappealing brown South American rodent, as it simultaneously searches for meals and tries to avoid predators. Over the next few minutes, just one sound comes from the table: a barely audible brew of jungle noises (they're actually sonic placeholders—developers are still trying to figure out what the jungle actually sounds like). Julian's eyes dart intently over the screen, his right forefinger moving nearly as quickly. Finally he looks up, dazed but with a whisper of a smile. A snake has eaten his agouti.

Not certain what to do, Julian timidly hands the tablet back to Mauriello, who takes it, puts it aside and begins quizzing the boy, moving quickly through a predetermined list of questions: *Were the buttons clear? Was the game fun? Do you want to keep playing? Would you play this game again?* And finally: *Would you recommend it to your best friend?* Julian, mildly affirmative on each question, says he liked the game just fine and yes, he would recommend it to his best friend. He hops down and walks away, in search of some other diversion.

As it happens, the next play-tester is John. Mauriello hands the boy a tablet and now Julian's actual best friend is playing the game, once more in silence: here's the unappealing agouti, here are the predators. John slides the animal across the screen, back and forth, up and down, and like Julian's, his agouti is inevitably eaten. He hands back the tablet and the questions begin. His feet dangle in oversized sneakers as Mauriello asks, *Do you want to keep playing?*

John adopts a pained little smile. He's getting paid to be honest, but he doesn't want to hurt anyone's feelings.

"A little."

Mauriello makes a note, then asks: *Would you play this game again?*

"A little."

Would you recommend it to your best friend?

The boy bites his lip. "A little."

If this were a commercial video game studio, scenes like this would be literally unremarkable—no one would notice them or have a thing to say. Play-testing, hour after hour, week after week, happens all the time in the video-game world—it's part of its DNA. While it looked like a typical play test, what was unfolding in Dumbo was taking place on an entirely different level. Mauriello was testing the user experience of school, shaping it as tightly as he would the best-designed PlayStation game. A researcher as well as a designer, he was soliciting detailed customer feedback about what amounts to a middle-school biology lesson. When completed, *Food Web* would appear in a wireless digital textbook, supplementing a lesson on predators and prey.

Mauriello recalled that as he and his colleagues brainstormed science ideas, another arose, for a game about reproduction. Someone suggested creating a digital facsimile of a 4-H animal husbandry lesson, which puts children in the role of raising their own livestock. "Every time somebody said '4-H,' we were like, 'Yeah!'" Mauriello said. The logic was simple. If you're thirteen years old, would you rather read a textbook about a cow's reproductive system, or play a tablet game in which you're a little bovine sperm swimming toward an egg to inseminate it? Of course you'd want to play the game. They hired the British games studio Preloaded, which created a game called *Repro Hero*. Like *Food Web,* it got a thorough vetting during play-testing.

The hipster banquet hall, rented three days a week, is just around the corner from the world headquarters of Amplify, the improbable entity created in 2010 when Rupert Murdoch's News Corp. bought a 90 percent stake in the educational technology startup Wireless Generation, or "Wireless Gen," as it's known. The tablets, in a way, come courtesy of Murdoch, the polarizing Australian who helped bring us Fox News and spent $360 million on the Wireless Gen purchase. Strictly speaking, though, the benefactor is Amplify's CEO, the equally polarizing former New York City Schools chancellor Joel Klein. Just as Murdoch found a way, nearly thirty years ago, to disrupt the big-three television networks, Klein is hard at work disrupting what has become a big-three textbook market. In Klein's vision, his new textbooks—actually, much of his school day—will live on a tablet, giving teachers access to sophisticated data analytics about how well students are doing every minute: what lessons and materials they're accessing, how much time they spend on the material, and even how far they've read in a given assignment. "If you have a tablet-based approach, you can get a whole lot smarter a whole lot more quickly, because you're getting a lot of clicks from kids and teachers," Klein told me recently.[1]

Perhaps no media conglomerate looms larger and more darkly in the public imagination than News Corp. Before Murdoch split it in two in 2013, it was one of the largest media companies on the planet. In the United States, News Corp.'s ties to Fox News make it radioactive for good liberals. Over two years, nearly everyone I spoke to on the creative side of Amplify recounted the awkward conversations they had with friends and family after they broke the news that, as one person put it, "Rupert Murdoch signs my paychecks."

Actually, from the start the digital textbook effort has displayed nothing if not a palpable sense of social justice. Its creators say technology can help erase the nagging achievement gap between rich and poor children by offering the equivalent of one-to-one tutoring in nearly every subject. Rich kids get that level of personal attention every day, they say. If we want true equality, shouldn't everyone?

Early on, Klein's team realized that without the help of video games to back up the lessons, equality was probably an empty promise. The revelation came in 2011, around nine months after the Wireless acquisition, when Amplify's top managers held a series of in-house meetings and brainstorming sessions at corporate apartments nearby. The sessions ultimately produced the largest corporate investment ever into educational games: a suite of forty full-feature, commercial-quality games, many brought to you by the same studios who created the alluring iPhone and iPad games you reliably turn to for challenge, companionship, and comfort. By any measure, the effort is unprecedented, and it represents the best hope of video-game advocates in the fight for brainshare in schools.

At a basic level, the idea makes sense, since both teachers and game designers have a similar problem: how do you persuade people to do something new and spend time doing it, even if they don't believe it's in their own best interest? Most institutions—schools, workplaces, families—use one of two simple but mostly ineffective methods: bribes or threats. Want your kid to take out the trash? Hand him a lollipop. Want your schools to raise test scores? Hand out pink slips to the teachers whose kids perform worst.

Julian and John, the two young play-testers, were at the center of a multimillion-dollar effort to develop a third way: If you want school to work, don't bribe or threaten people. *Show* them what it's like to succeed. Give them a taste of the work required and let them play with it. If kids need to learn about predators and prey, among a million other things, let them *be* the predators and prey. Let them make mistakes and help one another. Eventually they'll figure it out for themselves and take pleasure in it.

The idea may seem a flaky, anything-goes holdover from the 1960s, but it's rooted in a well-researched principle known as *self-determination theory*. Developed at the University of Rochester in the late 1970s and early 1980s by psychologists Edward Deci and Richard Ryan, the theory holds that extrinsic carrot-and-stick motivators may work in the short term, but they rarely help people achieve their long-term goals. Simply put, people are not machines. They can't be controlled by flipping their psychological switches like rats in a cage, fed pellets when they perform a task. As tempting as that metaphor might seem—and modern psychology has helped make it nearly gospel—Deci and Ryan have long held that if we want people to be productive and happy, we've got to find ways to help them own and enjoy doing what needs to be done.

Actually, people do respond to extrinsic motivators, but in a way that strengthens the importance of intrinsic motivators. If you're faced with getting an A in organic chemistry and you don't like organic chemistry, about the only way you'll succeed is if you see how it fits into your long-term goal. If you want to be a doctor, you'll put up with it. At home, if you're forced each week to take out the trash, you may actually come to accept and appreciate the task's value, but not because you get a lollipop each week. Associating trash-taking with lollipops only gets you to do it when lollipops appear, or for as long as you *believe* they'll appear. But you'll take out the trash forever if you believe that taking out the trash has value, if you can tie it to the feeling of contributing to the upkeep of the household, even when there are no lollipops in sight.

Video games may seem all gold stars, lollipops, bells, and whistles, like playing a Las Vegas slot machine. But what learning theorists are discovering is that good, well-designed games are powerful learning tools for just the opposite reason: They *don't* reward casual effort, mindless repetition, or rat-in-a-cage responses. Instead they reward practice, persistence, and risk-taking. They give the brain a way to filter out distraction and get to the task at hand. Most of all, they implicitly reward those who learn to enjoy the tasks they offer. They forge expertise.

Amplify's new tablet computer was scheduled to debut in the fall of 2014, with each game extending the lessons of its middle-school curriculum. What set the effort apart wasn't just its size or scope, but its stubbornly counterintuitive philosophy: play must be voluntary. Its creators cite the writings of Johan Huizinga, the Dutch theorist and one of the godfathers of play theory, who in the late 1930s wrote, "Play to order is no longer play."[2] To him, the most important feature of play is not necessarily that it's fun but that it's chosen. The player can step out at any time and say, "I don't want to play anymore." Without that, it's not a game but a job. Mark Twain expressed a similar sentiment when in *The Adventures of Tom Sawyer* he said of the title character, "If he had been a great and wise philosopher, like the writer of this book, he would now have comprehended that Work consists of whatever a body is *obliged* to do, and that Play consists of whatever a body is not obliged to do."[3] Simply put, the Amplify games are optional. Ideally, they're not to be assigned as homework, extra practice, or summer enrichment. They're not to be relied on at all, actually. Kids are invited to play them—or not—as they wish. A few of the games may hold the key to understanding cell biology or *Tom Sawyer,* but they are, at least in theory, off limits to teachers.

The unlikely idea comes courtesy of two men who met at Yale in 1989 and who for the past twenty-five years have wandered into and out of each other's orbits. One pursued a career in writing, politics, and diplomacy, the other in business. But every few years, one would find the other and hire him. The last time that happened, in 2008, the pair eventually created, almost by accident, Amplify's games effort, a project so improbable that even those involved often wonder whether it will ever work. The man at the head of the enterprise initially offered his best guess: just ten percent of their ideas for games would likely ever make a difference. If that happened, he'd be satisfied.

In 1992, Justin Leites was a Yale graduate philosophy student, an hour and a half from his home on the Upper West Side of Manhattan. A friend's invitation to volunteer for Bill Clinton's presidential campaign got him an introduction that summer to Brooke Shearer, a former journalist and friend of the Clintons who had taken on the role of Hillary Clinton's aide and personal advisor. For a time during the campaign, Leites served as Tipper Gore's personal secretary, a Jewish kid from Riverside Drive channeling the voice of a southern politician's wife as he ghost-wrote endless thank-you notes. After the campaign, Leites returned to Yale, but he soon got a call from Shearer, who by then was running the President's Commission on White House Fellowships, a kind of high-powered internship for political wonks. She wondered if he would like to work at the White House for a while.

At Yale, one of the students in the class Leites taught had been a hard-charging senior from upstate New York with a shock of brown hair and an irrepressible smile. Larry Berger was semi-famous even before he'd arrived in New Haven. Four years earlier, he'd persuaded two classmates at Ithaca High School to help him write a guidebook to the SAT. *Up Your Score: The Underground Guide to the SAT* appeared in 1987, when he was nineteen. Updated annually for more than twenty-five years, it has never gone out of print. Berger is now pushing fifty, but an image of his teen-aged self still appears on the cover, dressed in a purple Oxford shirt and blue jeans, one of five "kids who aced the SAT."

Berger recalled that Leites was a brilliant thinker, more challenging than many of Yale's tenured celebrity professors. That fall, when the teacher went off to work for Clinton, the student went to Oxford as a Rhodes Scholar (one of Berger's housemates was David Coleman, who'd later go on to head the College Board). Eventually, Leites persuaded Berger to apply for a White House fellowship. Berger titled his application "Lanes for Children on the Information Superhighway" and believed his idea was suited to the U.S. Department of Education. But NASA administrator Daniel Goldin read it and told him, "If you go to Education, they'll let you talk about it. If you come here, I will let you actually do it."

Berger spent a year developing *BioBlast,* an early computer-based biology curriculum. "I wouldn't swear that the taxpayers got as much out of it as I did," he said. For the next five years he dabbled in writing and educational technology, and in 2000 he and a partner founded Wireless Generation, based largely on an idea in an obscure 1972 essay by Alan Kay, the tech pioneer who has compared computers to pianos. A researcher at Xerox's Palo Alto Research Center (known widely as Xerox PARC), Kay proposed a device he called the DynaBook, a $500 "personal computer for children of all ages." What he had in mind—a flat, handheld "carry anywhere" computer about the size and shape of small-town phone book—looks and feels remarkably like an iPad. At a time when most computers "weighed over a hundred pounds and ate punch cards,"[4] Kay envisioned a thin, lightweight device with a pressure-sensitive keyboard and the visual appeal of TV, but "controllable by the child rather than the networks." Thirty years before the dawn of wireless Internet, Kay anticipated books being "instanti-ated" on the device. Libraries, he wrote, "are very useful, yet one neither wants to put up with their schedules nor locations (or con-tent) one hundred percent of the time."[5]

Though he was entrenched in computer research—Xerox PARC is the lab from which a twenty-four-year-old Steve Jobs in 1979 stole the idea for the Macintosh's elegant user interface and mouse—Kay was interested as much in education as in hardware. He shared "constructivist" beliefs with a few educational theorists of the era, most notably MIT's Seymour Papert, who called per-sonal computers "the children's machine." Kay saw the DynaBook as a kind of multimedia, interdisciplinary piano that would allow children to "play" with schoolwork. "If we want children to learn any particular area, then it is clearly up to us to provide them with something real and enjoyable to 'do' on their way to perfection of both the art and the skill," he wrote in 1972. Schools generally don't work this way, he said, especially with subjects like math, which children "do" mostly through memorization and dull repeti-tion. Fortunately, he wrote, "kids don't have to learn their native tongue under these circumstances."

Berger wanted to build a DynaBook, or something like it, but his work with teachers had shown him that first he had to build a dif-ferent device—for *them*—one that streamlined paperwork and cut down on the time they spent analyzing kids' skills. If you could build something that teachers would love to use, it would be easy to layer student applications on top of that. Student data, he realized, was everywhere, but schools weren't using it efficiently. They gave read-ing tests every day, but the results were in paper folders all over the school district. If schools could streamline their data collection and make the results available to teachers on demand, "suddenly it was much more valuable and interesting to the teacher—and much more valuable and interesting to the system as a whole." Desktop comput-ers, by then omnipresent in schools, were too cumbersome to check on the fly. Even laptop computers were inadequate. Teachers, he said, "don't really have laps because they don't get a chance to sit down."

Berger and his team raised $17 million from investors—among the first was Irwin Jacobs, who at the time was CEO of the San Diego tech firm Qualcomm. Jacobs listened to a pitch by Berger and a few days later sent over a $250,000 check. Attached was a Post-it note that read, "Let me know what percent of your company I bought."[6] Berger admits that the company, in its early years, was "desperate for scale" as it competed with the sales forces of the big publishers already on the ground. Berger and one of his vice presidents would later tell of getting "disturbingly good" at a little game they'd play during nighttime airline flights: They'd look out the window and assign numbers to each cluster of lights they saw. During one flight, he recalled, they decided that the city out the left window was a "37." Another, an hour later, clustered by a river, was a "54." When they landed, Berger checked Google Earth. The first city was Little Rock, with forty elementary schools, the second Wichita, with fifty-one.[7]

On January 8, 2002, President George W. Bush signed the No Child Left Behind law, a massive reauthorization of the federal Elementary and Secondary Education Act, which lays out much of Washington's commitment to public school funding. Congress would soon hand over nearly $50 billion for education, and that night Berger's employees pored over the massive bill looking for potential business. Berger would later write that they found "a rare opportunity" in the law's $1 billion-per-year Reading First program. Though 80 percent each year went to schools, the rest went directly to states, "an unusual amount of liquidity centralized at the state level that did not already have a bureaucracy designed to spend it."[8] They realized that Wireless Gen could win the reading assessment contract for an entire state without having to visit the thousands of districts those contracts comprised. They'd simply have to persuade a few bureaucrats in the state capital to buy its products. Unlike the big publishers who traditionally sold directly to districts and retained sales teams numbering in the thousands, Berger could count his national sales force on one hand. The law eventually earned him eighteen state contracts.

Wireless's first breakout product was a low-cost handheld computer that ran DIBELS, a popular diagnostic reading test for kindergartners. Soon Berger was shipping the devices to thousands of districts—and collecting reams of data on student performance. By 2007, Wireless Gen had 300 employees and was gathering diagnostic information for more than 2.5 million students, including most of the kindergarten-through-third-grade classrooms in New York,

Chicago, Miami, Houston, Washington, D.C., and more than a thousand smaller districts. As part of its agreements, Wireless had access to the information as well and was soon dabbling in data analysis for districts. Berger realized he needed someone to make sense of all of it.

By then, Leites was looking for a job. He'd spent seven years with the Clinton administration, but only a year at the White House. In February 1994, Clinton had tapped Strobe Talbott, his old Oxford roommate, to be deputy secretary of state. Like Shearer, Talbott was a former journalist. He was also Shearer's husband, and he quickly snapped up Leites, who moved from babysitting White House interns to promoting democracy abroad as a State Department speechwriter. After Clinton left office in 2001, Leites moved back to New York to work at the United Nations Development Program under Kofi Annan, where he helped a Danish colleague create and implement an audacious plan for modernizing the program's information technology systems. A consultant estimated that the new software would require a help desk of 200 technicians staffed around the clock. The UN's budget wouldn't allow it, so Leites set up online users' groups tying together each office. The users, he decided, would run their own help desk.

Why would career bureaucrats want to spend nights and weekends helping each other learn a new computer system? What Leites knew was that they worked for the United Nations for a reason: They wanted to be part of something big, international, and important. Because they'd also configured the software, they felt it was theirs. "It wasn't, 'Oh, the crappy software that the home office gave us,'" he said. "It was, 'Well, all right, this is *our* crappy software. We need to figure out how to make it better.'" It was self-determination theory 101: find what's worth doing and give people an opportunity to forge expertise. "We'd go home and go to sleep, and while we're all asleep you'd have the Vietnam office and the South Africa office and the Brazil office and the Russia office all helping everybody else," he said. "They really felt like they were part of professional communities, so it was really powerful."

After Annan left the United Nations in 2006, Leites fell into a funk. Suddenly the focus was less on collaboration than compliance, and he was soon spending his workdays online, playing fantasy sports. He loved the rich data sets that baseball offered—essentially every game ever played has been plotted on a spreadsheet—and he soon become one of the best fantasy baseball managers in the world. Simultaneously, he was calling friends, searching for a job. When he finally reached Berger, his former student offered to hire him on the spot. Leites agreed but later admitted, "I barely knew what he did."

He began working with Berger's biggest customers—Washington, D.C., and Chicago, among others—to help them understand how well their students were doing and how teachers could improve instruction. He decided that if schools wanted to do things differently, they had to figure out how to tap into teachers' desires to see their students succeed. He began poring over research on teacher effectiveness and what he found changed everything: teachers who somehow got kids to do *more work*—more pages of reading, more writing, more math problems—almost always outperformed their peers. A few teachers, the research found, were persuading their students to do twice as much work as the students in the next room. He wondered how they did that.

Meanwhile, the first iPads were appearing in stores and Berger immediately thought of Alan Kay. He saw that the tablet computer "was going to be a really compelling device for schools" and envisioned a new kind of curriculum on a new kind of textbook—not just a device that turned textbook pages into touchscreen PDFs. He wanted a DynaBook, and he began looking for someone who would help him create one. For years, publishers had come around asking Berger if he was ready to sell the company. He always balked. Most had deep pockets, but none were "the kinds of people who would make a big bet on things that were unproven." While talking to one of the big publishers, he learned that News Corp. was looking to get into the education publishing business. News Corp. CEO Rupert Murdoch has said that schools remain the last holdout from the digital revolution: "In every other part of life, someone who woke up after a fifty-year nap would not recognize the world around him. But not in education."[9] News Corp. wanted to challenge the textbook monopolies, and Wireless needed cash to develop its digital curriculum.

In November 2010, after months of negotiations, News Corp. bought 90 percent of Wireless Generation for $360 million in cash. Shortly after the sale, Berger began holding brainstorming sessions on the new curriculum. During one session, Leites raised his hand and volunteered that if Amplify could get kids excited about spending more time with the material through games, teachers would get excited too. He said he had experience developing games—in middle school and high school, he'd worked for the tiny New York board game company Simulations Publications Inc., producing titles like *Campaign for North Africa, Citadel of Blood,* and *Terrible Swift Sword.* Leites hadn't worked in games since he'd graduated high school, but for thirty years, through getting married and starting a family, he'd kept up with the industry. He could honestly say that most of the educational games on the market were crap. Leites said he'd write up a few ideas.

Berger was amazed. "It was clear that Justin had encyclopedic knowledge of games," he said, recalling the meeting. "He just started taking it and running with it." Before long, Leites was running the new games department.

The sweet spot for games, the two men decided, was in middle school, where many kids lose interest in school. They began calculating what it would take for the "big breakthrough" that Klein, their new boss, was seeking. If they wanted kids to play an educational game for half an hour to two hours a day after school, how much content did they need? There may be just 180 days in a school year, but if kids are to play the games over the summer, the stakes rise. The games had to cover multiple subjects: reading, math, science, history. And they had to work together seamlessly, strengthening kids' skills across different disciplines. The irony, Leites said, is that efforts like Amplify's are often lumped in with those built around teaching kids "twenty-first-century skills" like thinking critically and working together. While those are important, he said, "I actually think that what I'm trying to do is teach kids nineteenth-century skills." If you were lucky enough to be a white, wealthy young male in the nineteenth century, you likely got a great traditional education, complete with reading, writing, math, and scientific inquiry. "Those are not new skills," Leites said. "What's different is we want more people to have them. We don't want just 1 percent of our society to have those skills."

Leites insisted that there be games for different kinds of players. Those who spend every free minute playing *World of Warcraft* in their bedroom at home are different from those who pull out an iPhone at the bus stop and play *Cut the Rope,* but they may be sitting side by side on the school bus. Unless Amplify's games tapped into the abilities of both kids, the effort would fail. Forty games, they decided, was the least they could build. To do that, they needed help. Leites e-mailed Jesse Schell.

They'd never met, but Leites knew that Schell was one of the industry's most independent thinkers. The head of his own Pittsburgh game studio, Schell taught game design at Carnegie Mellon University and had written an influential game design textbook, *The Art of Game Design: A Book of Lenses.* Schell understood the challenges of designing educational games better than just about anyone. School, he'd once written, is simply a game. Indeed, our whole educational system is a game, with due dates standing in for countdown clocks, grades for scores, and final exams for boss levels. What's an honor roll but a sanctioned leader board?[10] The only reason school didn't feel like a game, he said, was because traditional education often features "a real lack of surprises, a lack of projection, a lack of pleasures, a lack of community, and a bad interest curve."[11]

Schell was perhaps most well-known by then for an infamous talk he gave at the 2010 Design, Innovate, Communicate, Entertain, or DICE, Summit, in which he warned of the dangers of rampant gamification and the psychological tricks of many casual games, including the "elastic velvet rope" of free games like *Club Penguin,* which bring in millions of dollars by tricking parents into underwriting their kids' online gaming habits. He warned that the convergence of inexpensive sensors and "points" systems would inevitably unleash a kind of dystopian world, in which just about everything we do is measured and rewarded. Schell envisioned a near future in which sensors track every aspect of our lives—how long we brush our teeth and how fast our heart beats on a walk—and award points for each achievement. It was a decidedly tongue-in-cheek talk, but it went viral. Within months more than a million people had seen it online. "This was shocking, especially to me," Schell later said, "because I'm a college professor and I'm not really used to people listening to what I say."[12] Leites loved the talk and, like many smart game designers, winced at the prospect of gamified toothbrushes. He decided that if he could bring Schell on board, building the rest of the team would be easy.

When Schell didn't respond to an e-mail, Leites began calling him. "It was like a six- to nine-month courtship," Leites said, "because he was like, 'You're from *where* and you want *what?* You have *money?*'" Finally Leites and Berger got on a plane and flew to Pittsburgh. "They were very serious," Schell recalled upon hearing their pitch. "They had a vision and they really believed in it right from the very beginning. My first thoughts were, 'I don't know if you guys know what you're getting into here.'"

One of Leites's biggest ideas, he told Schell, was an open-world, multiplayer reading game, then called *Librariana,* in which players would interact with characters from classic books—Tom Sawyer, Dr. Jekyll, the Cheshire Cat, Frankenstein's monster, and so forth—and go on adventures with them. At its core would be an electronic library of a thousand classic and modern books that would fit seamlessly with the game and that kids could read anytime. *Librariana* would keep a record of what books you'd read, how far you'd gotten and how well you understood them. If all went as planned, Leites hoped, a kid could pick up *Librariana* in sixth grade and not put it down until high school. He wanted Schell to be the lead developer and integrate several dozen mini-games throughout the main narrative, each developed by a different studio.

"They painted this big picture of what they wanted to do," Schell said, "and we thought, 'Well that's really big and that's really expensive.' And we talk to a lot of people with big, expensive visions who can't back them up." What Schell didn't know was that Leites had been talking to developers at other game studios for months about what it would take to make *Librariana* happen. Leites knew he had Klein's support, and he soon had a ballpark estimate of how much it would cost.

Schell had been burned before, by a big textbook company that had hired him to develop a new history game. They'd shelved the project after an upper-management reshuffle and never restarted it. But Schell saw promise in Leites's portfolio idea, as well as the patently experimental quality of *Librariana.* He especially liked Amplify's focus on middle school. "It's a time where kids are going through changes and sort of setting patterns that are going to last them a long time," he said. It's also a time when a lot of kids lose their way.

Schell finally signed on, and Leites remembered one of his early meetings with the Pittsburgh team, during the "get to know you" phase. Schell's designers, many of them still in their twenties, asked Leites which games he liked to play, so he mentioned, a bit sheepishly, that he loved *Dungeons and Dragons,* the nearly forty-year-old fantasy tabletop role-playing game. "I'm a little embarrassed to admit that," he recalled, "because it's going to make me seem like this total old fart. It's this game from 1974! And here are these young guys who are doing these cutting-edge things." After a pause, one of them said, "Well, we still play *Dungeons and Dragons* twice a week after work."

The partnership gave Leites a kind of instant credibility—and a way to recruit other studios. "I could sort of say I wasn't just some random guy from some company you'd never heard of." He moved quickly and soon had an international dream team of game designers on board, all of them pitching their own ideas and not the other way around. Austin, Texas, designer Adam Saltsman, who essentially created the "endless runner" genre with his 2009 game *Canabalt,* signed on to make a middle-school version of his iPad game *Hundreds.* The British studio Preloaded pitched *TyrAnt,* a science game set in an ant colony. Asymmetric Publications, a San Francisco studio with a cult following for their lo-fi game *Kingdom of Loathing,* pitched a version of their hand-to-hand combat game for vocabulary, *Word Realms.*

Even after they signed contracts, Schell remained skeptical that News Corp. would let the massive library game, now called *Lexica,* unfold as it should. For a while, he said, the game's in-house nickname was *Unicorn.* He'd tell his officemates, "A project like this shouldn't exist, but here it is and it's standing right there. Maybe if we just tiptoe up real quietly, maybe we can capture this thing. Or maybe the suit will come off and two guys will come out and beat us with clubs."[13]

Three years after his notorious 2010 gamification talk, Schell, by then in the thick of development for Amplify's games, took the stage again at DICE and offered an explanation—less apology than clarification—of his previous remarks. He said that after the original talk, dozens of companies sprang up—no fewer than three developing gamified toothbrushes. He told the crowd, "I have had dozens of people come to me and say, 'I started my company because of that talk you gave.' And I'm like, 'Man, don't blame *me* for that shit.' I don't want any part of that.'"

But he'd also discovered in the intervening three years that the hunger for gamification isn't a total boondoggle. One guy had come up to Schell and thanked him for saving his life—he'd weighed 350 pounds and after hearing the 2010 talk began giving himself points for losing weight. He'd dropped 200 pounds.

In the end, Schell realized, people want games that are going to make them better people. "If when I come out of the game on the other side, I feel like, 'Yes, I am more the person I want to be now,' if you can do those things, you're taking some good steps." All the same, he said, game developers must take seriously the power they wield to persuade people to *do* things: "We're shifting into an enjoyment-based economy, and nobody knows more about enjoyment than game developers." The world, he said, "is kind of looking to us to lead them into Utopia."[14]

Over the next several months, more than 1,000 kids like Julian and John would pass through Amplify's play-testing sessions. They'd change the direction of several games and effectively put the brakes on others. *Food Web* would undergo several iterations. Mauriello's team would tweak a similar title, *Habitactics,* after students complained that they didn't like it when foxes ate rabbits. "That always upsets them," Mauriello said.

When they finally put *Repro Hero,* the virtual 4-H bovine insemination game, in front of kids, Mauriello recalled that things didn't go as planned. The young play-testers "got all quiet—they wouldn't look at each other. They got very uncomfortable."

Seventh graders may have the opposite sex on their minds nearly all the time, but getting them to actually simulate insemination—even bovine insemination, even in a highly abstracted way—fell flat. "It was too much," he said. They ended up tabling the game indefinitely.

NINE

· ❭

A WALK IN THE WOODS

*How a First-Person Game
Based on Thoreau's* Walden
*Can Make Transcendentalism—
and Reading—Cool Again*

You awake in a field of wildflowers by the shore of a pond. The frame of an unfinished cabin sits nearby, a pile of boards at its side waiting to be cut. A campfire crackles a few feet from the front door. You are alone and unarmed and, within moments, hungry. The cabin needs walls and the fire needs tending, so you get to work. First you pick a handful of berries from a bush nearby, then you saw wood for siding. You walk to the pond and collect driftwood for fuel. Or perhaps this time you don't. Perhaps you stroll through the endless forest, a lovely, dreamlike, painstakingly rendered landscape that resembles nothing so much as a three-dimensional egg tempera painting. Perhaps you wander over to the train tracks at the top of the ridge and follow them into town. Or you simply sit by the fire, listen to birdsong and read *The Iliad*. It is summer. The year is 1845 and you are twenty-seven years old. Your name is Henry David Thoreau. The pond, it seems, is Walden Pond, and for the moment you are its only inhabitant.

If a good video game is, as the designer Sid Meier once said, "a series of interesting choices," then *Walden, A Game* is the ultimate game. In development for seven years as of this writing by a mostly volunteer team, the indie title is all about choices. But these are decidedly not the choices presented by most video games. There is no captured princess to rescue or alien invasion to repel, no zombie apocalypse, no war in a fictional Middle Eastern country and no real conflict of any kind. There is, strictly speaking, no power struggle except the one going on inside the player's head. As such, many of the verbs of this game are unlike those you'll encounter in other games. There is no fighting, no flying, no dancing, no driving, no cathedral-scaling. Instead, you gather, fish, sew, build, stroll, explore, think, talk, watch, listen, read, and rest. Even in failure there is no dying, only a bit of "fainting" that is over nearly as soon as it begins. There are no locks to pick or puzzles to solve. In place of levels are sunlit days and starry nights, four seasons and a journal that you fill with bits of Thoreau's actual meditations. There are no weapons, although you can borrow an axe from your friend and patron Ralph Waldo Emerson, who lives in nearby Concord, Massachusetts, and who has graciously invited you to live in his woods. But the axe is strictly for chopping wood. No homicides are allowed, even if, as Thoreau often declared, your fellow man drives you nuts.

Designed to be played on a laptop or home computer, *Walden, A Game* is not just a game. It is also an invitation to read and think about *Walden,* the book, to absorb its worldview and see for yourself what it's like to "live deliberately," as Thoreau would have said. The game's visionary and main creator, the veteran designer and educator Tracy Fullerton, calls it "my version, my translation, my sort of adaptation." As she has begun to move beyond creating commercial games, Fullerton, like others in the industry, has begun to see the potential of the form to breathe new life into the classics, those revered books that, as Mark Twain said, "everybody wants to have read and nobody wants to read."[1] She and others see games as a way to reinvent reading itself as a more active, embodied, social undertaking.

The book you're reading right now, you'll remember, began as an exploration of what was happening to reading in America, whether technology, in the form of texting, social networking, and games, was making books obsolete. How could mere ink on paper—even digital ink on digital paper—compete with moving, singing, swooshing, touchscreen *spectacle?* "The electronic impulse works against the durational reverie of reading," critic Sven Birkerts wrote twenty years ago. "And however much other media take up the slack—of storytelling, say—what is lost is the contemplative register."[2] Reading words like these, I was, at first, very discouraged. I remember standing between displays at the Los Angeles Convention Center during the Electronic Entertainment Expo, or E3, the earsplitting annual trade show of the video game industry. I remember taking in the lights, the music, the gunplay and explosions—journalist Jonathan Rauch once called it "one of the loudest places I have ever been"[3]—and thinking, *It's done. Books are done. Contemplation is done.*

Then, almost as soon as I began to lose hope, I began hearing about projects like *Walden.* I was surprised to find that, like Fullerton, nearly every game designer I met was already thinking about the same thing. Most were extremely well-read and intensely curious, though—and this is perhaps the most interesting part—many didn't do well in school. In fact, most were successful *in spite* of their formal education. In many cases they had taught themselves much of what they needed to know.

Many of them were thinking about the future of books.

I met Carla Engelbrecht Fisher, a New York game designer with a PhD from Columbia University's Teachers College, who in October 2013 persuaded Apple's App Store to release her $1.99 "endless runner" game. It resembled a kind of simplified *Temple Run,* with one key difference: in her version, a pixilated Elizabeth Bennet runs and jumps across the entire unabridged text of *Pride and Prejudice,* all 121,873 words of it, as the words stream by. Think of it as a Regency-era teleprompter. The little game might actually help focus readers' minds on the words, though stopping is not allowed, so it's hardly a practical solution—more of a lark and demonstration of the different kinds of reading that are possible on a smartphone. Almost by accident, Fisher said, she struck upon the app's name: *Stride and Prejudice.* "I love that pun," she told me. "That playfulness is what we need to be able to do to find other ways of doing education."[4]

I met Eoghan Kidney (his first name is pronounced "Owen"), an Irish screenwriter, who in July 2014 successfully crowd-funded the first portion of a planned virtual-reality version of James Joyce's *Ulysses*. To be played with special goggles that give players the peculiar impression that they're *in* a scene, the project—dubbed *In Ulysses*—is aimed at helping readers understand the "completely, utterly misunderstood" 1922 modernist epic by immersing them in an interactive digital rendition of Dublin on June 16, 1904, the day in which the book's events take place. The simulation would, eventually, stream the book's full text. "*Ulysses* is great," Kidney told potential funders. "Well, that's what we're told." When I spoke to him, he said he'd known about Joyce's epic "from when I was quite young," but admitted that he hadn't actually gotten around to reading it until two years earlier, with the help of extensive annotations and an interpretive podcast. The vast majority of Irish students, he said, "don't read *any* Joyce in school." Even the adults who helped him fund the project admitted that they like the idea "because they kind of see it as their opportunity to maybe *read* the thing," he said. "I get a lot of that. I get a lot of 'Yes! Yes! *Make* this thing!'"[5]

I met Laura Fleming, a New Jersey elementary school librarian who was working to get teachers interested in a digital serial novel called *Inanimate Alice*. Created by the British novelist Kate Pullinger and the British/Canadian multimedia artist Chris Joseph, *Alice* doubles down on spectacle—it blinks, buzzes, hums, sings, jitterbugs, plays games, and, on occasion, rains and snows. Whenever I'd ask Fleming about the story, she'd talk for half an hour, then e-mail me just to be sure I didn't have any questions. Her students, she said, were "absolutely enthralled" with *Alice* and had begun discussing it online through chat groups. The story was immersive like little else at school and the first piece of fiction that had gotten them to understand how a reader can see life through a character's eyes. Critics can't seem to agree on a name for the genre—they call works like *Alice* "episodic multiplatform stories" or "multimedia online novels," paratext or technotext. Someone even suggested "Franken-novel," though most often the *Rocky Horror*–sounding "transmedia" seems to have stuck. Digital pioneer and *Wired* magazine co-founder Kevin Kelly has called them "books we watch or television we read."[6] Fleming didn't much care what anybody called *Alice*. "It's a book," she said. Her students read it. They like it. The lines between different media "are so blurred for them" that there's nothing to discuss. The world of *Inanimate Alice,* she said, "is the world the kids are growing up in."[7]

I soon realized that I was not only outflanked in the fight over reading but, to my great mortification, very late to the battle. Many game designers—and, as it turned out, a few key writers, like Pullinger—were not only thinking about the future of books but had spent years strategizing about *what to do.* By the time I began feebly poking at what I imagined was the Corpse of Reading, these folks had already managed to hoist it onto a table, strap it down, and, electricity humming, shock the lovable old beast back to life. Far from seeing games as the opposite of books, they were beginning to see games as a way to save them.

As far back as 2004, editors and game designers at the children's publisher Scholastic, led by the young-adult novelist David Levithan, who is also its editorial director, were planning what was then a ten-book series that wove online games and trading cards into the novels' plots. The experiment was a response to what he and his colleagues saw as a misunderstanding about children's media habits. "Everybody, in common parlance, was seeing kids in terms of 'readers vs. gamers,'" he said. "You were one or the other. The majority of kids are actually readers *and* gamers. They don't see a dichotomy—they don't feel that they have to choose."[8] Scholastic, which publishes the Harry Potter and *The Hunger Games* books in the United States, began the effort as an experiment that placed Levithan's stable of writers in the same room as its group of in-house game designers and programmers, known as the Lab for Informal Learning. "Everything we did would draw kids back to the books," he said. The first title in the *39 Clues* series appeared in 2008, written by *Percy Jackson & the Olympians* author Rick Riordan, who told the *New York Times,* "Some kids are always going to prefer games over books. But if you can even reach a few of those kids and give them an experience with a novel that makes them think, 'Hey, reading can be another way to have an adventure,' then that's great. Then I've done my job."[9] The series took off among young readers, and its success encouraged Levithan to expand the idea into three series, comprising dozens of books. Eventually, the Lab for Informal Learning merged with the editorial department. "The gamers know much more about storytelling now," Levithan said. "And the storytellers know much more about gaming."

🌓⋯⋯⋯⋯⋯

When I met the novelist Matthue Roth in the summer of 2013, he was at work in his eighth-floor Brooklyn cubicle, writing dialogue for Tom Sawyer, the serial troublemaker, eponymous Mark Twain hero, and one of the main characters of Amplify's tablet-based, open-world reading game *Lexica,* which you heard about briefly in chapter 8. "I love the hell out of Tom Sawyer," he said, but admitted that he was having trouble tapping into the boy's voice. He was deleting lines of dialogue almost as soon as he had typed them. "His mission statement is that he wants to mess with the *status quo* in unexpected ways," Roth said. "When you're designing a game, the one thing that you *don't* want is to have unexpected ways."[10] Roth, a thirty-five-year-old Philadelphia native and observant Hasidic Jew, wears his beard full and his hair long in traditional *payot*. He had, he explained, invented the unusual spelling of his first name as a joke when he was nineteen, then bought the domain name www.matthue.com when he was twenty. "It turned semi-serious after that," he said. Already a noted young-adult novelist and father of two when he began working for Amplify, Roth had recently found that the only time he could find to get his own writing done was on the subway to and from work. The strategy seemed to be paying off: a month earlier, he had published his first illustrated children's book, *My First Kafka,* "a picture book about existentialism" that he'd written for his four-year-old daughter. She had since turned five and was "obsessed with death—she's not scared of death, she's really fascinated by it," he said. At the time, Roth and his wife, the Brooklyn restaurateur Itta Werdiger Roth, were expecting their third child, and he was also working on his first adult novel, about "seventy-year-old Jewish men who are secretly pirates." In some ways, he said, it was a complete shift from what he usually writes about. "In another way, I think it's all about the same thing."[11]

Roth's first novel, *Nevermind the Goldbergs,* came out in 2006—he jokes that he was the first writer to tap into the "Orthodox teenage punk rock" demographic. By then he had already written *Yom Kippur a Go-Go,* a memoir about becoming an Orthodox Jew. His second novel, *Losers,* appeared in 2008. Roth's publisher, Scholastic, marketed the book by calling it "*Borat* as directed by John Hughes." (As it turns out, Roth's editor at Scholastic is Levithan.) Roth's introduction to Amplify came in the spring of 2012, from two friends: Tom Bissell and Rob Auten, Los Angeles–based writers whose work on and about big "Triple-A" video game titles have helped define the field. The two co-wrote the script for the combat game *Gears of War: Judgment,* and Bissell's *Extra Lives* is probably the best book of video game criticism ever published. Bissell in particular has pushed to help his readers see games in a different light. "Spending the weekend in bed reading the collected works of Joan Didion is doing different things to your mind than spending the weekend on the couch racing cars around Los Santos," he wrote recently. "The human mind contains enough room for both types of experience. Unfortunately, the mental activity generated by playing games is not much valued by non-gamers; in fact, play is hardly ever valued within American culture, unless it involves a $13 million signing bonus."[12]

At the time, Bissell and Auten were doing early work on *Lexica,* but the game, they discovered, needed the voice of someone who could talk to kids. They recommended Roth, who showed up at Amplify's Dumbo headquarters and didn't even realize at first that it was a job interview. "I wasn't sure whether they wanted me to work there or whether they just wanted to show off ideas to me." Suddenly, he remembered, "we were plotting out the next year of my life."

The idea behind *Lexica* is pure hero's journey stuff: Inside an imaginary hidden library are more than a thousand classic books—real, actual e-books—that no one is reading. The problem, it seems, is that a rogue band of library guardians believes that in order to keep the books safe they must be kept out of the grubby hands of nearly everyone. Unless readers are smart enough to appreciate them—and of course no one is smart enough—the books stay off limits. But if no one reads them, the characters will die. So they start popping out of the books to get help. Players soon meet a handful of the most well-known literary characters— Tom Sawyer, Long John Silver, the Cheshire Cat—and go on a series of "quests" that result in more unlocked quests and more characters willing to join their party. Each character offers players special powers that can be used at key times throughout the game. The more characters from literature you get to know and the more books you read, the more powerful you become. The conceit is straight out of "mindset" research by the Stanford researcher Carol Dweck, who found that praising children for hard work encouraged them to work harder, while praising them for being smart actually had the opposite effect. It made children put the brakes on their academic risk-taking for fear of jeopardizing their "smart" label through academic failure. Like the other games on the tablet, *Lexica* is meant to be strictly optional, and the hope is that as kids play the game and read the books, they'll share their experiences with their friends, creating affinity groups around their favorite titles.

"You're checking in with these characters every week and coming to love these characters," Roth said, suggesting that the relationships might resemble those that many young people share with their favorite cult TV characters—Buffy the Vampire Slayer or the Doctor from *Doctor Who,* characters so compelling yet so familiar that viewers keep coming back to find out what will happen next. "I hope this doesn't sound really bad when it's written out," he told me, "but we want to bring books back to a point where they're like that."

As a child, he remembered being "terrified" of Robert Louis Stevenson. Books like *Treasure Island* seemed big and weighty, and Stevenson's characters "talked in a way that I didn't really recognize." The basic idea of *Lexica,* he said, is to drop players into so many interactions with characters like Long John Silver that their speech becomes familiar, their traits appealing, and their backstories irresistible. Eventually, adults can simply stand back and let students make their own connections. "Kids are incredibly curious and prolific creatures," he said. In a way, the scripts he and his team were writing amounted to a kind of fan fiction for each of the books, a strategy that he hopes will rub off on students. At some point, he said, *Lexica* will allow players to write their own scripts for the characters, bringing the game full circle.

Over lunch in a kosher restaurant, I worried out loud to Roth that *Lexica* had the potential to do to Tom Sawyer what Disney had done to Winnie-the-Pooh: pander to a modern pop sensibility and, well, dumb him down to move product. Maybe I was just imagining it, I told him, but I recalled sitting on a couch years earlier with one of my daughters and watching Winnie-the-Pooh ride a skateboard. I begged him not to fall prey to that sort of thing. Roth laughed. They had no plans to put *anyone* on a skateboard. But he said the team wasn't shying away from interpreting the characters in ways that might irk critics. He invoked a Hebrew word—and not an obvious one—to explain what they were trying to accomplish. *Gaiva*, he said, is a word with mostly negative connotations in the Hasidic community. It means "pride" or "ego," and he said he felt it now and then as he sat at his computer. He was bringing a kind of arrogance and irreverence to the task of getting kids interested in classic books, pushing to get them to pay attention to something so far outside of their normal media diet as to be almost alien. If critics got mad, he thought, let them. It was a sign that he'd succeeded. "As a writer, the worst thing is if your readers are indifferent. Sometimes you want them to be riled up." Even more so for school, he said, where students spend most of their day. "We're going into the place where indifference is born."

◖ ··············

"He is a singular character," wrote Nathaniel Hawthorne, "a young man with much of wild original nature still remaining in him; and so far as he is sophisticated, it is in a way and method of his own. He is as ugly as sin, long-nosed, queer-mouthed, and with uncouth and rustic, though courteous manners, corresponding very well with such an exterior. But his ugliness is of an honest and agreeable fashion, and becomes him much better than beauty."[13]

Henry David Thoreau made a big impression on Hawthorne, who in 1842 had just moved to Concord with his new bride Sophia. Waiting for the couple when they arrived was a wedding present from Thoreau: a vegetable garden that he'd planted. At the time, Thoreau was twenty-five and living in Emerson's house as a sort of handyman, gardener, and tutor to the family's four children. He was an oddball. Smart and well-read but socially awkward, the Harvard-educated son of a pencil maker loved poetry, looked after the town's trees, and considered himself the "self-appointed inspector of snow-storms and rain-storms," half-expecting to be offered a city job for his efforts. He was, Hawthorne wrote, "on intimate terms with the clouds, and can tell the portents of storms."[14] By 1845, when he built his cabin in the woods, he was principally known for two things: an uncanny ability to walk through a plowed field and stumble upon Indian arrowheads, and for having accidentally burned down a three-hundred-acre patch of woods near Walden the previous April while making fish chowder with a friend. Thoreau was, in other words, the most unlikely action hero in the history of video games.

But he was Tracy Fullerton's personal hero. Though she grew up in suburban Los Angeles, she could trace her family's roots back to Boston before the American Revolution, where an ancestor, "Baby John" Fullerton, ran away from home at the age of twelve to fight in the war. He eventually ended up joining the Massachusetts Navy and was among a group of soldiers court-martialed along with Paul Revere after the disastrous 1779 Penobscot Expedition to retake what is now Maine from the British. At war's end, the British gave it back anyway. Fullerton received a piece of land in the recovered territory and went into maritime trade. The Fullertons were "not any kind of Boston Brahmin family, but definitely New Englanders from way back."

She first encountered *Walden* as a child of twelve or so, on summer vacation, floating on a Massachusetts pond behind an aunt's home a few miles from Walden Pond. Her father, an engineer and "big reader," trained his four children to seek out books associated with the places they went each summer. "The sound of our family on vacation is the sound of pages turning," she told me.[15] At the time, Thoreau's harrowing description of a war between ant colonies gripped her. "I just thought of it as a storybook, just like all of the other storybooks I read."

The oldest of four siblings, Fullerton was born in 1965 in Los Angeles. She grew up in Mar Vista, west of downtown, where she remembered a childhood with "lots of making." Fullerton and her friends raided her father's tool cabinet to build forts, playhouses, spaceships, or whatever seemed worth constructing. They installed wooden mailboxes throughout the neighborhood and created their own shadow postal system. They built a battery-operated telegraph machine that they strung into the kitchen so that Fullerton's mother would know they were in the garage. "I don't know why we thought it was the neatest thing," she said. When I suggested that it was helpful for their mother to know where they were, she laughed. "She knew where we were anyway."

When they got tired of building things, they put on plays. They formed the "Summer Company of Amateur Stars," underwritten by nickels from recycled soft drink cans. Then Fullerton mail-ordered an EWA Backwinder for her Super 8 camera and became a filmmaker. The equipment allowed her to expose the same length of film twice and create homemade special effects. "This was extraordinary to me," she said. She and her friends shot stop-motion spinoffs of *Star Wars* and charged others to attend viewings. When they grew too old for sci-fi, "we started shooting the classics." Fullerton and her sister filmed their own adaptation of *The Iliad*, staging the burning of Troy in her sister's bedroom. They singed the rug. "We ended up cutting it and hiding it," she said.

Eventually the adulation that her film projects brought persuaded Fullerton to enroll in film school at the University of California. After seeing *WarGames*, the 1983 nuclear war–themed thriller starring Matthew Broderick, she commandeered a Commodore 64 and built her first computer game: a tic-tac-toe knockoff that produced a mushroom cloud whenever the player lost. "The picture was the big payoff," she recalled. Fullerton later realized how poorly designed it was because there was no real incentive to win, only to lose. She also reread *Walden* and this time she saw not just ant wars, but something larger: Thoreau's fiery political rhetoric.

Like many young people in her generation, Fullerton played early *Dungeons & Dragons* adaptations on her computer and loved them. But the seminal Cold War computer strategy game *Balance of Power*, one of the earliest "serious" games, changed everything. It was "crazy hard" and gripping. The Cold War was in full swing at the time, and Fullerton loved the game's implicit challenge: to prevent nuclear Armageddon. "If you tipped the world into war, then the whole thing would explode," she said. "And of course you always did." By the early 1990s, she was living in New York City and working as creative director for a startup called Interfilm that combined gaming and film—its most notable product was a tongue-in-cheek "cinematic game" named *Ride for Your Life*. Distributed to just forty-seven theaters, it starred former *Batman* leading man Adam West and required viewers to vote on what would happen next by pressing buttons on special three-button keypads that were installed in the armrests of their seats.

Then, within a few weeks in late 1993, two computer games arrived that would cleave the games industry in two. Both were technically unprecedented, but *Myst* and *Doom* could hardly have been more dissimilar. The first was a slow-paced, moody, photorealistic puzzler, "part Salvador Dali and part Jules Verne's *The Mysterious Island*," one critic wrote.[16] Conceived by two sons of a Spokane minister, *Myst* invited players to spend hours exploring, reading, fiddling, and thinking to unlock the secrets of a mysterious family on an abandoned island, all to a lush orchestral soundtrack. It essentially took a game genre that cut stories into pieces—the text adventure—and set it to music, sound, and pictures. In the process, it created, or at least popularized, the brainy video game. "People do not die in *Myst*, nor are they killed," reviewer Jon Carroll wrote in 1994, "yet it is sometimes a very scary game. There is no way to get trapped in *Myst*; yet it can induce uneasy feelings of panic in the unwary. It's as harmless as a walk in the woods, which is to say, not harmless at all."[17] By contrast, *Doom* was an unapologetic march through Hell, a lurid, blood-spattered, over-caffeinated survivalist romp set to a heavy-metal soundtrack. Developed by a rag-tag team of coders holed up in a suburban Dallas high-rise—they were co-led by John Romero, who would later tutor Stanford's Keith Devlin about math games—*Doom* essentially invented the first-person shooter game. Its creators even decided to name the company id Software, after the lowest part of the psyche, as per Sigmund Freud.

Fullerton and her colleagues loved both games and played whenever they could. "I remember turning the lights off to play *Myst,* to keep that mood," she said. *Myst* was a real, cinematic place, lovely and meditative. When *Doom*'s creators released special software that allowed players to create their own in-game scenarios, Fullerton and her colleagues recreated their New York office. She likened *Doom* to a sporting event, a "social sport," the fastest thing anyone had ever seen on a computer screen. Since then, the vast majority of popular game titles have looked, felt, and sounded very much like *Doom,* but she soon began wondering what things would have been like if *Myst* had provided the game world's DNA.

Fullerton went on to create Spiderdance, an interactive television game developer that created live multiplayer games for MTV, NBC, and The History Channel, among others, but in 2001, the September 11 attacks gutted networks' interactive budgets and in 2002, Spiderdance shut its doors. Fullerton climbed into her Jeep Cherokee and embarked on what would become a 10,000-mile road trip across America to think about what would come next.

She visited Walden Pond. It was summer, a popular time for swimmers, but she arrived on a rainy day and had the place to herself. She sat by the site of Thoreau's cabin, marked since 1872 by a cairn, or pile of stones, each one deposited by a visiting pilgrim— even Walt Whitman stopped by in 1881. Fullerton sat by the cairn and read *Walden.* This time, she realized, Thoreau was telling her how to live a balanced life. "He was talking a lot about how people just work themselves to death," she said.

By 1845, when Thoreau went into the woods, the world was indeed speeding up. The railroad had come through town just a year earlier, and workers would soon start laying thousands of miles of telegraph cable throughout the country. "That speed of life, that speed of communication, was causing someone like Thoreau to say, 'Hey, wait a minute, we need to regulate our own lives for what we think is important. We need to make choices so that when we come to the end of our lives we don't regret being swept away with the speed of our time." As she sat by the cabin site, thinking about Thoreau's words, "for some reason it just occurred to me that it would be wonderful to kind of *play out his experience.* Since we can't all take two years out of our lives to do that, wouldn't it be interesting if we could do it in a game?" So while other literate designers have built games based on the writings of Machiavelli, Sun Tzu, and Ayn Rand, Fullerton has spent much of the past decade figuring out how to extract game play from the writings of a man who urged his readers to "[c]ultivate poverty like a garden herb, like sage."[18]

Most gaming is built around acquisition and achievement, markers that Thoreau abhorred—he proposed working on the Sabbath and resting the other six days. "Do not trouble yourself much to get new things, whether clothes or friends," he wrote. "Sell your clothes and keep your thoughts."[19] As such, the game encourages players to live simply, working just enough to provide for essentials and spending the rest of their time enjoying nature, among other pleasures. "We need to break game players' expectations," Fullerton told the gaming website *Kotaku* in 2009,[20] shortly after development began in earnest.

When I met her, in the spring of 2012, Fullerton was working on the third edition of her textbook, *Game Design Workshop: A Playcentric Approach to Creating Innovative Games*. She also headed the game design program at the University of Southern California, holding the Electronic Arts Endowed Chair in Interactive Entertainment. *Walden, A Game* had received a flurry of attention, some of it unwanted, after her team won a $40,000 National Endowment for the Arts grant to move production along. A *TIME* article on the NEA grant warned its readers, "Get ready for some edge-of-your-seat 19th century transcendentalist action!"[21] On the conservative *CNS News* website, one commenter asked, "How can the government back something like this? They have made it impossible to do what Thoreau did. He would be penalized, er, I mean taxed for not having health insurance. Read the book and be inspired on [sic] what true freedom is."[22]

In April 2013, *Walden* changed again for Fullerton. She was diagnosed with breast cancer and underwent surgery, followed by radiation and chemotherapy. She dropped nearly everything except revising her textbook and working on the game. "Sometimes I feel a bit like *Walden* was my body trying to tell me to slow down," she said. "But that's the kind of place your mind wanders when they're pumping chemicals into your veins." She went for daily long walks, read books, grew tomatoes, listened to music, and spent time with her family. "I took care of myself. It was weird—in a way a lot of it was just stuff you should be doing—it's just that I had forgotten to take the time."

I first beheld a working prototype of *Walden* in February 2014, in a corner of Fullerton's USC studio. The game's art director, Luke Peterson, was guiding the onscreen avatar past a row of houses in the game's rendition of Concord, Massachusetts, as Fullerton sat nearby, eyes on the screen. "He wasn't a hermit," she said. "Much of the book is about society." Thoreau, she said, walked to town once or twice a week. He ate dinner in town. "In fact, you can go into this house here."[23] She pointed at the screen and Peterson approached Thoreau's family home. During his two-year experiment, he regularly got his laundry done there. As Fullerton spoke, an onscreen pop-up read, "This is your parents' house—there might be pie." Peterson turned a corner into the living room, and as if on cue, a pie appeared, cooling on a windowsill.

In virtually all video games, this is when the player reaches for the pie and collects it, without thinking twice. Pie good. But *Walden* forces players not only to think twice, but to make a habit of thinking twice. To Hungry Thoreau, the pie is food and that's good. But to Self-Reliant Thoreau, it's a giveaway. That's bad. Peterson dragged the mouse pointer to the windowsill and left-clicked. The pop-up read, "This is pie. I imagine it's delicious."

Wait, I said. *Not so fast.*

Fullerton grinned. "He's come to town, he's gotten his laundry done and he's gotten his food taken care of, and *that's a way to live,*" she said. "There's nothing wrong with that. But coming and going from town takes time, and it takes time away from finding inspiration. So the question becomes: How do you want to live your life? Do you want to have your mom do your laundry and make you pie?" When she began developing the game, friends would invariably ask her, "Will your mother do the laundry?" She decided to make it an option. "People kind of treat it like that sort of disavows his experiment, when in fact he wasn't doing an experiment in living in the wilderness. It wasn't *Survivor.*" Thoreau may have wanted to simplify his life, but he had little interest in ditching society, she said. He was simply sitting on the edge of it to see it more clearly.

"I had more visitors while I lived in the woods than at any other period in my life," Thoreau wrote, pointing out that he kept three chairs in his cabin: "one for solitude, two for friendship, three for society." He wrote of having "twenty-five or thirty souls, with their bodies, at once under my roof, and yet we often parted without being aware that we had come very near to one another."

Actually, players can spend most of their time in town, lecturing, writing articles and hanging out in Emerson's well-stocked library. Reading and writing are inspirational, but too much will jeopardize your relationship with nature, Fullerton said. Thoreau's main point was that life is not about not working or playing, but about finding the sweet spot between the two.

Peterson headed back to the pond and found Thoreau's bean field. During his Walden sojourn, Thoreau planted two and a half acres of beans a few yards from the cabin. Eventually he harvested twelve bushels of beans—"so many more than I wanted," he wrote in his journal. "I did not read books the first summer; I hoed beans." But he came away with $8.71 in profit from the endeavor. Players are invited to try and do the same. Actually, Fullerton said, they're free to plant as many beans as they like. They can sell their surplus and buy fancy suits and upgrade their house. "You could play this game to become a *Walden* millionaire." But to do that would take up most of your time each day, she said. You have to weed the plot, otherwise the field will turn to brush. You must also find a place to store the harvested beans. As she spoke, the in-game sun set, but Peterson continued toiling in the beanfield. "Luke's out farming at night, apparently," Fullerton said.

"When you want to be a millionaire . . ." he said.

"You've got to work at night," Fullerton replied with a broad smile.

⬤············

When we spoke by phone a few months later, I somehow persuaded Fullerton to send me a demo of the game so I could play at home. An opening tutorial sets up the experiment and follows the basic thematic lines of Thoreau's first chapter, titled "Economy." In it, he establishes that man has just four basic necessities: food, fuel, shelter, and clothing. "Once you've satisfied these things, really the whole project of life is to go out and experience nature, experience the more spiritual, the more inspirational aspects of life," Fullerton said. Players must work to meet their basic needs, but beyond that the game encourages them to wander and spend time as they will. On the other hand, if you don't finish the cabin, it starts to wear on you. The music changes. What moments earlier was a pastoral cello-and-piano duet turns to a solo piano death-march, the pianist perseverating on what sounds like the keyboard's lowest note. Movement also becomes more labored, and the colors of the game begin to wash out. Though she didn't realize it when she set out to create the *Walden* game, "I think now, looking back, that one of the things that attracted me to the book is that he sets out his experiment almost like a system, almost like a playable system," she said.

Playing the entire thing takes a few hours—they've compressed Thoreau's "two years, two months and two days" into twenty-four "days" of fifteen minutes apiece, six per season. The setting is a stunningly faithful reproduction of Walden, derived from U.S. Geological Survey data and Thoreau's own sketches—he was, among other things, a surveyor. Game play begins in summer and ends in spring, and it soon becomes clear that the amount of breathtaking scenery that the game generates moment-to-moment simply wouldn't have been possible on a home computer until recently. Nearly every item onscreen is "clickable," offering short descriptions of the pond's features, often in Thoreau's own writing.

Playing through the game one midsummer afternoon, I spoke on the phone to Alex Mathew, one of Fullerton's graduate students and part of the *Walden* team. He'd come to game design in high school, after encountering the PlayStation title *Shadow of the Colossus.* The game subverts the typical "boss" battle video game paradigm by commanding players to kill a series of giants in order to bring a loved one back to life. "You go off and you kill these majestic beasts that have done *nothing* to you," Mathew said. It was the first time he'd felt guilt while playing a video game and he wanted to learn how to make other players feel such powerful emotions. "It just changed everything."

Mathew told me to keep an eye on Walden Pond as I fished for perch. Whenever my avatar came near the shore, they'd circle beneath the pond's shiny surface, he said proudly. I tried it and he was right. As I moved away, they disappeared. He was also responsible, he said, for making sure that foxes, hares, mallards, mink, and "tons of birds" showed up on cue, in the right season, and behaved appropriately. After he learned that blue jays are historically linked to wisdom, he programmed them to lead players toward books found scattered throughout the game. He was also working on programming eye-tracking for owls. "I was thinking, 'This world isn't recognizing you enough.' So I've just got owls watching you as you walk by and recognizing you, to look *right at you*. That has something profound to it," he said.[24]

Michael Sweet, the game's sound designer and composer, told me I should be listening to the game through headphones. The sounds you hear are the actual sounds of Walden, said Sweet, who lives near the pond and has spent two years recording birds, insects, and other creatures in each of the four seasons. A friend of Fullerton's since the mid-1990s, he's most well-known for the score of the popular game *Diner Dash,* as well as the signature swooshing audio "logo" that plays each time anyone turns on an Xbox 360. Sweet also developed the video game scoring curriculum at Boston's Berklee College of Music, where he's on the faculty. Like the rest of the team, Sweet volunteers his time and energy for the project as he can fit it around his other jobs. He joined the team after Fullerton mentioned *Walden* three years earlier at the annual Game Developers Conference in San Francisco. He asked if he could help.

"If we were all working full-time on it we'd have definitely knocked the whole thing out by now," he said. "But I think also time allows us to shape the game differently than someone that's trying to knock something out really quickly. I get to listen to how the seasons and how the wildlife changes around me, and you couldn't do that if I had three months to build this game." Case in point: his recordings of cardinals ended up on the cutting room floor after he consulted with local birders, who told him that the species migrated north to the pond *after* Thoreau's era.

Sweet ended up living in Concord almost by accident. He'd wanted to live in Boston, but his wife preferred the countryside. Each time they moved, she kept saying, *Too close, too close, too close.* "I'm much more of an expert now that I'm living here and I get to experience the world around me at such a slow pace. It brings me closer to what Thoreau actually talks about."[25]

The cumulative effect of all of these details is powerful, resulting in true immersion. I know because after playing the game for just half an hour or so, the phone rang in my home office. I blinked at it for a second, unsure of exactly what the strange sound was. Then I was irked that I'd been pulled out of my nineteenth-century idyll. I turned the ringer off and continued the game.

I also began reading *Walden,* after realizing that I had never actually read the entire thing. Like just about everyone else, I'd been assigned sections of it in high school, but it occurred to me that, as with the wink-and-nod about Thoreau's laundry, most of us simply didn't understand the book very well. *Walden* was, I found, much more substantial and at times an angrier and funnier book than I'd ever believed, a heartfelt meditation that defies the "beat of a different drummer" refrigerator-magnet reductionism that most of us apply to it. I worried about a game's ability, in the long run, to rise above refrigerator magnets. Fullerton said I shouldn't. People get out of it what they put in. "The truth is, sure, you could simplify it—it could just be a nice walk in the woods if that's what you take away from it," she said. But if players dig a little deeper and test the system, "if they invest a little bit more in thinking about why Thoreau did what he did, why the game is the way that it is, if they allow the experience to affect them, they'll take away a lot more."

TEN

· ·>

THROW TRUCKS WITH
YOUR MIND

*How Video Games Can Help Heal
ADHD, PTSD, and Depression—
and Help Kids Relax*

The day is fine and the sun is high and the road goes on for-ever. A single lane wraps around the Technicolor landscape, a deep blue ocean sparkling in the distance. The music is a jaunty calypso ditty, and, like most video-game soundtracks, I fear I will never get it out of my head. I'm staring into the screen of a standard-issue laptop computer, but my hands are in my lap, touching neither keyboard nor mouse. Stretched around my head is a black elastic headband equipped with sensors that monitor electrical activity in the front of my brain and wirelessly transmit it via Bluetooth to the laptop. I look a bit like a laboratory subject in a psychology experiment, which I suppose I am. On the screen, in the middle of the road, stands a 3-D animated chicken. In cowboy boots.

I'm looking at her from above and slightly behind, as in a first-person shooter game or FPS. Let's call it an FCS—first-chicken shooter. Once I get over the nearly irresistible temptation to make stupid jokes about chickens crossing roads—it turns out that every-one who encounters this bird experiences the same baseline urge—I get to work. I breathe deeply, banish all distractions, and *focus on the chicken*. I'm not even sure how and I'm not given detailed instructions. I just tell myself: chicken, *run!*

Suddenly, as if by magic, she starts to move. Now I am really focused, and soon she shifts gears from a walk to a trot, her feet kicking up little clouds of dust as she clucks along. I am making the chicken run with my mind! The day is fine and the chicken is a bad-ass and we are running down the road together, our minds locked into one another's like some sort of Farmer Brown's Patented Olde-Time Vulcan Mind Meld. When the road turns left, she turns left, then straightens out on a section overlooking the ocean. Look at the way the sun hits the . . . wait, why is she stopping? Is it because I was looking at the ocean? I drag my gaze back to the chicken. She begins to move again.

Just to be sure, I try a little experiment: With the chicken once again running at a nice clip, I begin to think about that creamy latte I enjoyed on the way over here just a few minutes ago, at that French café down on Second Avenue. It's a chain, I know, but the barista, a heavyset, heavily pierced young man, did a fine job on my latte. The foam was sweet and light, and he even swirled it into a little . . . OK, my chicken has stopped. In the three seconds that my mind drifted, she lost her will to run. The calypso music keeps playing, but she is standing patiently in the road, awaiting instructions.

It turns out that my latte daydream, as brief as it was, simulated the basic symptoms of attention-deficit/hyperactivity disorder or ADHD, a neurobehavioral condition that affects at least 6 million children.[1] I'm sitting in a little room off the library of the Churchill School, a private day school in the Kips Bay section of Manhattan's East Side. Churchill specializes in educating children with attention problems, and as one of their therapies they're piloting this game, created by a Massachusetts outfit called Atentiv. Developed in collaboration with Duke University neuroscientist Ranga Krishnan, it's part of a burgeoning field called therapeutic neurogaming, which turns the mechanics of digital games into actual therapy that its proponents say can calm kids down, focus them, and help them overcome debilitating conditions like ADHD, anxiety disorder, depression, and even, in the near future, certain types of autism, so they can concentrate on schoolwork. It's built on two basic ideas: First, that the brain is "plastic" for far longer than scientists once believed, so healing can be achieved in schoolchildren of all ages without drugs, through basic neurofeedback therapy. Second, that therapy doesn't just *happen*—it requires work and patience and a regular dose of practice. Since games encourage people to spend time playing them, the theory goes, players will return to them regularly. Patients are more likely to make progress with a therapeutic game than with regular therapy that may be tiresome or dull. In medical terms, people who are playing an absorbing game will take all of their medicine.

The stakes are high. In 2011, the federal Centers for Disease Control and Prevention estimated that health-care providers had returned ADHD diagnoses for more than one in ten school-aged children and one in five high-school boys. The percentage of children taking medication for ADHD, as reported by their parents, grows about 7 percent each year. In 2011, an estimated 3.5 million children were taking ADHD medicine, 1 million more than in 2003.[2] The U.S. Food and Drug Administration has warned that side effects for Ritalin, one of the most popular ADHD drugs, can include high blood pressure, stroke, heart attacks, and, for users with heart problems, sudden death. The FDA also says Ritalin can stunt children's growth and give them blurred vision, headaches, seizures, decreased appetite, nausea, sleeplessness, and, for young men, "painful and prolonged erections." It can also cause psychiatric problems, including bipolar disorder.[3] Understandably, parents are willing to give almost anything to offer their kids a measure of nonpharmaceutical relief. So for the past few years, a small group of psychiatrists, researchers, educators, and game designers have run a quiet but intense footrace to become the first to earn FDA approval for a medically sound, prescription-strength video game for ADHD. That's not a metaphor. They are seeking approval for a game that a doctor can actually prescribe.

The problem with drugs like Ritalin or Adderall, researchers say, isn't just that they have side effects. It's that they're almost entirely hit or miss. They activate "your entire brain, in a very blunt way," said Dr. Adam Gazzaley, a psychiatrist and founding director of the Neuroscience Imaging Center at the University of

California–San Francisco. "We don't really have a selective way to target their effects, and because of that we have to increase their doses to very high levels," he said.[4] Most drug-prescription guidelines for doctors are entirely nonpersonalized, based on population data rather than the needs of the patient sitting in front of them. And once they've got the medicine, he said, there's an inherent delay between the time a patient takes it and the time that a doctor sees the effects, usually during the next office visit. "We have this very open-loop system, and I maintain that this is just really not good enough," Gazzaley said. A few years ago, he began searching for a new way to treat his patients, for a tighter feedback loop that was "targeted, personalized, multimodal, and closed-loop."

Gazzaley got interested in video games after reading medical literature that showed first-person shooters improved the cognitive abilities of players, both expert and naïve. He knew that as we get older, we have a harder time switching between different tasks, partly because of a phenomenon he calls "stickiness of perception."[5] Like doors hanging on rusty hinges, as we age our brain develops difficulty swinging from task to task, not only because it's hard to swing over to the new task, but because it's difficult to disengage from the old one. Gazzaley began wondering if he could develop a game to enhance this switching in older adults. At the time, a few of his friends were working for the game developer LucasArts, so he asked if they'd be interested in helping him out. They said they'd be delighted. "Their perspective was that they'd been teaching teenagers how to kill aliens for fifteen years now— most of their professional life—and they were looking forward to the opportunity to work on games that might have a different kind of impact."

Gazzaley's team developed *NeuroRacer,* an immersive 3-D cognitive trainer that, in many ways, resembles the Atentiv chicken game, though it predates it. *NeuroRacer* requires players to steer an animated racecar down a winding road while reacting to different colored shapes along the way. If players see a green sign, they press a button. If they see a red or blue sign, they try to ignore it. As they improve their multitasking skills, the game gets harder, but if players can't handle the simultaneous tasks, the game gets easier. That is its "special sauce," Gazzaley said. Unlike the real world, where as you get better at a task it gets easier, in *NeuroRacer,* reality is reversed in the name of science.

If the game were a dose of medicine, not only would patients be taking all of it—the medicine would be adjusting automatically, moment to moment, to their needs: When you make a decision, it impacts the game. The game shifts and feeds you a different challenge and you react to that. The feedback loop is closed. "The challenge scales to your skill level, so it holds you right in that sweet spot, which our game designers like to think of as a 'flow state,'" he said, referring to Mihaly Csikszentmihalyi. Brain scientists might call it "maximizing brain plasticity" or simply scaffolding learning more efficiently. "You're just pushing the system hard enough that it can change, but not pushing it too hard that people give up," Gazzaley said. Actually, a well-designed game could go one step further, using that feedback to map your cognitive strengths and weaknesses and feed you challenges that put just the right amount of pressure on them.

In a groundbreaking 2013 paper in the journal *Nature,* Gazzaley and his colleagues published their *NeuroRacer* results. They found that subjects in their early twenties were the best multitaskers, but that after the training, sixty- to seventy-year-olds performed just as well as twentysomethings, even a month after the sessions. Seniors' enhanced multitasking abilities remained as long as six months later.[6] Their working memory also improved, an unexpected and promising outcome that showed a positive effect of brain training at a time when many in the scientific community were souring on the idea. It's as if, Gazzaley said, you went to the gym for a month and were still as strong half a year later.

With the success, Gazzaley began working on a game about mindfulness, funded by the National Institutes of Health (NIH), and, through a company he co-founded, Akili Interactive Labs, another game for elementary-school-aged children that could treat ADHD, depression, and other disorders. One of the initial investors in the trials was the Irish drug company Shire Pharmaceuticals, makers of Adderall. "What we hope is literally in five years that we can drop those doses down, in some cases potentially remove them, and then use a game to selectively activate a circuit in your brain," Gazzaley said.[7] He also began working with researchers at the University of California–San Diego to develop a combination MRI/EEG brain-imaging device that connects to a game and feeds real-time images of players' brains into the game engine. Imagine, he said, watching your brain cells fire onscreen in a 3-D animation and having the ability to change the pattern as you watch. The device could someday allow researchers and game developers to tweak simulations so that they actually heal players' cognitive deficits—even injuries. "Video games are a really powerful way of changing the brain because what they do is activate circuits," he said. "We don't have drugs that do that—we don't have that level of selectivity and that's how games act. Because you interact with the environment in a targeted way, your brain acts selectively."

For all its science-fiction surreality, the development was inevitable. Though video games began as arcade amusements built almost entirely around quick reflexes and hand-eye coordination, forty years of rapidly improving computer technology and two generations of imaginative developers have pushed games into terrain that often borders on the therapeutic. In 2014, the Netherlands-based Playnice Institute developed *MindLight,* an EEG-powered game aimed at children as young as eight years old to help them with anxiety disorder. Puzzles and relaxation exercises teach kids how to face "fear events" and conquer them. In San Francisco, the startup Puzzlebox in 2012 began selling an EEG-controlled toy helicopter that only flies when users are calm and focused—it followed years of the company's founder working with elementary- and middle-school students on focusing techniques.

Another San Francisco startup, Emotiv, has developed a $399 EEG headband, designed for research, with fourteen brain-sensor points. It already allows users to see an onscreen 3-D visualization of their brain areas firing. Another utility guides users through the process of coaxing a photorealistic digital flower into blossoming. At a gaming conference in 2014, I sat at Emotiv's booth and watched as an employee squirted saline solution onto each of the contact points, then handed it to a co-worker who, as he lowered it onto my head, said, "This is going to feel a little cold." He was right, it felt a little cold. On the screen was a single white rose, but the bud was shut tight, almost unrecognizable as a flower. As I focused on the shape, silently willing it awake, then audibly saying,

"Open, open . . ." its papery petals began to peel apart, slowly and tentatively at first, then a little bit more confidently. In a few seconds it sat before me, fully open. Perhaps my brain was secretly gloating, because a moment later it quickly sealed itself shut, as if sensing danger. I told myself to relax a little more and stop gloating, and it opened again. Soon I was watching it open and close in tandem with my breathing. The rose and I were breathing together.

Game designer Robin Hunicke, who has worked on several genre-bending titles, said technologies like these point to a new direction for games. "We are at a place right now where this medium has the opportunity to expand in drastic and amazing ways," she said. "And if you are a designer, I would hope that you're curious enough to really push on that boundary and not just accept the status quo, not just work on a game because you know it will make money, but to really push yourself in your craft to design something new."[8] Improvements in technology have actually upped the ante for developers, she said, giving them greater responsibility for players' well-being. "You can't just make games about shooting people in the face because now you can see how people feel."[9]

A few independent developers have responded to exhortations like these, creating games that explore domestic violence and alcoholism, cancer, the loss of a loved one, and other fraught topics. The British game critic Andy Robertson has even proposed using games for worship, saying good, well-conceived titles have an almost mystical quality. They can transcend mere fun by putting players into altered states in which they can control their own destiny. Games, he said, "are about fun, but in a certain way. They're about fun in the same way that painting a picture is about putting pigment on a page. They're about enjoyment in the same way that prayer is about stringing words together."[10]

When it was released in 2012, exclusively for the PlayStation console, the meditative independent adventure game Journey quickly became the console's fastest-selling title.[11] In it, players wordlessly travel—sometimes through the air—from a cinematically rendered, windswept desert to a looming mountain, with no map, no instructions and no real backstory or narrative to speak of, all with a lush orchestral score. Jenova Chen, one of the game's creators (and a former student of Tracy Fullerton's) described Journey as a game that explores "our life's transformation and the crossing, the intersecting of our lives."[12] It won a trove of awards, including several "game of the year" honors, and its score was nominated for a Grammy—it lost to the soundtrack to *The Girl with the Dragon Tattoo*. One rapt reviewer called *Journey* "that rare breed of game storytelling that strikes the ideal balance between guiding you and allowing you to discover your own story."[13]

Though the game was not built explicitly for therapy, *Journey*'s developers soon began receiving letters from players who said spending hours with the game wasn't just fun or even mildly therapeutic—it helped relieve their post-traumatic stress disorder. Hunicke, whose work was instrumental in *Journey*, said the design team heard from players who said the experience was "transformative." A few players said they were able for the first time to process the loss of a family member who had recently died. "They felt a tangible sense of release from completing the narrative of the game," she told me. "The struggle in their own game reflected the struggles in their own lives."[14]

In one memorable instance, Chen stood up at a game design conference in 2013 and read a letter from a fifteen-year-old girl who had played *Journey* with her father after he'd been stricken with cancer. "It was the most fun I had with him since he had been diagnosed," she wrote. "My father passed in the spring of 2012, only a few months after his diagnosis. Weeks after his death, I could finally return myself to playing video games. I tried to play *Journey*, and I could barely get past the title screen without breaking down into tears. In my dad's and in my own experience with *Journey*, it was about him, and his journey to the ultimate end, and I believe we encountered your game at the most perfect time." She said she continues to play it, "always remembering what joy it brought, and the joy it continues to bring."[15]

C··············

In 1995, Yale University psychiatrist Bruce Wexler became one of the first researchers to use computerized cognitive remediation treatment, or CCRT, to help people suffering from schizophrenia. He published his results in 1997 and his approach was something of a revelation: instead of trying to treat the entire mess of the disease, he focused on strengthening specific cognitive functions, such as memory and attention tasks, that many think are the cause of other problems—it was, in a way, a kind of core conditioning regimen, CrossFit for the brain. Twenty-two schizophrenia patients practiced five times a week for ten weeks, with the tasks gradually becoming more difficult. After ten weeks, sixteen of the twenty-two performed as well as or better than members of a healthy control group on perceptual and memory tasks; eleven performed within the range of control subjects on a motor task. The training tasks got more complex and sophisticated, and in subsequent studies Wexler and his colleagues found that patients maintained the same high cognitive levels six months later. A year later, researchers found, the test subjects worked, on average, more hours and earned higher salaries than others with the condition, leading Wexler and his colleagues to conclude that patients with schizophrenia "appear to have greater potential for neurocognitive improvement, and potentially for employment, than generally appreciated."[16] At the time, Wexler remembered thinking that if you could show such promising results for adults with a "significant disease in their brain" like schizophrenia, imagine the kind of cognitive therapy you could offer to kids, whose brains are so much more plastic at that stage of life. "If it's not succeeding in children," he told me, "it's because we're not doing it right."[17]

A decade later, after teaching at Peking University, Wexler met Jinxia Dong, a former Chinese national gymnast and director of the university's Research Center for Sports Studies and Society. They developed an ADHD program that combined cognitive therapy and physical exercise to improve kids' abilities to "think, focus, learn, and socially interact." Their first trials took place in Beijing in 2010, and the following year they won a $4 million NIH grant in "transformative research" that funded two randomized control trials—one in Beijing and another in Hamden, Connecticut, near Yale. Like many in the field, Wexler complained that there are a lot of badly conceived products designed to make a buck. "It's a mixed bag in terms of what's out there," he said. "We have a lot more to learn. People who are trying to do it as carefully and seriously as possible have a long way to go to optimize this and I sometimes wonder what it will be like."[18]

When I spoke to Wexler in October 2014, his trials had expanded to 200 schools, learning centers, and clinics. In Brooklyn, an elementary school principal credited it with turning the school around. Students who got twenty-five or more sessions, he said, saw one year's worth of reading gains in three months. Wexler had also begun working with teachers at five elementary schools in Fairfax County, Virginia, near Washington, D.C. He'd just gotten promising results from more than 1,000 students there, including results from two urban schools where, for the first time, over half of the students saw their scores on standardized reading and math tests outpace those in the rest of the city. Perhaps in his exuberance, he dared to call the therapy "a school lunch program for the brain." Like the federal law that has fed millions of low-income children free meals since 1946, Wexler's therapy remediates a key deficit in poor kids' lives, he said. They're not stimulated enough, at home or in school, for normal executive function development, so they're less likely to succeed with the rigors of academic work. "They're put in a situation that, through no fault of their own, they're not neurocognitively prepared to meet the demands made of them," he said.

€ ··············

When they first catch a glimpse of the *Star Wars* movies, most young children sit spellbound, amazed by the sights and sounds of the strange new world. Those who love to tell stories might even feel the rumble of their true life's purpose, imagining themselves growing up someday to direct their own epic summer blockbuster. Lat Ware was six when he saw *Star Wars,* and his career path seemed clear: He would be a Jedi Knight. It didn't matter that he lived in Chapel Hill, North Carolina. Ware wanted to move things with his mind, like they did in the movies.

Once he started school, though, his grades were sub-Jedi level. He had trouble concentrating and was soon diagnosed with ADD, a less disruptive form of ADHD that is neurologically nearly identical. At a very young age, like millions of others before him, Ware found himself swallowing the usual pill each morning before school. "I was on some form of stimulant medication for most of my childhood," he told me.[19] First Ritalin, then Adderall. "The Ritalin worked, but it was not pleasant and it gave me migraines, like, once a month. Adderall was better, but still it felt like it wound me too tight. I could take it and focus and get the work done, but when it wore off, I crashed hard." He switched to a form of extended-release Adderall and found he didn't crash as hard, but hated the way he felt by the end of the day. "The main reason I wanted to get my ADD under control was to get off the medication," he said.

By then, like most kids, he had spent thousands of hours with video games and began thinking seriously about developing his own games. His dream of being a Jedi had been tempered by age, but he still thought a lot about Jedi powers, most notably how to move things with his mind. Then, one day when he was thirteen, his parents took him for a session of what was then a cutting-edge treatment: neurofeedback therapy. Clinicians showed him a helmet bristling with electrodes, connected by wires to an EEG machine. They were going to monitor his brain waves. All he really had to do, they said, was stare at a little electrical meter and try to control the strength of the signal. Technicians slathered gel on the contacts and pressed them to his head. It was, he remembered, "intrusive, kind of gross and boring," but he struggled through the task for an entirely different reason. He quickly saw that he was controlling a kind of rudimentary video game with his mind. "Kids have a way of finding fun in basically anything," he said, "and the fun I had was unrelated to the intended use."

Ware was told to focus as strongly as he could, to max out the meter and keep it there, but instead, he said, "I goofed around. No one yelled at me, but I can't imagine they didn't notice." This may have been a groundbreaking alternative therapy—he only tried it for a few weeks and readily admits that, had he applied himself, he'd have gotten more out of it. But more importantly, he saw that it was exactly the kind of hardware he needed to make his groundbreaking, never-before-seen Jedi Knights game.

Like many super-intelligent young tech impresarios, Ware speaks quickly—a few clicks too quickly. A cowlick of unmanageable dark brown hair hangs permanently above his right eye, and he never quite opens his mouth wide enough for the rush of syllables to properly emerge once his thoughts coalesce. "It's important to understand," he said, "I have always been 'that weird kid.'"

After high school, Ware ended up at DigiPen, the private college in Redmond, Washington, that specializes in video-game design and production, and he found, to his delight, that the demographics of DigiPen skewed strongly toward guys like him: smart, creative, pop culture savvy, and obsessed with video games. "It was very strange going from being 'that weird kid' to being average," he said. "At first it was this wonderful experience. 'Yay, I'm not alone anymore!' Gradually I started to become more keenly aware of the personality flaws that I was harboring." For the first time in his life, he wondered if he could be a different kind of person.

At eighteen, Ware was still taking daily ADHD medication, but he began to actively manage how he was thinking and feeling. Self-monitoring and mindfulness aren't as easy when you don't have a digital meter in front of you, but he gradually learned to focus and calm himself. To block out distractions in the computer lab, he'd open a large umbrella over himself—"my little portable programmer cave," he called it—and wear sound-muffling headphones. Then, in 2005, during spring break of his sophomore year, he and most of his classmates headed down to San Francisco for the annual Game Developers Conference, a raucous insiders' gathering of what's new, cool, and cutting-edge in the field. DigiPen always schedules spring break to coincide with the event. One day, Ware wandered into a demonstration by the San Jose, California, hardware maker NeuroSky, which was showing off its new EEG headsets. They'd hooked the headsets to the engine of a popular first-person shooter, *Half-Life 2*, and the demo was showing off the hardware's ability to allow players to . . . move objects with their minds!

Ware instantly noticed a few things. First, the headset was non-invasive, with no contact gel. Second, it didn't just measure brain function but more specifically how calm and focused users were. Unlike other EEG headsets at the time, it used only two contact points with the scalp. In the demo, players used their calm to lift large virtual items such as cars, chairs, and filing cabinets, and pull them with their focus. Ware was astounded. "I asked them, 'When are you going to *release* this game?' and they said, 'Never.' So I said, 'Can *I* make this game?' And they said they'd be happy for me to." His heart sank when they told him the price for a developer's kit: $5,000. He went back to Redmond, discouraged but determined to create his game once the price came down.

Ware graduated in 2007—he has to think twice to remember exactly when—and moved to Sunnyvale, in the heart of Silicon Valley, to work in the tech industry. He was, it turned out, in NeuroSky's backyard. Finally, in 2011, the company released a commercial version of the headset for a hundred bucks—Ware snapped up two and began coding, simultaneously developing the game and immersing himself in the latest research findings on ADHD. "My primary goal was not actually therapy," he said. It was to find a "masterable skill" that could be leveraged both to improve a player's mental powers and, more importantly, form the core of a fun game. "Ultimately it doesn't matter how therapeutic the product is. If it's not fun, nobody is going to use it." Ware spent two years creating the game on a laptop, occupying a table at a Philz Coffee shop in Palo Alto. Strange young men with laptops and Bluetooth headbands are not an unusual sight in Silicon Valley, nor was it considered strange when, periodically, he'd turn to a fellow customer and ask, "Would you like to throw trucks with your mind?" The response, he said, was almost universally positive, and soon the game's name was born.

Throw Trucks with Your Mind operates quite simply, so pay attention: calm lifts, focus throws. Rudimentary keyboard commands may move the player around the board and tweak her abilities—pulling objects rather than pushing them, for instance—but most of the important functions have no keyboard commands. Red and blue bars measure how calm and focused players are moment to moment, and the ability to stay that way determines success. "I'm giving you a clear video game representation of a muscle you didn't know you had," Ware said.[20] Get good enough at being calm and you can also activate a force field. Focus hard enough and you can become invisible or develop the ability to jump many times higher than normal.

Through play-testing, Ware found that his initial instinct about the game was correct: competition was a more powerful motivator for most players than self-improvement, so he developed a robust multiplayer version in which the items you lift and throw serve little purpose but to squash your opponent. "People really like to feel better than other people, so by hiding away all these therapy things and only telling you that the game is about crushing people with your mind, it's a lot more palatable," he said. *Throw Trucks*'s basic scenario is that of a series of comic gladiators' duels—the characters have evolved into an assortment of oddballs, including a sadistic cat who controls a giant wearable robot. Players run, jump, and fly while they wield their ever-developing calm and focus like weapons, crushing one another with objects strewn throughout the environment. Ware called it "the only game where you can kill your friends by thinking about puppies."[21]

Our minds are strange, complicated places, so perhaps it should come as no surprise that after years of tweaking and endless play-testing, Ware found that his little crush-a-friend game was also good at helping alleviate depression. At 29, Ware suffers from chronic depression, and he said the game has helped him control what is sometimes called the "anxiety spiral" or "worry spiral," in which one negative thought leads to a bigger one, and then an even bigger one, until the series of "what-ifs" becomes debilitating. The game, he found, can quickly nip the cycle in the bud by helping players visualize the negative effects of their doubts as they watch their focus diminish. "You see your power in the game fall, and you see it fall exponentially, as you allow the 'worry spiral' to continue." The more you play, the better you get at stopping the pattern. "For a lot of people with depression, this can give tremendous relief."

In early 2013, looking for cash to hire a few artists and developers, Ware launched a *Throw Trucks* Kickstarter campaign. He was seeking $40,000, but he raised $47,000. Perhaps more importantly, he got a lot of games journalists interested. A few of them were over the moon. After playing a demo in February 2013, Rus McLaughlin, a writer for the tech site *VentureBeat* crowed, "I am a motherfucking Jedi Master."[22] Another play-tester, Jonathan Nelson, creator of the Silicon Valley startup incubator Hackers and Founders, actually threw money at Ware. Nelson was playing *Throw Trucks* against an opponent on another laptop and his face "just lit up," Ware recalled. "He turned to me with this look: 'Oh my God; you have fulfilled all of my childhood dreams.'" As Ware stumbled to frame a response, Nelson opened his wallet, threw a crisp $100 bill at him and said, "Shut up and take my money." It was the first cash Ware had ever earned for the game—or for any game. To this day, he refuses to spend the bill.

The Kickstarter campaign allowed Ware to hire an actual staff, and he assembled a handpicked team of DigiPen graduates who were "awesome but between jobs." Development began on April 1, 2013, and Ware's company, Crooked Tree Studios, released a polished PC version eleven months later. I sat down and played it in San Francisco in May 2014, and it was everything Ware's fans loved: a funny, challenging, twisted little power fantasy that, somehow, really worked. As I sat at a crowded table filled with laptops, one of Ware's colleagues fitted me with a headset—no disgusting contact gel! Ware himself guided me through the basic keyboard commands, which follow those of your typical first-person shooter—arrow keys control your character's movement, for instance—but the core of the game play literally takes place in your head. EEG headband snugly affixed, I had to banish all other thoughts, get calm and focus, Ware said, or else I was dead meat. As I wandered through a kind of gladiators' salvage yard, I practiced a few times and found myself surprisingly able to concentrate. Using the arrow keys, I locked onto a junked car and, eyes on the matching calm/focus meters, I breathed deeply. The car rose with a kind of electrically charged vibration and hovered in midair. I easily tossed it into the distance with a satisfying crash.

I threw a few oversized metal cubes and decided I was getting the hang of it. Just then, Ware leaned in, pointed to a shape in the distance and asked me if I'd noticed the other character onscreen, over there in the corner. It belonged, he said, to the real-live man who was sitting to my right, just two feet away. He'd been there the whole time, another middle-aged white guy like me, probably another journalist who'd wandered into Ware's tangled web. He was wearing an identical headset and sitting in front of an identical laptop, practicing his moves. We nodded hello and Ware declared that it was time for us to crush one another to death. Thus began the strangest battle of wills I've ever experienced. We couldn't shoot, slash, stab, slap, strangle, kick, punch, stomp, or otherwise manhandle one another. We were, in strict video-game terms, almost entirely disabled. All we could do, other than some rudimentary running, jumping, and turning, was sit back and *relax*.

The battle was brief, as there were other people behind us clamoring to play Ware's demo, but we quickly maneuvered to either side of the arena, focused on a giant vehicle in the center and began, with self-conscious giggles, to try to will it into the air. I repeated the mantra: *calm lifts, focus throws . . . calm lifts, focus throws.* In a few seconds, our combined effort made the car rise, but then came the real test: Who was more focused? *I was.* I crushed him mightily, 2,000 pounds of concentration smashing my opponent against the far wall. Then he respawned and decked me with a monstrous metal cube, a silent, mindful sucker punch that knocked me silly. As I stood and removed the headset, I felt a kind of mental clarity that comes from a brisk walk or yoga session.

Throw Trucks makes no medical claims, but Ware has moved forward with a series of clinical trials, hoping someday to get it covered by insurers. "If my game works, this would actually be a good call for an insurance company," he said. Since he bought his first pair of headsets in 2011, the price has come down again, and at $99, the game *and* headset now cost less than a month's prescription for Ritalin—actually, he wants to get the total cost down to $60. But FDA approval could take a decade or more. "Ultimately this is for the best," he said, "because we don't want snake oil on the market."[23]

When I spoke to Ware in late June 2014, he was working with a Hong Kong company to test *Throw Trucks*'s effects on ADHD, and with the University of California–San Diego to test its efficacy for subjects on the autism spectrum. Like Wexler, he'd spent years watching as other neurogames made claims about their health benefits—he said he could goose sales quickly if he simply sold it as a vaguely beneficial, feel-good alternative therapy. "As much as I'd love to have marketing points like that, scientific rigor is important," he said. At the time, he was living in Redwood City, half an hour north of Sunnyvale, but he said he'd be back in Palo Alto in July. He wasn't getting a new apartment, he explained. He was couch surfing.

Before I sat down for my chicken-game demo at Churchill School in New York, I'd watched two nine-year-old students show me how it was really done. Both excelled at keeping their chicken running at a steady clip, concentrating with a kind of easy, sustained attention that kids with ADHD usually have trouble mustering. So far, Atentiv studies of the results at Churchill and other schools have shown that kids who go through a carefully planned, eight-hour series of sessions with the game show much higher math and reading fluency and better performance on math and grammar tests, more consistent planning and homework completion and better ability to complete written work in class, as well as other skills. They also have better attention and impulse control at home, their parents report, and they can control their emotions better. The game's inventors credit much of the improvement to a phenomenon they call "feed-forward," as opposed to feedback. The basic idea is that the game isn't so much reacting to you as it is waiting for you to push it forward. The more you do, the more efficient you get. "You're trying to manage focus for a sustained period of time and it's showing your actual attention levels, the highest levels of attention," said Eric Gordon, one of Atentiv's founders and a veteran of the medical-device business. He is convinced that it can be as effective as any drug or expensive therapy and he sits beside me as I try the game. More than once, as I try to concentrate on the chicken, he gently asks, "Are you feeding forward?"

After a few minutes I'm clearly not feeding much of anything, least of all my poor chicken, who seems a bit bored by the session. She stands in her cowboy boots, waiting patiently for my focus to return. At those moments when I'm really distracted, an animated bar at the bottom of the screen lets me know that my "focus force" is dangerously low. When it drains to zero, as it does several times, the screen reads: "Concentrate to move." Thanks for the suggestion!

Part of the problem could be my insatiable need to explain myself to Gordon and his young assistant, both of whom wait patiently, much like the chicken, as I make excuses. I'm stressed, I say. I'm tired, I'm over-caffeinated . . . I'm *trying* to lose focus to see what happens. They've heard it all, it seems, every excuse. They neither scold nor reassure me, just suggest I keep feeding forward.

Six minutes and four seconds after I begin, I get my results: my "focus force" averages forty-seven out of one hundred. In other words, I'm not very focused. Gordon says that's not bad for a beginner. By the time it's over—I also try out a classroom simulation, complete with the inexplicable sound of a crying baby—I can't quite put my finger on exactly what, moment to moment, I'm doing right or wrong. There are a few instances when I feel I'm focusing intently on the chicken but she simply stops in her tracks. Other times I zone out—why are the palm trees *blue?*—and she happily keeps up her pace, little puffs of dust trailing behind her. I decide that what works best is to breathe deeply and focus not on making the chicken move, but on *being* the chicken. Turn off my mind, relax, and float downstream, imagining that I'm the endless-runner hero of my own meaningless story. *The Zen of Motorchicken Maintenance, The Loneliness of the Long-Distance Chicken.* I am the Egg Man, forever feeding forward. That actually seems to work.

ELEVEN

THE OPPOSITE OF FIGHTING

*How Violent Video Games
Really Affect Kids*

On the morning of August 12, 2013, nearly eight months after twenty-year-old Adam Lanza shot his way into Sandy Hook Elementary School and killed twenty-six people, Michael Mudry, an investigator with the Connecticut State Police, drove to nearby Danbury to try to figure out a little mystery in the case. Police had found a Garmin global positioning system unit in Lanza's house, and its records showed that the gunman had driven to the same spot nine times in April, May, and June of 2012, arriving around midnight each time and staying for five hours.

The GPS readout took Mudry to the vast parking lot of a suburban shopping center off Interstate 84, about fourteen miles west of Lanza's home. When Mudry looked around, he realized that if Lanza had spent time there, it could have been in one of only three places: a Best Buy, a Lowe's home improvement store, or the AMC Loews Danbury 16 movie theater. When Mudry showed employees of the Best Buy and the Lowe's a photo of Lanza alongside his mother, no one could identify him. But at the movie theater, workers immediately recognized the kid in the photo. He was in there constantly, they told the investigator, but never to see movies. He came to the lobby to play an arcade game—the same one, over and over and over again, for hours on end.

Police had been scouring the Lanzas' home since the shootings and it didn't take them long to piece together the usual school shooter's profile: an obsession with guns, murder, and mayhem, and the time and space to indulge it. On Adam Lanza's computer hard drive they found, among other items, information on weapons magazine capacities, images of Columbine killers Eric Harris and Dylan Klebold, copies of the violent movies *Bloody Wednesday* and *Rampage,* and a list of ingredients for TNT. Like many teenaged boys, Lanza owned the typical first-person shooters and action games: *Call of Duty, Dead or Alive, Grand Theft Auto.*

But more than any of these, the game at the movie theater seemed to possess him. He had a home version for his Xbox too, police noted, and his hard drive held videos in which Lanza put himself through the game's paces. At the theater, a supervisor named Corey Davidson told Mudry he'd seen Lanza "pretty much every weekend for the past four years."[1] For a while, a girl came with him, but then she disappeared. Then an Asian boy, but he disappeared too. Lanza, on the other hand, showed up reliably, every Friday, Saturday, and Sunday, and stayed for four hours, always playing the same game and challenging others to beat him. In August 2011, said Darren Price, another theater employee, Lanza began spending even more time playing the game—eight to ten hours a night.

The title that so obsessed the Sandy Hook shooter? *Dance Dance Revolution.*

Also known as *DDR,* the Japanese import had been an arcade staple for fifteen years. The state police report, which described the game as well as anyone, called it "a music video game in which the player stands on a platform, watches a video screen and moves his feet as directed by the video."[2] At the theater, Price told Mudry, everybody referred to Lanza as "*DDR* Guy." He was always dressed the same: gray hoodie and cargo pants. And the kid had stamina. Lanza "never appeared winded unless really exhausted," one witness told police. The unnamed girl who for a time joined him was known as "*DDR* Girl." A subsequent report from the state Office of the Child Advocate noted that Lanza's medical records showed he'd been playing the game as far back as 2003. He would "whip himself into a frenzy," witnesses said, dancing to the point of physical exhaustion, "a behavior consistent, possibly, with a need to contain anxiety-producing impulses and thoughts." Some days, Lanza would do nothing else. One witness said the theater manager on occasion had to unplug the game to get Lanza to leave.[3]

Mudry filed his report and the police dropped the inquiry. So did the mainstream press. Though instinctively drawn to any promising lead in a story this big, everyone understood that a nine-year obsession with competitive dancing on colored squares to the rhythm of Asian techno pop hadn't somehow turned the twenty-year-old into a stone-cold killer. Just because Lanza, all 6 feet and 112 pounds of him,[4] played *DDR* endlessly for nearly a decade doesn't mean that the game had much of anything to do with his deadly outburst.

Though it might seem like a big cognitive leap, we need to apply that same understanding to more troublesome video game titles as well. We need to understand that shooting virtual opponents turns players into killers about as often as dancing on colored squares does. It's a complex and counterintuitive argument, and it will take some explaining, but it's important to understand. Along with books, magazines, comics, terrible YouTube videos, pop music, and Tumblr posts, video games are just media. We misunderstand kids' relationship to their media in dangerous ways, and we need to start rethinking it.

For a long time this line of inquiry seemed beyond the scope of my investigation—after all, I was looking at educational games, many designed by teachers and most of them certainly approved by teachers. As groundbreaking a game as the open-world, adult-rated *Grand Theft Auto: Vice City* is, few teachers would assign students to play it, either in class or for homework. But whenever I told people that I was writing a book about games, they wanted to talk about violence and what they saw as their kids' addiction to certain titles. They wanted to talk about *Hitman* and *Halo, Resident Evil, The Walking Dead*. They wanted to talk about Columbine and Virginia Tech and why their sons couldn't tear themselves away from *Minecraft*[5] to finish their homework. Parents wanted to know: were they being bad parents by indulging their kids' love of games, some of them violent?

The short answer is *no* and the slightly longer answer is *it depends*. More on that in a moment. But the most important thing to remember is this: decades of research have turned up no reliable causal link between playing violent video games and perpetrating actual violence. A few statistical studies actually find that violence goes *down* when you add violent video games to the mix. This is not to say that games have no effect. As we've seen, they're *built* to have an effect. It's just not the effect most people think.

The implicit link between violent media and violent behavior is so old and affixed to our understanding that, like an old barnacle, it's hard to chip off. The basic notion dates back at least 150 years to the Victorian era, when educators, tastemakers, and clergymen began criticizing what was then a fairly raucous popular culture. Violent, sex-soaked "dime novels" and penny magazines were immensely popular, and upstanding publications such as *Harper's* and the *Atlantic Monthly* took delight in denouncing them. In one editorial cartoon, a publisher handed out trashy stories to children in front of a sign that read, "A nice pistol!!! Given with every year's subscription!"[6] Author and critic Harold Schechter, whose 2005 book *Savage Pastimes* lays out a social history of violent entertainment, noted that the trend actually divided the literati of the time. Ralph Waldo Emerson complained about his countrymen "reading all day murders & railroad accidents" in penny papers, but Nathaniel Hawthorne loved them so much he had a friend ship stacks of them to Liverpool while he lived abroad as United States Consul. The Belle of Amherst herself, Emily Dickinson, loved to read stories of "those funny accidents where railroads meet each other, and gentlemen in factories get their heads cut off quite informally."[7] In Britain, readers thrilled to the serial exploits of Sweeney Todd, "the Demon Barber of Fleet Street." The character would later appear on Broadway in the 1979 Stephen Sondheim musical and in a 2007 movie adaptation directed by Tim Burton, but in 1846, the revenge-seeking London barber debuted in a popular magazine aimed at "the whole family, children included," Schechter wrote. To get a sense of what that signified, he suggested, "imagine the Hallmark Channel replacing *Touched by an Angel* with a weekly show about Jeffrey Dahmer."[8]

The twentieth century brought even more robust criticism. In 1936, Catholic scholar John K. Ryan laid out what he called the "mental food of American children, young and old" as seen through the media they consumed. It was a very, very long menu: "Sadism, cannibalism, bestiality. Crude eroticism. Torturing, killing, kidnapping. Monsters, madmen, creatures half-brute, half-human. Raw melodrama; tales of crimes and criminals; extravagant exploits in strange lands and on other planets; pirate stories; wild, hair-raising adventures of boy heroes and girl heroines; thrilling accounts in words and pictures of jungle beasts and men; marvelous deeds of magic and pseudoscience. Vulgarity, cheap humor, and cheaper wit. Sentimental stories designed for the general level of the moronic mind. Ugliness of thought and express."[9] He was talking about daily newspaper comic strips.

In 1947, critic and actor John Houseman, who would later define the image of starchy academia in *The Paper Chase,* lodged similar complaints about the cartoons most kids watched on TV. "The fantasies which our children greet with howls of joy run red with horrible savagery," he wrote. "Today the animated cartoon has become a bloody battlefield through which savage and remorseless creatures, with single-track minds, pursue one another, then rend, gouge, twist, tear, and mutilate each other with sadistic ferocity."[10]

Into this fray entered Stanford psychologist Albert Bandura (at this writing now in his late eighties). With a series of experimental studies in the early 1960s, he established the theoretical basis for limiting kids' access to violent media. By then, Bandura had already been puzzling over childhood aggression for nearly twenty years. In 1961, he was trying to determine if the effects of punishments and rewards meted out to children after they've performed an aggressive act could be extended to include punishments and rewards they watched others receive after performing similar acts. The idea was, for its time, revolutionary. B. F. Skinner and others had demonstrated that humans react predictably to positive and negative reinforcement—if I smack my sister, I'll get yelled at, so perhaps I shouldn't smack my sister. But what if I simply *watched* someone get punished for such an act? Would that deter me? More to the point, what if they *didn't* get punished for it?

Bandura gathered up seventy-two preschoolers at the Stanford University Nursery School, kids as young as three and as old as five years and nine months. The median age was about four and a half.[11] He had lab assistants lead the kids, one at a time, into a playroom, where they sat at a small table and received instruction on how to make potato-print pictures. Soon another adult entered the room and settled into the opposite corner with a tinker toy set, a mallet and a five-foot inflated "Bobo" clown doll, the kind that's weighted at the bottom so it rights itself if knocked over. The adult then either assembled the tinker toys "in a quiet subdued manner," ignoring Bobo, or turned to the doll and spent nearly the rest of the time "aggressing toward it." The adult punched the doll, laid it on its side and sat on it, struck the doll on the head and kicked it around the room, all the while saying things such as, "Sock him in the nose," "Hit him down," "Kick him," and "Pow."[12] After ten minutes of this, each child was led into another room that held "relatively attractive toys" such as a fire engine, a locomotive, a colorful spinning top, and a complete doll set. Kids were invited to play with these toys, but after just two minutes a lab assistant announced that these were "her very best toys," that she didn't let just anyone play with them, and that she'd decided to reserve them for other children. The kids were swept into a third room that held more toys, both "aggressive and non-aggressive": a tea set, crayons, dart guns, a mallet . . . and a three-foot Bobo doll. You see where this is going.

Faced with the frustration of having nice new toys suddenly snatched away, preschoolers who'd watched Bobo get mistreated were more likely than the others to take out their aggression on the mini-Bobo. Boys were about twice as likely to be aggressive if the adult who'd punched Bobo in that first room was a male. Bandura repeated the experiment in 1963, adding film and cartoon versions of the Bobo mistreatment, with similar results. The conclusions seemed clear: watching unchecked aggression in real life, on film, or in cartoons makes us more aggressive because it provides us with "social scripts" to guide our behavior. Bandura's conclusions opened a floodgate of "media effects" research that continues today.

The problem is that many of the findings, especially when applied to children's media and play, are misleading at best. Critic Gerard Jones, whose 2003 book *Killing Monsters* makes a persuasive case for giving kids access to "fantasy, super heroes and make-believe violence," put Bobo in perspective: "There is no evidence to suggest that punching an inflatable clown has any connection to real-life violence," he wrote. "There is no evidence that kids who love to punch inflatable clowns are more prone to playground aggression or later delinquency. There is anecdotal evidence that clown-punching is beneficial when it has any effect at all. And yet incidents of clown-punching have been jotted down by generations of researchers as evidence of "'heightened aggression.'"[13] In many cases, he and others said, researchers tap into subjects' temporary aggression but mislabel it as behavior that holds the potential for violence. In other cases, they tap into natural competitiveness and call it aggression. In still others, they simply interpret the results of discomfort as aggression. In an often-quoted study conducted more than a decade after Bandura's first Bobo trials, researchers found that preschoolers who watched *Mister Rogers' Neighborhood* were three times more aggressive afterward. Jones suggested that the experiment itself may have made kids anxious or even angry by compelling them to watch TV on cue. "I love Fred Rogers," Jones wrote, "but I suspect if I were forced to sit in a hard plastic chair in a strange room and stare at him when I'd rather be out playing, I'd act aggressively too."[14]

The link between media violence and real-world violence is drawn "from bad or irrelevant research, muddleheaded thinking and unfounded, simplistic news reports," wrote child psychologist Lawrence Kutner and media researcher Cheryl K. Olson.[15] In one case, they found that the American Academy of Pediatrics (or AAP, which has put forth sensible media-use guidelines) asserted in 2001 that "more than 3,500 research studies have examined the association between media violence and violent behavior," with all but eighteen showing a positive relationship.[16] The figure is taken as gospel in the world of media research, but when Kutner and Olson went searching for its source, they found it not in a research study but in a footnote of *Stop Teaching Our Kids to Kill*, a 1999 book that compared violent movies, TV, and video games to the military's Vietnam-era desensitization drills. Its author, retired U.S. Army sergeant Dave Grossman, famously called video games "murder simulators." He had found the 3,500 figure in a 1998 article, published in Sweden, by the United Nations Educational, Scientific, and Cultural Organization. It offered no information on the "positive relationship" assertion or how anyone even arrived at the 3,500 figure.[17] Yet today if you Google the phrase "3,500 research studies," you'll get a quarter million results, most of them uncritically offering up the AAP declaration.

Schechter, who traced the history of penny papers and Sweeney Todd, said the Baby Boomer generation watched so much violence on TV as children that you'd expect them all to be killers. In 1958, he found, there were no fewer than seventeen westerns on prime-time TV, all of them "rife with gunplay."[18] While researching his book, Schechter tracked down a DVD of the 1955 Disney series *Davy Crockett at the Alamo,* a show whose "level of carnage remains unsurpassed in the history of children's entertainment." Watching it again after nearly fifty years, he recalled, "I was stunned by the sheer brutality of the battle sequences, which featured more deaths by sword, bayonet, knife, pistol and rifle than can possibly be counted."[19] Critics of the day warned that watching all that violence would turn Schechter's generation into sociopaths. "Instead, we grew up to be the generation that preached (however sanctimoniously) peace, love and flower power, and believed we could end the Vietnam War by surrounding the Pentagon and chanting 'Om.'"[20]

It was the 1999 Columbine High School shootings that got many Americans thinking about violent video games. After the attacks, victims' families sued more than two dozen game makers, saying games such as *Doom,* a first-person shooter that the two teen gunmen played, desensitized them to violence. A judge dismissed the lawsuits because the games weren't subject to product liability laws—they didn't "fail" like a badly wired toaster or bottle of poisoned aspirin. But the lawsuits and the post-Columbine uproar in Congress pushed the industry to adopt a ratings system similar to that of movies. It also effectively brought cognitive research on all games to a halt, wrote Duke University researcher

Cathy Davidson. Since then, she said, fear of video games has made them "virtually off limits to educators even as adults have benefitted profoundly from them."[21] Instead, researchers began dissecting games, much as Bandura did TV, in search of the roots of aggression. "The language," she wrote, "was all about containment." In a 2010 experiment, researchers at the University of Sussex and Ludwig-Maximilians University in Germany asked subjects to play one of three video games for eight minutes—either a "prosocial" game, an "aggressive" game, or the "neutral" game *Tetris*. After eight minutes, the experimenter reached for a stack of questionnaires but "accidentally" knocked a cup of pencils off the table and onto the floor. Participants who had played the prosocial game were twice as likely to help pick up the pencils as those who played the neutral or aggressive game, researchers found. Of the eighteen people who played the prosocial game, twelve helped to pick up the pencils. Only six of the eighteen who'd played the neutral game helped, and just five of the aggressive players helped.[22]

In a 2012 study, researchers at the University of Luxembourg found that inexperienced players felt a need to "cleanse" themselves after playing a violent video game. Dubbed "the Macbeth effect" from the Shakespeare tragedy, it comes from the memorable "Out, damned spot" speech of Lady Macbeth, who goes insane following her husband's murder spree. In the experiment, researchers asked subjects to play either a driving game or *Grand Theft Auto* for fifteen minutes, then asked them to pick out four gifts from an assortment of ten, half of them "hygienic" (shower gel, deodorant, or toothpaste, for example) and half non-hygienic (gummi bears, Post-it notes, or a box of tea). Inexperienced players who played *GTA* were more likely than experienced players to pick out hygienic products. They were also more likely to pick out hygienic products than other inexperienced players who'd played the driving game.[23]

Enough is enough, wrote British media researcher Guy Cumberbatch. "While tests of statistical significance are a vital tool of the social sciences, they seem to have been more often used in this field as instruments of torture on the data until it confesses something which could justify publication in a scientific journal," he said. "If one conclusion is possible, it is that *the jury is not still out.*

It's never been in. Media violence has been subjected to a lynch mob mentality with almost any evidence used to prove guilt."[24]

A year after Columbine, the U.S. Secret Service and U.S. Department of Education began looking at the habits of forty-one school shooters, including Harris and Klebold. They found that five of them were interested in violent video games, but that twice as many liked violent movies and books. The largest group, more than one in three, exhibited an interest in a different kind of violent media: their own writings, such as poems, essays, or journal entries.[25]

Well, that was then. Video games have grown explosively in the past several years, with sales more than doubling since 1996. With their rise in popularity, youth violence has more than doubled as well, right? Actually, just the opposite: The number of violent youth offenders fell by more than half between 1994 and 2010, according to government statistics.[26] Michael R. Ward, an economist at the University of Texas, Arlington, decided that if short-term aggression is a problem, it should show up quickly in crime rates. Ward in 2011 had already shown that as the number of video-game stores in a county rises, there are "significant" reductions in both crime rates and mortality. He found either a smaller effect or no effect at all when new sporting goods stores or movie theaters open.[27] When Ward and two colleagues looked at game sales, they found that higher rates of violent game sales actually coincided with a drop in crimes—especially violent crimes. On the other hand, crime rates were not affected by the sales of nonviolent games.[28]

Yes, but everybody knows that we have a gun problem. Video games must be making matters worse, right? A 2012 analysis by the *Washington Post* found that the United States has by far the highest gun-related murder rate in the developed world, about twenty times the average.[29] But our per-capita video-game spending lags behind that of most other countries. Every single one of them—the ones who spend more and the ones who spend less—have lower gun-related murder rates. The *Post*'s Max Fisher concluded that video-game consumption "does not seem to correlate at all with an increase in gun violence." Countries where video games are popular, he wrote, "also tend to be some of the world's safest (probably because these countries are stable and developed, not because they have video games)."[30]

What about the U.S. military and their Vietnam-era "desensitization drills"? They actually spend millions of dollars developing sophisticated video games and simulations to train soldiers in combat—how are similar commercial games *not* "murder simulators"? Media scholar Henry Jenkins put it into perspective. The military, he wrote, uses games "as part of a specific curriculum, with clearly defined goals, in a context where students actively want to learn and have a need for the information being transmitted. There are consequences for not mastering those skills."[31] The military itself has concluded that there is no direct correlation between playing video games and an increased urge to kill. For the kinds of hands-off killing called for in modern combat, "homicidal rage is hardly a requirement," noted journalists Heather Chaplin and Aaron Ruby. Actually, they found, the military's 2003 manual *Training for Future Conflicts* states, "In short, everybody must think."[32] Case in point: A decade ago, the U.S. Marine Corps developed *Marine Doom* by adapting the seminal first-person shooter *Doom* to train four-man fire teams. The two Columbine killers, you'll recall, played the original game. Far from fostering rage, the military says, *Marine Doom* "teaches concepts such as mutual fire team support, protection of the automatic rifleman, proper sequencing of an attack, ammunition discipline, and succession of command."[33]

But if media can teach us to be better people, can't it teach us to be worse? It can't simply be a one-way street, can it? Whatever we practice repeatedly affects the brain, wrote psychologist Douglas A. Gentile of Iowa State University. If we practice aggressive ways of thinking, feeling, and reacting, "then we will get better at those."[34] While it's difficult to attribute causality, he said, when we "practice being vigilant for enemies and then reacting quickly to potentially aggressive threats, we are rehearsing this script." In a 2008 study, he and a colleague found that violent video games "appear to be exemplary teachers of aggression." Playing lots of violent video games, they found, "appears to lead to better transfer of aggressive cognitions and behaviors" than playing a mix of violent and nonviolent games or just nonviolent games. They also found that eighth and ninth graders who played violent games more frequently displayed greater "hostile attribution bias" (being vigilant for enemies) and got into more arguments with teachers.[35]

Cognitive scientist Daphne Bavelier and psychologist C. Shawn Green might concede this point but look at the problem holistically. Violent video games alone, they wrote, "are unlikely to turn a child with no other risk factors into a maniacal killer." But in children with many risk factors, the size of the effect "may be sufficient to have practical negative consequences."[36] The larger question might be: why don't we stop worrying about the media the child is consuming and do something about the many risk factors first?

Actually, decades of research have shown that one type of media *does* cause more school shootings: media coverage of school shootings. Since most of the young perpetrators are suicidal, "intensive reporting" on suicides in general and school shootings in particular may "tip the balance and make the at-risk individual feel that suicide is a reasonable, acceptable, and in some instances even heroic, decision," the U.S. Surgeon General reported in 1999.[37]

By themselves, games are neither good nor bad, said games scholar James Paul Gee. It depends what you do with them. Played in moderation, with an assist from adults and friends, they're beneficial, with lasting cognitive and social effects. "Played as babysitters by children from violent homes, they are bad," he said.[38] Asked how many people have ever been killed because of a video game, his best guess is perhaps none, perhaps half a dozen. We don't really know, which is remarkable since nearly all young men play video games. Meanwhile, billions have been killed because of what's in books, and no one but the most spit-flecked zealot wants to ban books, "an infinitely more powerful technology for good and evil" than video games, said Gee. "Loads of people across the world believe God wrote a book—they just don't agree which one. No one thinks he designed a video game."[39]

Jenkins offers perhaps the best answer to the violence question. "Media is most powerful in our lives when it reinforces our existing values," he wrote, "and least powerful when it contradicts them.[40] If I *actually believe* I need to be vigilant for real-life enemies, a game will work on me quite effectively. If I don't, it's not going to work on me at an elemental level. It won't change my personality. Actually, Jenkins wrote, a child who responds to a video game the same way he or she responds to a real-world trauma could be showing symptoms of being emotionally disturbed. In that sense, a violent game could actually serve as a kind of affordable and efficient diagnostic tool—more about this in the next chapter. But beyond that, media effects research, with its Bobo dolls as markers of real-world aggression, is problematic. "The kid who is punching a toy designed for this purpose is still within the 'magic circle' of play and understands her actions on those terms," Jenkins wrote. "Such research shows us only that violent play leads to more violent play."[41]

In the 1960s, as Bandura conducted his media effects research, the British folklorists Iona and Peter Opie spent years observing and studying children's outdoor play. They watched children play games—many of them made up—with names like *Underground Tig* and *Witches in the Gluepots* and concluded, "A true game is one that frees the spirit. It allows no cares but those fictitious ones engendered by the game itself." When children commit to the games, they opt out of the ordinary world and "the boundary of their existence becomes the two pavements this side of a pillar-box, their only reality the excitement of avoiding the chaser's touch."[42] It may seem a stretch, but we should apply the same understanding to the first-person shooter games that teenagers enjoy. "In games a child can exert himself without having to explain himself," the Opies wrote, "he can be a good player without having to think whether he is a popular person, he can find himself being a useful partner to someone of whom he is ordinarily afraid."[43]

To be perfectly clear, what looks from the outside like killing is not. In a way, said Brian Sutton-Smith, the renowned play theorist, it's the opposite. The kind of fighting kids do when they're playing—either in a physical game or a video game—is always just a simulation, with "inhibited" outcomes not meant to hurt one's real-life opponent. "This may be a display of fighting," he wrote, "but it is also *the opposite of fighting,* seeing as it is carried on by those who are not enemies and who do not intend to harm each other, and always accompanied by the special faces and signals that different species use to convey that their intent is only to play. Play-fighting as an analogy to real fighting seems more like displaying the meaning of fighting than rehearsing for real combat. It is more about meaning than about mauling."[44]

In a sense, we're pointing fingers at the wrong people. When we worry that a violent game is going to turn our kids into killers, aren't *we* the ones who fail to grasp the difference between fantasy and reality? Kids already know the difference. We're the ones having trouble separating the two.

TWELVE

••••••••••••••••••••••••→

THE LUDIC LOOP

*How to Talk to Your Kids about
Their Gaming Habits*

The kid was twenty-three years old, still living at home and chronically unemployed. He'd been playing online role-playing games since high school, and though he'd kept up with schoolwork, his gaming had since overwhelmed just about everything else. He somehow found a job at a software-development company, but then quit after just three months. "I'm not looking for any job," he told his father. "I want to take some time to find one that suits me." The father, in China's Shaanxi Province, began searching for a way to sour his son on the games and discourage him from playing any further. So he hired higher-level players of several multiplayer games as "hitmen" to find his son's avatar online and assassinate him, over and over again, wherever they found him.[1] A gambling and addiction expert who heard the story remarked, "It's not going to do much for family relations."[2]

Parents rightfully worry about the large chunks of time that their kids spend on computers, and games have become a big part of screen time. Words like "addicted" certainly seem to describe what happens to kids. Games, after all, are designed to keep us playing, incorporating what one scholar has called "the ludic loop"—a never-ending procession of play. But there's play and there's *play*.

Games often require players to test and improve their skills, follow a narrative, take part in teamwork, and interact with other people, but sometimes games don't. In that sense, those that pull us away from others and into hours of solitary, uninterrupted play—especially if they don't require much in the way of skills—can be considered neurological cousins to Las Vegas slot machines and their "machine zone" draw. "It's just you and you're interacting with the screen," said Natasha Dow Schüll, the sociologist who has studied slots. "You're not waiting for other people. It's just pure repetition, pure procedure."[3] So the difference between playing *Just Dance* with a group of friends and *Candy Crush* alone in your room (or *Newton's Gravity* in your hotel room) is akin to the difference between eating a fresh apple and an apple-flavored lollipop. Both are sweet, but the latter is a purer, more concentrated form of sweetness that hits our pleasure center more directly, that more reliably and quickly triggers our dopamine response.

However, in all but the worst cases, "addiction" is probably not the appropriate term. Children aged eight to eighteen, after all, now spend about seven and a half hours daily in front of screens, but only about eighty minutes playing video games, recent surveys have found.[4] When we use words like "addicted," we're misspeaking about what's happening in the minds of most players—and we fail to put their play into context.

Other media rarely get saddled with the same pathological description, said games journalist Tom Chatfield. "A book is described as 'impossible to put down,' and this is high praise. A television series is described as 'compulsive viewing' and this—a term borrowed from a behavioral disorder—is a testament to its quality and the skill of its makers. Yet most people don't worry that books or television series are, of themselves, so appealing that they represent a hazard to consumers."[5]

Stanford researcher Nick Yee, who has made a career of studying massively multiplayer online games, recently suggested this exercise: Imagine a multiplayer social game that takes place in a "cordoned-off portion of reality," a kind of virtual world where different rules apply. Players take on fantasy roles that have functional meaning *only* in the game world. Arbitrarily defined tasks earn points, and both teamwork and intense competition are key.

The game, of course, is football, though it could just as easily be *World of Warcraft*.[6] Yet when things go wrong in football—when a player is injured or even when a player drops dead from heat stroke—we tend to think about it holistically, he said. "And in no time during all this introspection does anyone suggest football is addictive and that a new pathological designation should be created for football."[7] Invoking the word "addiction" usually has one function: to shut down conversation about broader issues. It's a "rhetorical sleight of hand that distracts us from the actual psychological problems" from which gamers might suffer, such as depression or social anxiety, said Yee. Taking away the technology, he wrote, "won't resolve these underlying psychological problems."[8]

As we saw in the last chapter, playing with aggression can help blunt its real-life force. But a game can also help people face down their fears. Experiencing mediated fear "gives us the opportunity to experience fear in a controlled way, where we have the potential, at least, to master our fears, to control threats, in a way that we can't in real life," wrote Indiana University's Andrew Weaver.[9] Putting oneself at the center of violent fantasy play, often in the guise of an alternate identity—a fifteen-year-old boy playing as a woman or vice-versa—can be a healthy exercise. "Playing with rage is a valuable way to reduce its power," wrote *Killing Monsters* author Gerald Jones. "Being evil and destructive in imagination is a vital compensation for the wildness we all have to surrender on our way to being good people."[10]

Our fear of our kids' aggression comes from our justifiable anxiety over real-life violence, but it comes at a cost, Jones found. We're stifling kids' power fantasies in ways we wouldn't dream of when it comes to fantasies about money, love, adventure, and the like. "We don't usually ask whether game shows predispose our children to greed, or whether love songs increase the likelihood of getting stuck in bad relationships. But when aggression is the topic, we try to puree a million games and dreams and life stories into statistical studies."[11]

Children, he concluded, need to feel strong and powerful "in the face of a scary, uncontrollable world." When something troubles them, he wrote, "they have to play with it until it feels safer." Media—violent, explicit, and otherwise—can help.

"Superheroes, video-game warriors, rappers and movie gunmen are symbols of strength. By pretending to be them, young people are being strong."[12]

Connecticut psychologist Eric Schleifer, who specializes in treating young teenaged boys, said many of his patients are heavy gamers—and many are struggling with anxiety about the world and their place in it. The more anxious they are, he told me, the more interested they are in violent content, almost as a way to test how brave they are. They'll try to one-up him when it comes to consuming violent games or movies, asking if he has seen all of the horror movies they have seen or played the same first-person shooter games. One boy with severe anxiety about his mother was fascinated by the *Saw* horror movies, saying during one session that he wasn't afraid of what happened onscreen—but when his mother was late to pick him up from the appointment, the boy was sure that she'd gotten into a car accident. The session took place during a thunderstorm, and after waiting for just five minutes, he was convinced she'd been struck by lightning. A passing ambulance siren, Schleifer recalled, was all the proof the boy needed that his mother was hurt. "This is in the same session where he's telling me all of these scary movies he's watched. On the one hand, he's telling me, 'I'm not scared of anything, I'm less scared than you are.' And on the other side it's this really frightened other side of himself," Schleifer said. "It was a constant dialogue around those things."[13]

What most adults fail to realize, he said, is that as safe as they are, kids today are dealing with anxieties that previous generations didn't. "We're exposed to things going on all over the world," Schleifer said. "A hundred years ago, children were only exposed to what was on the block, what was around the corner. Maybe something bad would happen in the neighborhood, but if it wasn't in the neighborhood, then *nothing happened*." Now, he said, they've got access to news of the world, to bad things happening everywhere. "How does a child get their head around something like a tsunami? How would you *deal* with that? For *adults* there's no way to deal with it."

Schleifer actually uses games diagnostically. "If I come across a boy who is really into the violent content, that almost assures me that there's something going on, that they're struggling with something, that they have a high degree of anxiety," he said. "The more that boys are interested in violent content, the more they're trying to work through anxieties they have—or the more anxious they are, and they're trying to work it out that way. So it's a really good indication for parents: If you have that kid who is pressing, pressing, pressing, 'All the other kids are playing,' and the game that they're focused on just happens to be the most violent game out there, then that might be an indication that there are things that are going on, that they're scared of things and they're trying to work it out."

To parents who blanch at their children shedding virtual blood, a game designer might ask, *Have you ever thought about blood-as-feedback?* For twenty years, since the dawn of the first-person shooter game, designers have been programming red pixels as place-holders for success. "The reason there are so many guns in games is because guns provide a very abstract, useful shorthand way of pro-jecting power over a distance," said designer Chris Hecker. Shoot-ing a virtual gun creates an efficient feedback loop. "You know when you missed, especially if there's a pock mark on the wall."[14] If your kid is playing a video game that requires a gun—or, for that matter, a spear, knife, chainsaw, or bow and arrow—the only way she knows if she hit her target is if it bleeds.

As we saw earlier, whatever game your child loves, she loves it in large part because it reacts instantaneously to her input ev-ery time, shows whether she's improving, and encourages her—actually, it requires her—to improve her skills. When the rest of life is unsatisfying, indifferent, or worse, think about the pleasure a kid can take from something that responds to her every gesture and that holds her accountable for results. The pleasure that Atari founder Nolan Bushnell felt fifty years ago when he first played *Spacewar!* has changed little. It's immediate and unambiguous, wrote psychologist Jamie Madigan. In the case of shooter games, "You see opponents stagger, see blood fly off them, and ultimately see them collapse."[15]

Moment to moment, the game is supplying three kinds of feed-back, wrote Rigby and Ryan. They break it down along three lines: granular competence (you wander off the path and the controller rumbles, or you shoot a rocket at a distant enemy and it flies off into space—you missed your target); sustained competence (you're getting better at staying on the path and figuring out how to hit enemies with rockets); and cumulative competence (you covered three miles on the path today and your rocket launcher hit forty-seven enemies).[16]

But even though today's parents grew up in the golden age of video arcades, modern games' sophistication, complexity, and, in many cases, brutality, have blindsided them. When I meet these folks, I often ask two questions:

1. Have you sat down and played the game with your kid?
2. Have you asked her what she's getting out of it?

This idea is an adaptation of a concept that was born in the early 1970s. Children's media advocates found that "co-viewing" TV with kids helped them get more from the shows. Research showed that kids who watched *Sesame Street* with their parents and talked about what they were watching understood more. In one early study, low-income Israeli children who watched the show with their mothers got as much educational benefit as middle-class children who watched alone. Sometimes, the study showed, the low-income kids got *more* benefit.[17]

Advocates now call for a different kind of co-viewing around video games, dubbed "joint media engagement." Essentially it's a fancy term for sitting on the couch, playing with your kids and *talking about what's happening onscreen*. Though you don't have to be the best video gamer, you should think about the *kind* of gamer you are. How do you react to being killed every time by the same bad guy, in the same spot? Do you keep trying? Do you take failures in stride, or complain that the controller must be broken, the game has a glitch, or the mission is stupid? Do you play silently? Do you trash talk? Do you ask for help? When you win, do you do a little victory dance? Do you gloat? As with real life, your kids are watching, though they may not always seem to be. They're going to learn as much about you from your failures as from your successes, so fail well.

Parents should also realize that games with adult ratings carry them for a reason. Online interactions with other players can also be decidedly adult. Writer Rosalind Wiseman learned that while researching her 2013 book on boys, *Masterminds and Wingmen*. Video games, she realized, don't cause violence, but they can "normalize humiliation, degradation and senseless violence—as do a lot of things in our culture that we fully or tacitly accept."[18] Putting games in their proper context gives parents more credibility when talking to their kids about them, she wrote. But what to do if your son enjoys playing the role of a bully? In September 2013, after he spent four days straight playing through the latest *Grand Theft Auto* game, critic Tom Bissell concluded that *GTA* "is basically the most elaborate asshole simulation system ever devised, a game based on hurting people and doing whatever you like."[19] If your son is playing a lot of *GTA,* maybe, just maybe, he wants to try out being an asshole. Maybe you should try it alongside him and talk about the experience.

If your children are very young, you should think twice about handing them a screen of any sort. American Academy of Pediatrics guidelines say children under two years of age shouldn't have access to screens—no iPad, no iPhone, no PlayStation, no TV. In fact, recent research shows that even watching TV *in their presence* or leaving the TV on when no one is watching can affect their development. So-called "secondhand television" hurts their language development and interrupts their natural play, said the pediatrics group, which in 2011 included warnings about the practice in its guidelines on children's media. It pointed to several studies, including one from 2008 that found background TV reduced the length of time they played and caused their focus on play to stray. Recent surveys find that about one family in three leaves the TV on most of the time, even though this keeps young children and their parents from interacting—a key way, as we've seen, that children develop the working vocabulary they'll need in school. "If you're trying to connect with your kids, you've got to turn the screens off," said Ari Brown,[20] an Austin, Texas, pediatrician and lead author on the recommendations.

Other pediatricians are beginning to warm up to touchscreen devices such as the iPad, saying they open new possibilities, not just for learning but for engagement between children and parents. But the interactive possibilities of real life should be the default setting for the very young, said *Children's Technology Review* editor Warren Buckleitner. "I've pretty much dedicated my last twenty years to trying to understand interactive media and kids, and my standard line is, if you've got an under two-and-a-half-year-old, get a cat."[21]

For a few players, addiction is real. Douglas Gentile, the Iowa State researcher, in 2009 applied criteria normally reserved for diagnosing pathological gamblers to determine whether gamers had "a problematic relationship" with games. He surveyed 1,178 young people ages eight to eighteen and found that 8.5 percent met six or more criteria of "pathological patterns of play."[22] One in five admitted doing poorly on a school assignment or test because he or she spent too much time playing video games. Nearly one in four admitted to sometimes skipping homework to play games. Other research has shown that heavy gamers spend less time doing homework—but often simply complete it faster than non-gamers. "Gamers may actually be more effective in completing homework assignments, and as a result, they spend less time doing homework. We need to look deeper into what is going on," said the University of Michigan's Hope Cummings.[23]

Rigby and Ryan, the psychologists, have pointed out one more key attribute of games, one that can have a magnetic effect: games offer *density of experience* that few interactions do. Much as Jane McGonigal found that *World of Warcraft* is "the single most powerful IV drip of productivity ever created," Rigby and Ryan found that while real life often seems sparse, "games are there to offer us this density as well as instant feedback that makes us feel effective and even important."[24] As a result, they found, people who don't have this kind of feedback loop in real life may be susceptible to "over-involvement" in games, sometimes at the cost of time with families or dealing with the more difficult challenges and issues that "the molecular world" presents. One gamer told them, "I missed the first five years of my kid's childhood because of games, and I don't want that to continue."[25] They suggest that once players cross the twenty-five-hours-per-week mark, their gaming could be problematic and deserves another look.

Psychologists Hilarie Cash and Kim McDaniel, who specialize in treating young people whose video game habits have created havoc in their lives, said any child who plays more than two hours a day has entered the "slippery slope of misuse" and could slide into addiction.[26] All children, they said, need to feel "securely nestled in their families. When this security is absent, a child feels a desperate longing for the attachments that are missing. For a person feeling a lack of emotional security, safety, and love, screen time provides a distraction and a substitute. *On-line communities substitute for real-life communities.* Stimulating/medicating video games dull the pain of what is missing from real life."[27]

The American Academy of Pediatrics now recommends that pediatricians take a detailed "media history" of patients—especially those who show aggressive behavior; are overweight or obese; use tobacco, alcohol, or other drugs; or have difficulties in school. The group says pediatricians should ask parents two key questions at every well-child visit: "How much recreational screen time does your child or teenager consume daily? Is there a television set or Internet-connected device in the child's bedroom?" They also recommend that pediatricians take a look at their own media use, saying those who watch more TV are less likely to advise families to follow AAP recommendations.[28]

In the end, what may be most important is helping kids maintain a sense of balance, of not letting games become the only safe, reliable, and rewarding part of their lives. When children ask for his autograph, Shigeru Miyamoto, the legendary Japanese designer who created the *Super Mario* games for Nintendo, often signs notes: "On a sunny day, play outside."[29]

EPILOGUE

Games Everywhere

As the opera's Mozart-inspired overture plays, the camera pans over an underground, post-apocalyptic landscape, then swoops down the length of an impossibly tall tower, through deserted streets and into a home lit by a blazing fireplace. Inside, a brother and sister sing about their long-lost parents, who fled to the surface eleven years ago to explore the land that people once inhabited. The siblings long to reunite with their parents, but an evil emperor keeps everyone below. So the duo hatch a plan to escape.

In most respects, *The Surface: A World Above,* hews to the conventions of your typical opera, except for one: its five roles are performed in a virtual world. Projected onto an enormous screen are five full-body digital avatars controlled by five offstage actors, each wielding a laptop computer. On either side of the screen, five singers, each paired with one of the actors, stand at microphones. Created by a group of teenaged boys at an after-school music class at Virginia Tech University, the work is set entirely inside the massively popular online world-building game *Minecraft.*

The project's roots lay in a familiar artists' dilemma: its director couldn't afford a set. In the spring of 2013, Ariana Wyatt, a redheaded operatic soprano, Juilliard alumna, and thirty-two-year-old assistant professor of voice in Tech's School of Performing Arts, won a $25,000 in-house grant to stage an opera with local teens. She wanted to focus on the music and the drama, so she asked a colleague, Ico Bukvic, if there was some sort of virtual world in which her students could build a set at little to no expense. "There *has* to be a way, right?" she asked him.[1]

Wyatt was not a gamer. Growing up in Ventura County, California, she never came closer than dabbling in an online "shoot-'em-up game"—she doesn't remember which one—for a few months as a college freshman. She played it so she could spend time chatting over the Internet with her high-school sweetheart—she was at the University of Southern California and he was 400 miles away, at the University of California–Davis. They broke up that year and she never returned to the game.

By the time Wyatt came to Bukvic, a Tech instructor and composer, both of his children, aged eight and twelve, were gone on *Minecraft*. He knew immediately that the blocky, retro-feel open-world building game was what she was after. With millions of players—at last check, more than 50 million copies were circulating worldwide—he realized that Wyatt's students would surely be familiar with it, perhaps even skilled at building. They'd be coming from several communities across southwestern Virginia, so they could collaborate on the set without even having to be in the same zip code. The students could work on it any time of day or night, as long as they were online and signed in. "It was one of those things that was just staring right in your face," he said.[2]

Not quite knowing what she had gotten into, Wyatt printed up fliers asking, "Do you like *Minecraft?* Do you like music?" She tacked up them in high schools throughout the region. Another colleague suggested they call it *OPERAcraft*.

A few weeks later, eight teenaged boys showed up, and what followed was a burst of invention as they quickly designed and built the set while Bukvic hacked *Minecraft's* code to make its blocky avatars more expressive. He also figured out a way to sync movement of the avatars' mouths with the sounds coming from singers' microphones. It was a kind of two-person digital operatic karaoke, relying upon music "just totally stolen" from five Mozart operas and a symphony. Wyatt knew that the boys would love building the set but fretted that their excitement wouldn't extend to the rest of the enterprise.

They were interested in all of it. The set, the music, the libretto, everything. They got into heated discussions—fights, actually—about where the story was headed and eventually settled upon the post-apocalyptic theme with missing parents. Over the next six months, Wyatt and her colleagues coached the group through writing a book and libretto, then staging and (no pun intended) blocking the performance. They named one of the main characters Markus, after Markus "Notch" Persson, *Minecraft*'s Swedish designer.

The opera's first act debuted in December 2013 in a theater at Virginia Tech. A small crowd of friends and family watched as a pianist played the overture and the game's "camera"—really just a player sitting in the third balcony and controlling the view from a laptop—opened onto a projected view of the massive 3-D underground world that the students had created. The first time I saw it, I got a lump in my throat. No, I did not write a poem, as per Robert Frost, but I did think about what made it such a moving experience. Maybe it was the Mozart talking, or the fact that a bunch of teenaged boys had somehow gotten excited about opera. I finally decided that *The Surface* is exciting for another reason: the little drama in a digital sandbox represents one of the most promising applications of games and learning that I've seen since I began reporting this book.

This isn't the same old thing done more efficiently or, heaven forbid, the same old *stupid* thing done more efficiently. These aren't better flash cards or gamified toothbrushes with points attached. This is cutting-edge technology applied to something totally new and strange and beautiful. It offers kids the chance to create something no one has ever seen, something keyed to their passions but with an eye toward broadening them. They start with one foot in a familiar world and end up somewhere new and different. In this case, of course, they're stepping from the digital world back into ours. Our gamers became students.

Forty years ago, the educator Herbert R. Kohl wrote that most failing students "know all kinds of things that are never considered important in school or used as the foundation upon which to learn new things." He recalled hearing teachers—himself included—say things like:

"Put that comic book away. It's time to do reading."

"Stop playing cards. It's math period."

"Shut off your transistor. It's interfering with the choral music lesson."

Translation:

"Stop reading. It's time to study reading."

"Stop using math. It's time to study math."

"Stop listening to music. It's time to study music."

Kohl put his finger on something that the new games-in-school movement has actually underplayed, but which Wyatt discovered: the importance of getting to know students *as they are* in the real world. Kohl suggested spending time in the community and learning what parents teach their children, what games kids and parents play, both "verbal games" and jump rope. "In other words," he said, "to know the culture not as an anthropologist from an outside community but as a participant and celebrant."

If teachers looked around, he said, they'd find games everywhere. "By beginning the learning process in school with the games of the community, a teacher permits the students to remain in contact with a familiar world while they reach out to more abstract issues," he said. "The teacher is not a judge of his or her students but rather a worker whose role is to serve their needs and broaden their options. The community and the classroom must help each other."[3]

Wyatt may simply have been trying to build an inexpensive stage set, but her need tapped into Kohl's directive. She was smart enough to see what was happening and let it unfold. She also saw another advantage, aside from the cost, in building an opera set in a virtual world: Future productions, she told me, could access the set and stage their own performances simply by persuading her to send them a link to its *Minecraft* location.

The possibilities didn't end there. When I spoke to him in the summer of 2014, Bukvic, Wyatt's Tech colleague, was experimenting with ways to invite audience members to watch the opera from their own computers. Actually, he was taking it further than that. Since each player in *Minecraft* sees the virtual world from his or her own perspective, Bukvic has proposed giving audience members the opportunity to take in the action not from behind a virtual proscenium but from *within the set itself*. Audience members would be invisible avatars, ghosts that watch and listen from anywhere on the set but can't interact with the actors or be seen or heard by them. Bukvic had even begun imagining a more boldly experimental work in which audience members wandered around a future set during the performance and simply began dismantling scenery. "Any time you can engage your audience to be more than just an audience, they become a stakeholder in the experience and that can have a profound effect on how they perceive an experience," he said.

Oddly, a little glitch on opening night brought home the point that, for all its digital reality, the opera was still a human endeavor. At the climax of the first act, when—spoiler alert!—Markus's sister Regina was supposed to charge the evil emperor, grab him, and hurl the two of them off the balcony at the top of the tower, Regina's digital avatar froze. Instead of throwing the emperor off, she watched helplessly as he hesitated for a split-second, then threw himself over the edge. She had no choice, once her avatar unfroze, but to follow him moments later. The glitch made her character's heroic act—in the script, she sacrifices herself to allow Markus to escape to the upper world—look like a strange double suicide.

The boys, so used to living in a digital world where they could control every little detail, hadn't been prepared for that. Afterward, Wyatt found herself consoling the performers, telling them not to take the hiccup too hard. Little mess-ups like that have always been part of live performance, she said, and they always will.

More than fifty years ago, you'll recall, hackers at MIT played around with a nearly priceless computer and invented the video game. Twenty-five years ago, an eight-year-old boy playing with LEGOs at MIT's Media Lab coined the phrase "hard fun." Last September, while teaching an upper-level course called Games and Social Change, Scot Osterweil, a game designer, researcher, and creative director of MIT's Education Arcade, challenged his students to take a deeper look at play. "To get into MIT, you get there one of two ways," he told me. "You either get there because you're innately playful and inventive, or you get there because you're really good at doing what you're told."[4]

Class discussions showed that his students understood the importance of play, but they balked at the notion that *work* could be more playful. "There was some sense that play is great as play, but it's not work, and sometimes you have to knuckle under and do your hard work. Which I think we should be challenging."

In the mid-1990s, before most academics even dreamed of video games in school, Osterweil was co-creating a series of logic games that helped create a genre: the smart, strange, entertaining puzzle game, a category that lives on with *DragonBox, Wuzzit Trouble,* and similar titles. If you are a young person of a certain age— perhaps by now a parent—you probably played *Logical Journey of the Zoombinis,* a candy-colored adventure game that essentially took players through the steps of learning to create and use a database. Osterweil watched as the game and others like it took off, then crashed and burned when they were rebranded as "educational," reflecting the anxieties of parents struggling to give their kids a leg up. He sees the same pattern playing out now. "The notion that simply forcing your kid into a STEM field is going to get them a job is, well, we know historically that people always guess wrong on what the future is going to need in terms of skills or careers," he said. "What we really need are people who are creative and flexible and inventive and who will figure out how to make the future regardless of what changes technologically."

Over generations, the U.S. education system has gotten very good at producing "an acceptable average as efficiently as possible," he said. But if a young person wants to be a scientist now, "you need to be the inventive kind of scientist, the creative kind of scientist—not the one who has memorized all the parts of the cell. They're not the ones who make the great discoveries—it's the ones who have figured out how to ask interesting questions. Scientists, engineers, every field. Lawyers? The ones who are creative are going to be the good lawyers, not the ones who have memorized all of the case law."

Kids want to please us, but there's a natural limit to their patience. The MIT students who initially do what they're told often shake that off after they've been there a while. "There's always the obedient path, even at MIT," Osterweil said, "and there are kids who excel at that." But many more of them, he said, soon discover that other classmates are doing more interesting things with their time. "The good news is that here I think kids frequently figure out how to be more inventive with their own learning. I try to make it explicit to them and say, 'The fact that you got into MIT means that you may not really understand education, because it was always so easy for you. You may not really be aware of what the real challenges are.'"

Reporting this book, I often felt a bit of despair for our educational system. It often seems designed by the people for whom school was easy, who have always done what they're told. In spite of this—or perhaps because of it—the system seems to mess up everything it touches, even the great ideas. But each time I sat down to watch a child work, I came away more hopeful. Again and again, I was reminded of one key fact: young people are naturally, unpredictably creative and resilient, and most of the time they're merely tolerating our input. They live inside the magic circle and know how powerful it is.

Most of the time it's the adults who are holding them back, even when we're guiding them in what we feel is the right direction. We need to step back. We need to give them better tools, then trust their creativity. Giving them a chance to explore, to fail, to pick themselves up and try again, will yield great results. "Nobody," said games scholar Jim Gee, "has successfully underestimated a child."

ACKNOWLEDGMENTS

I began reporting this book as a Spencer fellow at the Columbia University Graduate School of Journalism, and I owe a debt of gratitude to everyone who made that wonderful year possible: Michael McPherson, Nicholas Lemann, LynNell Hancock, Marguerite Holloway, Samuel Freedman, Kelly McMasters, Arlene Morgan, and Barbara Kantrowitz, among others. Thanks also to several Spencers who offered invaluable help, timely advice, and, in a few cases, their agents' phone numbers: Alexander Russo, Dana Goldstein, Annie Murphy Paul, Peg Tyre, Sarah Garland, Elizabeth Green, Sarah Carr, Liz Bowie, and Trey Kay.

Thanks as well to my Columbia classmates who offered help, suggestions, and support, including Jaime Joyce, Shira Dicker, Delaney Hall, Philip Eil, and a great little writers' group: Dana Goldstein, Suzanne Mozes, Kitty Hoffman, Tanya Paperny, and Arturo Conde.

Inspiration, direction, and invaluable assistance came from dozens of people: Susan Maushart, M. T. Anderson, Katherine Paterson, Melanie Stegman, Peggy Kidwell, Radu Burducea, Lyndsay Lewman, Connie Yowell, Andy Solomon, Michael Levine, Jessica Millstone, Jim Gee, Alan Gershenfeld, Jessica Lindl, Michael John, Kristen DiCerbo, Bob Mislevy, Katie Salen, Ilena Parker, Robert Gehorsam, Diana Rhoten, Valerie Shute, Mizuko Ito, Lisa Nielsen, Michelle Luhtala, Justin Hamilton, Jane Dornemann, Mike Gallagher, Erik Huey, Dan Hewitt, Howard Yoon, Margery Mayer, Kyle Good, Tyler Reed, Sarah Trabucchi, Alex Sarlin, Ted Hasselbring, David Dockterman, Daniel Willingham, Ingrid Ellerbe, Rafi Santo, Liz Willen, Henry Jenkins, Marc Prensky, Joey Lee, James Tracy, Joel Levin, Kate Ho, Lisa Dawley, Will Richardson, Lucien Vattel, Luis von Ahn, Nancy MacIntyre, Larry Cocco, Karen Novak, Doug Levin, Sharon Sloane, Stone Librande, Jessie Woolley-Wilson, John Danner, Preston Smith, Charlie Bufalino, Richard Whitmire, John Merrow, Ulrich Boser, John See, Ian Hopper, John Studt, Tom Vander Ark, Andy Bowman, Celia

Pearce, Caroline Hendrie, Lori Crouch, Emily Richmond, Cornelia Grumman, Stephanie Banchero, Linda Perlstein, Bror Saxberg, Rick Hess, Michelle Byrd, Asi Burak, Nolan Bushnell, Tom Butt, Drew Davidson, Jesse Schell, Kellian Adams, Zoran Popovich, Girlie Delacruz, Ryan Baker, Sandra Okita, Trip Hawkins, Robin Hunicke, Nicole Lazzaro, Erik Klopfer, Scot Osterweil, Susannah Gordon-Messer, Jodi Asbell-Clarke, Teon Edwards, Jamie Larsen, Mat Nicholas, Casey Carlin, Elizabeth Rowe, Erin Bardar, Barb MacEachern, Zack Lynch, Elizabeth Olson, Jamie Madigan, Ali Carr-Chellman, Christopher Ferguson, Brad Lewis, Brock Dubbels, Jane McGonigal, Leslie Redd, Lisa Guernsey, Jamie Horwitz, Steven Hood, Mary Brophy Marcus, Tina Barseghian, Jordan Shapiro, Constance Steinkuehler, Jack Buckley, Mark DeLoura, Richard Culatta, Erik Martin, Seth Andrew, Dorie Turner, David Coleman, Kevin Carey, Ed Metz, Linda Faber, Roy Rodriguez, Amy Stefanski, Adam Renard, Ben Bertoli, John Bailey, Elena Bertozzi, Beth Fertig, Lou Kesten, Brooke Donald Gorlick, Steven Southall, Amanda Ripley, Lori Lewman, and Becky Scroggy Gould, among many others.

Thanks as well to my editors at *USA Today* for their great patience during this project: Susan Weiss, Dennis Kelly, Leslie Miller, Chris Cubbison, Glenn O'Neal, Dave Teeuwen, and Mike James, among others. Thanks also to Elizabeth Weise, Michelle Healy, Mary Beth Marklein, Dan Vergano, Liz Szabo, Haya El Nasser, Paul Overberg, Sharon Jayson, Gregg Zoroya, Brett Molina, and Mike Snider for keeping me in mind when video game news broke, and to Marisol Bello for a bit of key translation.

Thanks to Amanda Urban and Amelia Atlas at ICM Partners for taking a chance on this book, and to the team at Palgrave for their clear-eyed editing and infinite patience: Elisabeth Dyssegaard, Donna Cherry, and Ryan Masteller, among others.

Thanks as always to my family for their love and support during this intense period, including my parents, Silvia and Marshall Toppo; the Port Chester Toppos: Marshall Jr., Sue, Emily, and Sophia, for their hospitality and company; my Riverside Drive cousins Luigia, Herbie, and Bianca Miller and Bill Hopkins for countless late-night discussions; and to my wife, Julie, mother-in-law Mary Neidorf, and my remarkable daughters, Ava and Mairin, for all of their love, patience, and understanding.

NOTES

PROLOGUE: HARD FUN

1. Raymond students increased their math proficiency level by 15.28 percentage points in 2014, putting them in the top five among all elementary schools citywide in percentage gains. District of Columbia Public Schools, 2014 DC CAS Results by Sector, July 31, 2014, http://osse.dc.gov/sites/default/files/dc/sites/osse/publication/attachments/CAS%20Classification%202014_FOR%20POSTING_FINAL.pdf (accessed November 9, 2014).
2. I am indebted to Harvard's David Dockterman for sharing with me the manuscript of his important book, *Tools for Teachers: An Historical Analysis of Classroom Technology.*
3. Kurt Squire, *Video Games and Learning: Teaching and Participatory Culture in a Digital Age* (New York: Teachers College Press, 2011), 59.
4. Sara Corbett, "Learning by Playing: Video Games in the Classroom," *New York Times Magazine,* September 15, 2010, MM54.
5. Nicholas Negroponte, *Being Digital* (New York: Knopf, 1995), 196.
6. Michael John, presentation, Education Writers Association, Stanford University, May 4, 2013.
7. This is my modification of an idea that comes from motivational psychologists Scott Rigby and Richard Ryan. In their 2011 book *Glued to Games,* they lay out the difference between traditional stories and games. In stories, they say, readers can, at best, "vicariously enjoy the hero's exploits." But in video games, the heroic narrative supports in their minds the idea that they *are* a hero. "The game believes in them and their ability (i.e., competence)." Scott Rigby and Richard Ryan, *Glued to Games: How Video Games Draw Us in and Hold Us Spellbound* (Santa Barbara, CA: Praeger, 2011), 33.
8. James Paul Gee quoted in Corbett, "Learning by Playing."
9. Arana Shapiro, interview with author, May 15, 2014.
10. Nicole Lazzaro, presentation, Neurogaming Conference, San Francisco, May 8, 2014.
11. Joachim Liebschner, *A Child's Work: Freedom and Guidance in Froebel's Educational Theory and Practice* (Cambridge, UK: Lutterworth, 2006).
12. Vivian Gussey Paley, *A Child's Work: The Importance of Fantasy Play* (Chicago: University of Chicago Press, 2004), 36.

13. Quoted in Stuart Brown, *Play: How It Shapes the Brain, Opens the Imagination, and Invigorates the Soul* (New York: Avery, 2009), 185.

14. Jodi Asbell-Clarke, interview with author, December 14, 2012.

15. Steven Johnson, *Everything Bad Is Good for You: How Today's Popular Culture Is Actually Making Us Smarter* (New York: Riverhead, 2005), 187.

16. Marshall McLuhan and George B. Leonard, "The Future of Education: The Class of 1989," *Look,* February 21, 1967, 23-24, http://learning spaces.org/files/mcluhanfs.html.

17. Marc Prensky, *Teaching Digital Natives: Partnering for Real Learning* (Thousand Oaks, CA: Corwin, 2010), 2.

18. High School Survey of Student Engagement 2010, Indiana University, November 9, 2014, p. 7, http://www.indiana.edu/%7Eceep/hssse/images /HSSSE_2010_Report.pdf.

19. John M. Bridgeland, John J. DiIulio Jr., Karen Burke Morison, "The Silent Epidemic: Perspectives of High School Dropouts," report by Civic Enterprises in association with Peter D. Hart Research Associates for the Bill & Melinda Gates Foundation, March 2006, iii.

20. Amanda Ripley, "What It Takes: Keeping up with the Competition, Part I—K 12," *Education Nation,* February 12, 2014, http://www.nbcnews .com/feature/education-nation/commentary-it-takes-keeping-competi tion-k-12-n11836 (accessed November 9, 2014).

21. Megan McArdle, *The Up Side of Down: Why Failing Well Is the Key to Success* (New York: Viking, 2014), 23.

22. Gabe Newell, presentation, Games for Change, New York, June 22, 2011.

23. Stuart Dredge, "Angry Birds Playground: Rovio catapults gaming into the classroom," *The Guardian,* September 16, 2013.

24. "Learning Math through Video Games: An Interview with Keith Devlin," *Math Mirror,* March 2, 2012, http://www.mathmirror.org /perspectives/entry/learning-math-through-video-gamesan-interview -with-keith-devlin/.

1: A KIND OF ULTIMATE DECADENCE

1. Ransom Riggs, "Who Reads Books?" *Mental Floss,* April 25, 2011.

2. U.S. Department of Education, *Fifty Years of Supporting Children's Learning,* March 2005, 17, http://nces.ed.gov/pubs2005/2005311.pdf.

3. From 9 percent to 27 percent according to the U.S. Department of Education, *National Assessment of Educational Progress Long-Term Trend, Reading Classroom Context: Reading for Fun,* 2012, http:// www.nationsreportcard.gov/ltt_2012/context_read.aspx#2-0 (accessed November 9, 2014).

4. Nicholas Carr, *The Shallows: What the Internet Is Doing to Our Brains* (New York: W. W. Norton, 2010), 138.

5. David Trend, *The End of Reading: From Gutenberg to Grand Theft Auto* (New York: Peter Lang, 2010), 9.

6. Wendy Griswold, Terry McDonnell, and Nathan Wright, "Reading and the Reading Class in the Twenty-First Century," *Annual Review of*

Sociology 31 (August 2005): 127–41; first published online as a Review in Advance on March 11, 2005.

7. Kelly Gallagher, *Readicide: How Schools Are Killing Reading and What You Can Do about It* (Portland, ME: Stenhouse, 2009), 59.

8. Ibid., 5.

9. M. T. Anderson, interview with author, October 22, 2010.

10. Will Richardson, *Why School?: How Education Must Change When Learning and Information Are Everywhere,* TED Conference, 2012, e-book location 270.

11. Robin Hunicke, "Now Is Beautiful," May 4, 2012, https://www.you tube.com/watch?v=Gp7aAvtimaU.

12. Erik Martin, interview with author, September 15, 2014.

13. Tom Bissell, *Extra Lives: Why Video Games Matter* (New York: Pantheon, 2010), 121.

14. Alex Hutchinson, interview with author, March 28, 2012.

15. Kurt Squire, *Video Games and Learning: Teaching and Participatory Culture in a Digital Age* (New York: Teachers College Press, 2011), 1-2.

16. You can watch a video of the touchdown on YouTube: https://www.you tube.com/watch?v=I74BG0YFKUc (accessed November 9, 2014).

17. Patrick Hruby, "The Franchise," *ESPN,* August 5, 2010, http://sports .espn.go.com/espn/eticket/story?page=100805/madden.

18. Dennis Baxter and Peregrine Andrews, "The Sound of Sport," *Falling Tree Productions,* April 30, 2011, http://www.fallingtree.co.uk /broadcast_history/2011/the_sound_of_sport.

19. Jim Rossignol, *This Gaming Life: Travels in Three Cities* (Ann Arbor: University of Michigan Press, 2008), 200.

20. Dale Russakoff, "Schooled," *The New Yorker,* May 19, 2014, http:// www.newyorker.com/magazine/2014/05/19/schooled.

21. Paul Saettler, *The Evolution of American Educational Technology* (Charlotte, NC: Information Age Publishing, 2004), 100.

22. David Dockterman, *Tools for Teachers: An Historical Analysis of Classroom Technology,* unpublished dissertation, Harvard Graduate School of Education, 1988, 25, 99.

23. Randall Davidson, *9XM Talking: WHA Radio and the Wisconsin Idea* (Madison: University of Wisconsin Press, 2006), 266.

24. Larry Cuban, *Teachers and Machines: The Classroom Use of Technology Since 1920* (New York: Teachers College Press, 1986), 34.

25. Seymour Papert, *Mindstorms: Children, Computers, and Powerful Ideas* (New York: Basic Books, 1993), 9.

26. Saettler, *The Evolution of American Educational Technology,* 457.

27. Cuban, *Teachers and Machines,* 88.

28. David Langendoen and Spencer Grey, interview with author, May 3, 2012.

2: TO THE MOON AND BACK IN FIVE MINUTES

1. John Markoff, *What the Dormouse Said: How the Sixties Counterculture Shaped the Personal Computer Industry* (London: Penguin, 2005), xi.

2. Stewart Brand, "We Owe It All to the Hippies," *TIME* 145, no. 4 (Spring 1995).

3. Walter Isaacson, *Steve Jobs* (New York: Simon & Schuster, 2012), 30.

4. Douglas Engelbart, "Augmenting Human Intellect: A Conceptual Framework," Stanford Research Institute, October 1962, http://www.dougengelbart.org/pubs/papers/scanned/Doug_Engelbart-AugmentingHumanIntellect.pdf.

5. Markoff, *What the Dormouse Said*, 67.

6. Heather Chaplin and Aaron Ruby, *Smartbomb: The Quest for Art, Entertainment, and Big Bucks in the Videogame Revolution* (Chapel Hill: Algonquin Books of North Carolina, 2005), 41.

7. Steven Levy, *Hackers: Heroes of the Computer Revolution* (Sebastopol, CA: O'Reilly Media, 2010), 10.

8. W. A. Higinbotham, "The Brookhaven TV-Tennis Game," Brookhaven National Laboratory, http://www.bnl.gov/about/docs/Higinbotham_Notes.pdf (accessed November 9, 2014). Years after the video game industry took off, Higinbotham wrote, "I agree that I should have applied for a patent, but I would not have been any the richer. The patent would have belonged to Uncle Sam."

9. J. C. Herz, *Joystick Nation: How Video Games Ate Our Quarters, Won Our Hearts, and Rewired Our Minds* (New York: Little, Brown and Company, 1997), 8.

10. Steward Brand, "*Spacewar:* Fanatic Life and Symbolic Death Among the Computer Bums," *Rolling Stone,* December 7, 1972.

11. Bushnell recalled testing a driving video game once for three or four hours, then getting into his car and driving to his home in the canyons west of Los Angeles. "I found myself driving up the canyon in a four-wheel drift a couple of times around the corner, and then all of a sudden I said, 'Oh shit! This is real! If I go over the edge here, I can't just hit the reset button.' It was a real wakeup call to me." Nolan Bushnell, interview with author, March 4, 2014.

12. Markoff, *What the Dormouse Said*, 221.

13. Scott Cohen, *Zap! The Rise and Fall of Atari* (New York: McGraw-Hill, 1984), 23.

14. Lazowska and two computer architecture colleagues—Luis Ceze of the University of Washington and Mark Hill of the University of Wisconsin—looked at advances in microprocessors from the introduction of Intel's 4004 in 1971—widely regarded as the first microprocessor—to today's Intel Xeon with fifteen cores. They found a million-fold increase in density, comparable to fitting "a mid-size jet inside a matchbox"; in operations per second, he said, the improvement has been about 100,000-fold; the improvement in efficiency has been about 6,750 times, equivalent to a single laptop battery being able to power an average household for a week; the improvement in cost-effectiveness equals about 2,700 times, making it possible, for instance, for someone to earn enough money to buy a house by working for about three hours—the house, he said, would be as cheap as "a nice bottle of wine." Ed Lazowska, e-mail to author, August 9, 2014.

15. David Williamson Shaffer, *How Computer Games Help Children Learn* (New York: Palgrave Macmillan, 2006), 11.

16. David Greelish, "An Interview with Computing Pioneer Alan Kay, *TIME*, April 02, 2013, http://techland.time.com/2013/04/02/an-interview-with-computing-pioneer-alan-kay/.
17. A. A. Lumsdaine, "Teaching Machines: An Introductory Overview," in *Teaching Machines and Programmed Learning: A Source Book*, eds. R. Glaser and A. A. Lumsdaine (Washington, DC: National Education Association of the United States, 1960), 6.
18. You can see B. F. Skinner describe how teaching machines work in a 1956 instructional film uploaded on December 20, 2011, to YouTube: https://www.youtube.com/watch?v=jTH3ob1IRFo.
19. Peggy Aldrich Kidwell, Amy Ackerberg-Hastings, David Lindsay Roberts, *Tools of American Mathematics Teaching, 1800-2000* (Washington, DC, and Baltimore, MD: Smithsonian Institution and Johns Hopkins University Press, 2008), 72.
20. You can see Sidney Pressey demonstrate the machine in a 1964 instructional film uploaded on October 29, 2013, to YouTube: https://www.youtube.com/watch?v=n7OfEXWuulg.
21. Kidwell, et al., *Tools of American Mathematics Teaching*, 80.
22. James Paul Gee, *Situated Language and Learning: A Critique of Traditional Schooling* (New York: Routledge, 2004), 1.
23. James Paul Gee, interview with author, November 15, 2013.
24. James Paul Gee, *Good Video Games + Good Learning: Collected Essays on Video Games, Learning, and Literacy* (New York: Peter Lang, 2007), 61.
25. Marc Prensky, *Digital Game-Based Learning* (St. Paul, MN: Paragon House, 2001), 69.
26. Gee, *Good Video Games + Good Learning*, 112.
27. Center on Education Policy, *NCLB: Narrowing the Curriculum?* July 2005, http://www.cep-dc.org/displayDocument.cfm?DocumentID=239.
28. James Paul Gee, *Why Video Games Are Good For Your Soul: Pleasure and Learning* (Australia: Common Ground, 2005), 84.
29. Gee, *Situated Language and Learning*, 8.
30. Gee, *What Video Games Have to Teach Us About Learning and Literacy*, 216.
31. James Paul Gee, in Cynthia L. Selfe, Gail E. Hawisher, eds., *Gaming Lives in the Twenty-First Century: Literate Connections* (New York: Palgrave Macmillan, 2007), xi.
32. Gee, interview with author, November 15, 2013.
33. Constance Steinkuehler, interview with author, December 2, 2011.
34. Ibid.
35. James Paul Gee, *The Anti-Education Era: Creating Smarter Students through Digital Learning* (New York: Palgrave Macmillan, 2013), 7.
36. James Paul Gee, presentation, Hechinger Institute, May 20, 2011.

3: "DON'T KISS THE ENGINE, DADDY, OR THE CARRIAGES WON'T THINK IT'S REAL"

1. Tom Bissell, *Extra Lives: Why Video Games Matter* (New York: Pantheon, 2010), 34-35.
2. Boris Johnson, "The Writing Is On the Wall—Computer Games Rot the Brain," *The Telegraph*, December 28, 2006, http://www.telegraph

.co.uk/comment/personal-view/3635699/The-writing-is-on-the-wall
-computer-games-rot-the-brain.html.

3. Daphne Bavelier et al, "Interactive Media, Attention, and Well-Being," Washington DC: National Science Foundation, August 21-22, 2012, http://www.bcs.rochester.edu/games4good/GameWellBeingAttention _NSFReport.pdf.

4. Ibid.

5. Sandro Franceschini, et al., "Action Video Games Make Dyslexic Children Read Better," *Current Biology,* March 18, 2013, http://dx.doi.org /10.1016/j.cub.2013.01.044.

6. Sandra Blakeslee, "Video-Game Killing Builds Visual Skills, Researchers Report," *New York Times,* May 29, 2003.

7. Irving Biederman and Edward A. Vessel, "Perceptual Pleasure and the Brain," *The American Scientist* (May-June 2006): 248-55.

8. Jaak Panksepp, *Affective Neuroscience: The Foundations of Human and Animal Emotions* (New York: Oxford University Press, 1998), 145.

9. Biederman and Vessel, "Perceptual Pleasure and the Brain," 248-55.

10. Lynne A. Isbell, "Snakes as agents of evolutionary change in primate brains," *Journal of Human Evolution* 51 (2006): 1-35.

11. Noah Falstein, "Natural Funativity," *Gamasutra,* November 10, 2004, http://www.gamasutra.com/view/feature/130573/natural_funativity .php.

12. Raph Koster, "*A Theory of Fun* Ten Years Later," talk at 2013 Game Developers Conference, *Gamasutra,* October 18, 2013, http://www.gama sutra.com/view/news/202607/Video_Raph_Koster_revisits_A_Theory _of_Fun.php.

13. Raph Koster, *A Theory of Fun for Game Design* (Sebastopol, CA: O'Reilly Media Inc., 2004), 96.

14. Michael Apter, *Danger: Our Quest for Excitement* (Oxford, UK: Oneworld Publications, 2007), 43.

15. David A. Raichlen, et al., "Wired to run: exercise induced endocannabinoid signaling in humans and cursorial mammals with implications for the 'runner's high,'" *The Journal of Experimental Biology* 215 (April 15, 2012): 1331-36.

16. Mark A. Smith, et al., "Aerobic Exercise Decreases the Positive-Reinforcing Effects of Cocaine," *Drug and Alcohol Dependence* 98, no. 1-2 (November 2008): 129-35.

17. Natalie Angier, "Job Description Grows for Our Utility Hormone," *New York Times,* May 2, 2011.

18. Ibid.

19. Panksepp, *Affective Neuroscience,* 144-45.

20. Lennart Nacke, quoted in Maria Konnikova, "Why Gamers Can't Stop Playing First-Person Shooters," *New Yorker,* November 26, 2013.

21. Credit Noah Falstein, in *Natural Funativity,* for this observation. In fact, several smartphone exercise applications have leveraged our instinctual predator/prey trigger. *iRun from Dogs* encourages runners by simulating the sound of "angry dogs chasing you" in your device's earbuds. Its developer notes, "The closer dogs get to you, the louder you will hear them in your headphones." The app includes a "Steady Chase" workout as well as a "Challenge of Death." Another app, *Zombies, Run! 5k*

Training is an eight-week "training program and audio adventure" that promises more than twenty-five workouts "combined with a gripping story delivered straight to your headphones."

22. Roger Caillois, *Man, Play and Games,* trans. Meyer Barash (New York: The Free Press of Glencoe Inc., 1961), 36.

23. Winifred Gallagher, *New: Understanding Our Need for Novelty and Change* (New York: Penguin, 2011), 10.

24. Koster, *A Theory of Fun,* 40-42.

25. Elizabeth Hellmuth Margulis, "One more time: Why do we listen to our favourite music over and over again? Because repeated sounds work magic in our brains," *Aeon Magazine,* March 7, 2014, http://aeon.co/magazine/altered-states/why-we-love-repetition-in-music/.

26. As if to emphasize the combat underlying many sports, Dutch neuroscientist D. F. Swaab calls boxing "neuropornography," noting that since World War II, about 400 boxers have died from brain injuries in the ring. "You can watch boxers inflicting permanent brain damage on one another in prime-time television," he wrote, "yet no one seems to get very upset about it." D. F. Swaab, *We Are Our Brains: A Neurobiology of the Brain, from the Womb to Alzheimer's* (New York: Spiegel & Grau, 2014), 234.

27. Annie Murphy Paul, "Your Brain on Fiction," *New York Times,* March 17, 2012.

28. Stanislas Dehaene, *Reading in the Brain: The New Science of How We Read* (New York: Viking, 2009), 4.

29. Ibid., 42.

30. Ibid., 139.

31. Ibid., 302.

32. Paul Bloom, *How Pleasure Works: The New Science of Why We Like What We Like* (New York: W. W. Norton, 2010), 155-56.

33. Ibid., 187.

34. Kathryn Y. Segovia and Jeremy N. Bailenson, "Virtually True: Children's Acquisition of False Memories in Virtual Reality," *Media Psychology* 12 (2009): 371–93.

35. Tamar Szabo Gendler, "Alief and Belief," *Journal of Philosophy* 105, no. 10: 634-63.

36. Chris Bateman, *Imaginary Games* (Alresford, UK: Zero Books, 2011), 63.

37. Johan Huizinga, *Homo Ludens: A Study of the Play-Element in Culture* (London: Routledge, 1950), 11.

38. Katie Salen and Eric Zimmerman, *Rules of Play: Game Design Fundamentals* (Cambridge: Massachusetts Institute of Technology, 2004), 304.

39. Bernard Suits, *The Grasshopper: Games, Life and Utopia* (Peterborough, ON: Broadview, 2005), 22.

40. Robert Krulwich, "There's a Fly in My Urinal," *NPR Weekend Edition Saturday,* December 19, 2009, http://www.npr.org/templates/story/story.php?storyId=121310977.

41. *Urinal Fly,* http://www.urinalfly.com/product-category/stickers/ (accessed November 13, 2014).

42. Huizinga, *Homo Ludens,* 8.

43. Daniel Cook, "Games Are Designer Food for Infovores," *Lostgarden,* July 24, 2006, http://www.lostgarden.com/2006/07/games-are-designer -food-for-infovores.html.

44. Scott Rigby and Richard Ryan, *Glued to Games: How Video Games Draw Us in and Hold Us Spellbound* (Santa Barbara, CA: ABC-CLIO, LLC, 2011), 11.

45. Alex Sarlin and David Dockterman, "The 'Gamification' of Math: Research, Gaming Theory and Math Instruction" presentation, National Council of Teachers of Mathematics, April 30, 2013.

46. Tom Chatfield, *Fun Inc.: Why Gaming Will Dominate the Twenty-First Century* (New York: Pegasus, 2011), 40.

47. Tim Schafer, interview with Critical Path, http://criticalpathproject .com/?v=38442883 (accessed November 13, 2014).

48. Ken Levine, interview with Critical Path, http://criticalpathproject .com/?v=38407124, (accessed November 13, 2014).

49. Britt Myers, interview with author, January 23, 2014.

50. Janet Murray, *Hamlet on the Holodeck: The Future of Narrative in Cyberspace* (New York: The Free Press, 1997), 98-99.

51. Jamie Madigan, "The Psychology of Immersion in Video Games," *The Psychology of Video Games,* July 27, 2010.

52. Mihaly Csikszentmihalyi, *Flow: The Psychology of Optimal Experience* (New York: Harper & Row, 1990), 3.

53. Henning Boecker et al., "The Runner's High: Opioidergic Mechanisms in the Human Brain," *Cerebral Cortex* 18, no. 11 (2008): 2523-31.

54. Amby Burfoot, "Runner's High, *Runner's World,* April 28, 2004.

55. Csikszentmihalyi, *Flow,* 83.

56. David Sudnow, *Pilgrim in the Microworld* (New York: Warner Books, 1983), 46. Thanks to Jane McGonigal for pointing out Sudnow's book.

57. Ibid., 74.

58. Ibid., 45.

59. Ibid., 114.

60. Ibid., 102.

61. Natasha Dow Schüll, *Addiction by Design: Machine Gambling in Las Vegas* (Princeton, NJ: Princeton University Press, 2012), 12.

62. Jesper Juul, *The Art of Failure: An Essay on the Pain of Playing Video Games* (Cambridge: Massachusetts Institute of Technology, 2013), 12.

63. Niklas Ravaja et al., "The Psychophysiology of Video Gaming: Phasic Emotional Responses to Game Events," proceedings, DiGRA Conference, 2005.

64. *We the Giants,* http://www.arcadeplay.com/game/we-the-giants (accessed November 13, 2014).Thanks to Anna Antropy for pointing out *We the Giants* in her book *Rise of the Videogame Zinesters: How Freaks, Normals, Amateurs, Artists, Dreamers, Drop-outs, Queers, Housewives, and People Like You Are Taking Back an Art Form* (New York: Seven Stories, 2012).

65. *We the Giants (latest sessions),* February 7, 2010, http://www.youtube .com/watch?v=4sY7i_yTaqI.

4: THE GAME LAYER

1. Tim Kelley, interview with author, March 10, 2013.

2. Steve Dunbar, interview with author, March 12, 2013.
3. Tim Kelley, interview with author, Nov. 12, 2014.
4. Eric Nelson, interview with author, March 30, 2014.
5. Aaron Dignan, *Game Frame: Using Games as a Strategy for Success* (New York: Free Press, 2011), 49.
6. Ian Bogost, "How I Stopped Worrying about Gamers and Started Loving People Who Play Games," *Gamasutra*, August 2, 2007, http://www.gamasutra.com/view/feature/1543/persuasive_games_how_i_stopped_.php.
7. Adam Penenberg, *Play at Work: How Games Inspire Breakthrough Thinking* (New York: Portfolio, 2013), 181-82.
8. Jonathan Schultz, "Speed Camera Lottery Wins VW Fun Theory Contest," *New York Times*, November 30, 2010, http://wheels.blogs.nytimes.com/2010/11/30/speed-camera-lottery-wins-vw-fun-theory-contest/?scp=3&sq=speed%20and%20lottery&st=cse.
9. Penenberg, *Play at Work*, 158.
10. Quoted in Penenberg, *Play at Work*, 158.
11. James S. Coleman, "Academic Achievement and the Structure of Competition," *Harvard Educational Review* 29, no. 4 (Fall 1959): 337.
12. Ibid., 343.
13. Ibid.
14. Ibid., 347.
15. Ibid., 350. The findings would eventually become the core of Coleman's 1961 book *The Adolescent Society*.
16. Sarah Garland, *Divided We Fail: The Story of an African American Community That Ended the Era of School Desegregation* (Boston: Beacon Press, 2013), 77.
17. Ibid., 78.
18. Barbara J. Kiviat, "The Social Side of Schooling," *Johns Hopkins Magazine*, April 2000.
19. Greg Toppo, "Thousands of Black Teachers Lost Jobs," *USA Today*, April 28, 2004.
20. Shawn Young, interview with author, March 4, 2014.
21. Quoted in Raymond E. Callahan, *Education and the Cult of Efficiency: A Study of the Social Forces That Have Shaped the Administration of Public Schools* (Chicago: University of Chicago Press, 1962), 9.
22. Ibid., 62.
23. Ibid., 73.

5: MATH WITHOUT WORDS

1. Andrew Elliot-Chandler, interview with author, September 19, 2012.
2. Lyndsey Layton, "Is a charter school chain called Rocketship ready to soar across America?" *Washington Post*, July 29, 2012.
3. Richard Whitmire, *On the Rocketship: How Top Charter Schools Are Pushing the Envelope* (San Francisco: Jossey-Bass, 2014), 74.
4. Ibid., 104.
5. Matthew Peterson, interview with author, November 14, 2012.
6. Rocketship *Sí Se Puede* Academy School Accountability Report Card, 2012-13, http://rocketship.schoolwisepress.com/reports/2013/pdf/rocketship/sarce_en_43-10439-0119024e.pdf.

7. Peterson, interview with author, November 14, 2012.
8. Amy Bruckman, *Can Educational Be Fun?* paper, Georgia Institute of Technology, http://www.cc.gatech.edu/~asb/papers/bruckman-gdc99.pdf, March 17, 1999 (accessed November 13, 2014).
9. Jacob Habgood and Shaaron Ainsworth, "Motivating Children to Learn Effectively: Exploring the Value of Intrinsic Integration in Educational Games," *Journal of the Learning Sciences* 20, no. 2 (2011): 169-206.
10. Annie Murphy Paul, "What's the Secret Sauce to a Great Educational Game?" *Mind/Shift*, April 26, 2012.
11. Matthew Peterson, TED Talk, June 8, 2011, https://www.youtube.com /watch?v=2VLje8QRrwg.
12. Keith Devlin, *Mathematics Education for a New Era: Video Games as Medium for Learning* (Natick, MA: A. K. Peters, 2011), 2.
13. "Martin Gardner, Genius of Recreational Mathematics," *Weekend Edition Saturday,* April 12, 2014, http://www.npr.org/2014/04/12/302166 509/martin-gardner-a-genius-of-recreational-mathematics.
14. Keith Devlin, "The Music of Math Games," *American Scientist* 101, no. 2 (March-April 2013): 87-91.
15. Terezinha Nunes, David William Carraher, Analucia Dias Schliemann, *Street Mathematics and School Mathematics* (Cambridge, UK: Cambridge University Press, 1993), 28.
16. Quoted in Don Tapscott, *Grown Up Digital: How the Net Generation Is Changing Your World* (New York: McGraw-Hill, 2009), 19.
17. Devlin, "The Music of Math Games," 87-91.
18. Jordan Shapiro, "Video Games Are the Perfect Way to Teach Math, Says Stanford Mathematician," *Forbes,* August 29, 2013.
19. Devlin, *Mathematics Education for a New Era,* 6.
20. Ibid., 48.
21. Keith Devlin, interview with author, July 24, 2013.
22. Devlin, *Mathematics Education for a New Era,* xii.
23. Ibid., 6.
24. Devlin, interview with author, July 24, 2013.
25. Devlin, *Mathematics Education for a New Era,* 6.
26. David Kushner, *Masters of Doom: How Two Guys Created an Empire and Transformed Pop Culture* (New York: Random House, 2003), x.
27. Keith Devlin, interview with author, March 14, 2014.
28. Jean-Baptiste Huynh, interview with author, April 18, 2013.
29. Ibid.
30. Ibid.
31. Jonathan Liu, "*DragonBox* Beats *Angry Birds*," *Wired,* June 13, 2012, http://archive.wired.com/geekdad/2012/06/dragonbox/all/.
32. Greg Toppo, "White House Office Studies Benefits of Video Games," *USA Today,* February 2, 2012, http://www.usatoday.com/news/washing ton/story/2012-01-26/edcuational-video-games-white-house/529080 52/1.
33. Julia Greenberg, "Kids Like to Learn Algebra, If It Comes in the Right App," *Wired,* November 23, 2013.
34. Washington State Algebra Challenge, http://wa.algebrachallenge.org (accessed November 13, 2014); Minnesota Algebra Challenge, http:// mn.algebrachallenge.org. (accessed November 13, 2014).

35. Nova Barlow, "Looking to the future with Algebra Challenge," University of Washington Center for Game Science, May 28, 2014, http://centerforgamescience.org/2014/05/.

36. Jordan Shapiro, "Can Video Games Make Your Kids Smarter?" *Forbes,* December 11, 2012, http://www.forbes.com/sites/jordanshapiro/2012/12/11/can-video-games-make-your-kids-smarter/.

6: RUBE GOLDBERG BROUGHT US TOGETHER

1. Tyler Spielberg, interview with author, June 24, 2014.

2. Katie Salen, interview with author, August 4, 2014.

3. Ibid.

4. John D. Sutter, "The School Where Learning Is a Game," *Gaming Reality, CNN,* August 2012, http://www.cnn.com/interactive/2012/08/tech/gaming.series/teachers.html.

5. You can watch it online: http://vimeo.com/102239371.

6. Don Rawitsch, interview with author, November 3, 2011.

7. Jessica Lussenhop, "*Oregon Trail:* How Three Minnesotans Forged Its Path," *City Pages,* January 19, 2011.

8. Dan White presentation, Games for Change Festival, New York: June 19, 2013, https://www.youtube.com/watch?v=HziGw50w8es.

9. Karaoke Ice Press Release, August 8, 2007, https://lace-media.s3.amazonaws.com/files/Karaoke_Ice_press_release.pdf.

10. Katie Salen, interview with author, November 21, 2013.

11. Salen, interview with author, August 4, 2014.

12. Robert Torres, interview with author, July 16, 2014.

13. Susan Aud, Mary Ann Fox, and Angelina KewalRamani, *Status and Trends in the Education of Racial and Ethnic Groups* (Washington, DC: U.S. Department of Education, National Center for Education Statistics, July 2010), http://nces.ed.gov/pubs2010/2010015.pdf.

14. New York City Department of Education, *New York City Graduation Rates,* http://schools.nyc.gov/NR/rdonlyres/723B1E9A-B35E-4C25-9D48-4E18E0BA90A5/0/2013GraduationRatesPublicWebsite.pdf.

15. Yasmeen Khan, "Most Eighth Graders Matched to a High School of Their Choice," *SchoolBook,* March 15, 2013, http://www.wnyc.org/story/301978-high-school-admissions/.

16. J. M. Bridgeland, J. J. DiIulio, and K. B. Morison, *The Silent Epidemic: Perspectives of High School Dropouts* (Washington, DC: Civic Enterprises, 2006).

17. Donald Roberts, Ulla Foehr, and Victoria Rideout, "Generation M: Media in the Lives of 8–18 Year-Olds," report by the Henry Kaiser Family Foundation, March 2005, http://kaiserfamilyfoundation.files.wordpress.com/2013/01/generation-m-media-in-the-lives-of-8-18-year-olds-report.pdf.

18. Eric Klopfer, Scot Osterweil, Jennifer Groff, Jason Haas, "Using the Technology of Today, in the Classroom of Today: The Instructional Power of Digital Games, Social Networking, Simulations, and How Teachers Can Leverage Them," paper, Massachusetts Institute of Technology, *Education Arcade,* 2009, 1, http://education.mit.edu/papers/GamesSimsSocNets_EdArcade.pdf.

19. Eric Klopfer, Scot Osterweil, Katie Salen, "Moving Learning Games Forward: Obstacles, Opportunities, and Openness" (paper, Massachusetts Institute of Technology, *Education Arcade,* 2009), 5-6, http://education.mit.edu/papers/MovingLearningGamesForward_EdArcade.pdf.

20. Katie Salen, Robert Torres, Loretta Wolozin, Rebecca Rufo-Tepper, Arana Shapiro, *Quest to Learn: Developing the School for Digital Kids* (Cambridge, MA: MIT Press, 2011), x-xi.

21. Al Doyle, interview with author, August 12, 2014.

22. Rocco Rinaldi-Rose, interview with author, July 20, 2014.

23. Ibid.

24. Salen, interview with author, August 4, 2014.

25. Sara Corbett, "Learning by Playing: Video Games in the Classroom," *New York Times Magazine,* September 15, 2010.

26. "Reframing Failure as Iteration Allows Students to Thrive," *Edutopia,* November 12, 2013, http://www.edutopia.org/made-with-play-game-based-learning-iteration-video.

27. Shula Ehrlich, interview with author, August 15, 2014.

28. Alicia Iannucci, interview with author, March 25, 2014.

29. Joel Rose, interview with author, June 20, 2014.

30. Richard Arum, Patrick Inglis, Kiley Larson, Max Meyer, Alexis Pang, Jane Park, Rafael Santana, and Michelle Williams, *Quest Schools: Formative Program Assessment Report,* September 2012, New York University.

31. Rose, interview with author, June 20, 2014.

32. Richard Arum, interview with author, August 14, 2014.

33. Rebecca Rufo-Tepper, interview with author, June 24, 2014.

34. Herbert R. Kohl, *Math, Writing and Games in the Open Classroom* (New York: Random House, 1973), 97.

35. Salen, *Quest to Learn,* ix.

7: "I'M NOT GOOD AT MATH, BUT MY AVATAR IS"

1. Peggy Sheehy, interview with author, October 25, 2011.

2. Yee found that "gender-bending" is much more common among male than female players—about seven to eight times more common; out of a hypothetical 1,000 players encountered in *World of Warcraft,* he estimated, 348 would be female characters—of those, 193, or 55 percent, would be played by males. Nick Yee, "WoW Gender-Bending," *The Daedalus Project* 7-1, 2009, http://www.nickyee.com/daedalus/archives/001369.php.

3. Nick Montfort and Ian Bogost, *Racing the Beam: The Atari Video Computer System* (Cambridge, MA: MIT Press, 2009), 51.

4. "Q&A: *Pac-Man* Creator Reflects on 30 Years of Dot-Eating," *Wired,* May 21, 2010, http://www.wired.com/2010/05/pac-man-30-years/.

5. Sherry Turkle, *Alone Together: Why We Expect More from Technology and Less from Each Other* (New York: Basic Books, 2011), 198.

6. Ibid., 191-92.

7. James Paul Gee, *What Video Games Have to Teach Us about Learning and Literacy* (New York: Palgrave Macmillan, 2003), 63.

8. Annette Lareau, *Unequal Childhoods: Class, Race, and Family Life* (Berkeley: University of California Press, 2003), 2-3.

9. When she tells this story, as an aside, Sheehy says of MacNaughton, "This is the kind of man we need at the helm, not this knee-jerk, fear-based crap." Peggy Sheehy, interview with author, November 19, 2013.

10. Peggy Sheehy, interview with author, July 12, 2014.

11. Nick Yee, *The Proteus Paradox: How Online Games and Virtual Worlds Change Us—and How They Don't* (New Haven, CT: Yale University Press, 2014), 150-54.

12. Hal Hershfield, "You Make Better Decisions if You 'See' Your Senior Self," *Harvard Business Review,* June 2013.

13. Nick Yee and Jeremy Bailenson, "The Proteus Effect: The Effect of Transformed Self-Representation on Behavior," *Human Communication Research* 33, no. 3 (July 2007): 271-90.

14. Leon Festinger and Henry W. Riecken, *When Prophecies Fail* (Minneapolis: University of Minnesota Press, 1956), 171.

15. Peggy Sheehy, "ISTE 2011," August 17, 2012, https://www.youtube .com/watch?v=5CL9M—_bgI.

16. Constance Steinkuehler and Sean Duncan, "Scientific Habits of Mind in Virtual Worlds," *Journal of Science Education and Technology* 17, no. 6 (December 2008): 530-43, http://website.education.wisc.edu/stein kuehler/blog/papers/SteinkuehlerDuncan2008.pdf.

17. Jane McGonigal, *Reality Is Broken: Why Games Make Us Better and How They Can Change the World* (New York: Penguin, 2011), 61.

18. Ibid.

19. Mareesa Nicosia, "Ramapo Central Cuts Programs, Staff in Adopted $128M Budget," *The Journal News,* April 26, 2013.

20. Sugata Mitra, "Method—ELSE, For Schools Where Children Teach Themselves," *School of Education, Communication and Language Sciences,* Newcastle University, May 2010.

8: PROJECT UNICORN

1. Joel Klein, interview with author, February 22, 2013.

2. Johan Huizinga, *Homo Ludens: A Study of the Play-Element in Culture* (London: Routledge, 1950).

3. Mark Twain, *The Adventures of Tom Sawyer,* 12.

4. Brian X. Chen, "The Laptop Celebrates 40 Years," *Wired,* November 3, 2008.

5. Alan Kay, "A Personal Computer for Children of All Ages," *Proceedings of the ACM National Conference,* Boston, August 1972, http://mprove .de/diplom/gui/kay72.html, (accessed November 19, 2014).

6. Julie Landry Petersen, "For Education Entrepreneurs, Innovation Yields High Returns," *Education Next,* Spring 2014, 9-16.

7. Larry Berger and David Stevenson, "K-12 Entrepreneurship: Slow Entry, Distant Exit," conference, "The Supply Side of School Reform and the Future of Educational Entrepreneurship," American Enterprise Institute Conference, Washington, D.C., October 25, 2007.

8. Ibid.

9. Stephanie Mencimer, "Fox in the Schoolhouse: Rupert Murdoch Wants to Teach Your Kids!" *Mother Jones,* September 23, 2011.
10. Jesse Schell, *Art of Game Design: A Book of Lenses,* 443.
11. Ibid.
12. Jesse Schell, Design, Innovate, Communicate, Entertain (DICE) Summit, Las Vegas, 2010.
13. Jesse Schell, interview with author, July 23, 2013.
14. Schell, DICE Summit, 2010.

9: A WALK IN THE WOODS

1. Mark Twain, "Address at the Dinner of the Nineteenth Century Club," speech, 1900, http://www.pbs.org/marktwain/scrapbook/06_connecti cut_yankee/page3.html (accessed November 16, 2014.
2. Sven Birkerts, *The Gutenberg Elegies: The Fate of Reading in an Electronic Age* (New York: Faber and Faber, 1994), xv.
3. Jonathan Rauch, "Sex, Lies, and Videogames," *The Atlantic,* November 1, 2006, http://m.theatlantic.com/magazine/archive/2006/11/sex-lies-and -videogames/305293/.
4. Carla Engelbrecht Fisher, interview with author, November 8, 2013.
5. Eoghan Kidney, interview with author, August 1, 2014.
6. Kevin Kelly, "Reading in a Whole New Way," *Smithsonian Magazine,* August 2010.
7. Laura Fleming, interview with author, March 1, 2011.
8. David Levithan, interview with author, August 6, 2014.
9. Motoko Rich, "Scholastic Plans to Put Its Branding Iron on a Successor to Harry Potter," *New York Times,* December 18, 2007, http://www .nytimes.com/2007/12/18/books/18scho.html?pagewanted=print&_r=0.
10. Matthue Roth, interview with author, July 22, 2013.
11. Ibid.
12. Tom Bissell, "Poison Tree: A Letter to Niko Bellic about *Grand Theft Auto V,*" *Grantland,* September 25, 2013, http://grantland.com/features /tom-bissell-writes-letter-niko-bellic-grand-theft-auto-v/.
13. From Nathaniel Hawthorne's journal, September 1, 1842, http://tran scendentalism-legacy.tamu.edu/authors/thoreau/hawthorneonhdt.html, (accessed November 16, 2014).
14. Ibid.
15. Tracy Fullerton, interview with author, January 18, 2013.
16. Harold Goldberg, *All Your Base Are Belong to Us: How Fifty Years of Videogames Conquered Pop Culture* (New York: Three Rivers Press, 2011), 109.
17. Jon Carroll, "Guerrillas in the *Myst,*" *Wired,* August 1994.
18. Henry David Thoreau, *Walden, a Fully Annotated Edition* (New Haven, CT: Yale University Press, 2004), 319.
19. Ibid.
20. Stephen Totilo, "*Walden: The Game* Is in Development," *Kotaku,* May 29, 2009, http://kotaku.com/5272278/walden-the-game-is-in-development.
21. Erik Hayden, "Thoreau's *Walden:* The Video Game," *TIME,* April 30, 2012, http://newsfeed.time.com/2012/04/30/thoreaus-walden-the-video -game/.

22. Eric Scheiner, "Thoreau-ly Virtual: Gov't Grant Gives Rise to 'Walden' Video Game," *CNS News,* October 2, 2012, http://cnsnews.com/news /article/thoreau-ly-virtual-gov-t-grant-gives-rise-walden-video-game.

23. Tracy Fullerton, interview with author, February 21, 2014.

24. Alex Mathew, interview with author, July 19, 2014.

25. Michael Sweet, interview with author, July 28, 2014.

10: THROW TRUCKS WITH YOUR MIND

1. Susanna N. Visser, Melissa L. Danielson, Rebecca H. Bitsko, Joseph R. Holbrook, Michael D. Kogan, Reem M. Ghandour, Ruth Perou, Stephen J. Blumberg, "Trends in the Parent-Report of Health Care Provider-Diagnosed and Medicated Attention-Deficit/Hyperactivity Disorder: United States, 2003–2011," Journal of the American Academy of Child & Adolescent Psychiatry, November 19, 2013, http://jaacap.org/web files/images/journals/jaac/visser.pdf.

2. Ibid.

3. Food and Drug Administration, Ritalin Medication Guide, http:// www.fda.gov/downloads/Drugs/DrugSafety/ucm089090.pdf (accessed November 16, 2014.

4. Adam Gazzaley, "Harnessing Brain Plasticity: Video Games and the Future of Cognitive Enhancement," presentation, Games for Change, New York, April 22, 2014, https://www.youtube.com/watch?v=P5ILcdhvuNI.

5. Douglas Foster, "How to Rebuild an Attention Span," *The Atlantic,* September 4, 2013, http://www.theatlantic.com/health/archive/2013/09 /how-to-rebuild-an-attention-span/279326/.

6. J. A. Anguera, J. Boccanfuso, J. L. Rintoul, O. Al-Hashimi, F. Faraji, J. Janowich, E. Kong, Y. Larraburo, C. Rolle, E. Johnston, and A. Gazzaley, "Video game training enhances cognitive control in older adults," *Nature* 501 (September 5, 2013): 97-101.

7. Gazzaley, "Harnessing Brain Plasticity," https://www.youtube.com/wa tch?v=P5ILcdhvuNI.

8. Robin Hunicke, interview with author, July 29, 2014.

9. Robin Hunicke, presentation, NeuroGaming Conference and Expo, San Francisco, May 7, 2014.

10. Andy Robertson, "Geek Sermon: Join the Church of the Gamer (Part 1)," presentation, July 29, 2013, https://www.youtube.com/watch?v=UX 8J5ORkcUo#t=226.

11. Jenova Chen, "Journey Breaks PSN Sales Records," PlayStation.Blog, March 29, 2012, http://blog.eu.playstation.com/2012/03/29/journey -breaks-psn-sales-records/.

12. "Journey: The making of–Official video game trailer," March 8, 2012," https://www.youtube.com/watch?v=dzwSL6zQbX4.

13. Leigh Alexander, "In-Depth: Journey's Rare and Magical Success," *Gamasutra,* March 1, 2012, http://gamasutra.com/view/news/163143 /InDepth_Journeys_rare_and_magical_success.php.

14. Hunicke, interview with author, July 29, 2014.

15. Brian Crecente, "Journey and the search for emotional gaming," *Polygon,* February 7, 2013, http://www.polygon.com/2013/2/7/3965342/jou rney-and-the-search-for-emotional-gaming.

16. B. E. Wexler, K. A. Hawkins, B. Rounsaville, M. Anderson, M. J. Sernyak, M. F. Green MF, "Normal neurocognitive performance after extended practice in patients with schizophrenia," *Schizophr Res* 26, no. 2-3 (August 29, 1997): 173-80.

17. Bruce Wexler, interview with author, June 10, 2014.

18. Ibid.

19. Lat Ware, interview with author, June 29, 2014.

20. "Graduate Focuses on Brain-Powered Game," *Digipen,* April 15, 2013.

21. Justin Davis, "Throw Trucks with Your Mind Developer Demo," May 23, 2013, https://www.youtube.com/watch?v=mmmJOcSSSrI.

22. Rus McLaughlin, "Throw Trucks with Your Mind is the best Star Wars game ever (preview)," *VentureBeat,* February 25, 2013, http://venturebeat.com/2013/02/25/throw-trucks-with-your-mind-is-the-best-star-wars-game-ever-preview/view-all/.

23. Ware, interview with author, June 29, 2014.

11: THE OPPOSITE OF FIGHTING

1. Connecticut Department of Emergency Services and Public Protection, Sandy Hook Elementary School Shooting Reports, 26, http://cspsandy hookreport.ct.gov/.

2. Ibid., 31-32.

3. State of Connecticut Office of the Child Advocate, Shooting at Sandy Hook Elementary School report, November 21, 2014, 98. http://www.ct.gov/oca/lib/oca/sandyhook11212014.pdf (accessed January 4, 2015).

4. Ibid.

5. Or *Temple Run, Tiny Wings, DragonVale, Uncharted, Sim City,* etc.

6. Harold Schechter, *Savage Pastimes: A Cultural History of Violent Entertainment* (New York: St. Martin's, 2005), 32.

7. Ibid., 60.

8. Ibid., 40.

9. Ibid., 126.

10. Ibid., 131.

11. Albert Bandura, Dorothea Ross, and Sheila A. Ross, "Transmission of Aggression Through Imitation of Aggressive Models," *Journal of Abnormal and Social Psychology* 63 (1961): 575-82.

12. Ibid.

13. Gerard Jones, *Killing Monsters: Why Children Need Fantasy, Super Heroes, and Make-Believe Violence* (New York: Basic Books, 2002), 38.

14. Ibid., 35.

15. Lawrence Kutner and Cheryl K. Olson, *Grand Theft Childhood: The Surprising Truth about Violent Video Games and What Parents Can Do* (New York: Simon & Schuster, 2008), 8.

16. American Academy of Pediatrics Committee on Public Education, "Media Violence," November 2001.

17. Kutner and Olson, *Grand Theft Childhood,* 78.

18. Schechter, *Savage Pastimes,* 23.

19. Ibid., 25.

20. Ibid., 25-26.
21. Cathy Davidson, *Now You See It: How Technology and Brain Science Will Transform Schools and Business for the 21st Century* (New York: Penguin, 2011), 155.
22. Tobias Greitemeyer and Silvia Osswald, "Effects of Prosocial Video Games on Prosocial Behavior," *Journal of Personality and Social Psychology* 98, no. 2 (2010): 211–21.
23. Mario Gollwitzer and André Melzer, "Macbeth and the Joystick: Evidence for Moral Cleansing after Playing a Violent Video Game," *Journal of Experimental Social Psychology* 48 (Impact Factor: 2.22) (July 2012): 1356-60, doi:10.1016/j.jesp.2012.07.001.
24. Quoted in Kutner and Olson, *Grand Theft Childhood*, 7.
25. Bryan Vossekuil, et al., *The Final Report and Findings of the Safe School Initiative: Implications for the Prevention of School Attacks in the United States,* report, U.S. Secret Service and U.S. Department of Education, May 2002, 22.
26. Benedict Carey, "Shooting in the Dark," *New York Times,* February 11, 2013.
27. Michael R. Ward, "Video Games and Crime," *Contemporary Economic Policy* 29, no. 2 (April 2011): 261–73, http://ssrn.com/abstract=1021452 or http://dx.doi.org/10.2139/ssrn.1021452.
28. Scott Cunningham, Benjamin Engelstätter, and Michael R. Ward, "Understanding the Effects of Violent Video Games on Violent Crime," April 7, 2011, http://ssrn.com/abstract=1804959 or http://dx.doi.org/10.2139/ssrn.1804959.
29. Max Fisher, "Chart: The U.S. Has Far More Gun-Related Killings Than Any Other Developed Country," *Washington Post,* December 14, 2012, http://www.washingtonpost.com/blogs/worldviews/wp/2012/12/14/chart-the-u-s-has-far-more-gun-related-killings-than-any-other-developed-country/.
30. Max Fisher, "Ten-Country Comparison Suggests There's Little or No Link Between Video Games and Gun Murders," *Washington Post,* December 17, 2012, http://www.washingtonpost.com/blogs/worldviews/wp/2012/12/17/ten-country-comparison-suggests-theres-little-or-no-link-between-video-games-and-gun-murders/.
31. Henry Jenkins, "Reality Bytes: Eight Myths about Video Games Debunked," *The Video Game Revolution, PBS,* http://www.pbs.org/kcts/videogamerevolution/impact/myths.html.
32. Heather Chaplin and Aaron Ruby, *Smartbomb: The Quest for Art, Entertainment, and Big Bucks in the Videogame Revolution* (Chapel Hill, NC: Algonquin Books, 2005), 210.
33. Maj. Kelly P. Houlgate, "Urban Warfare Transforms the Corps," *The Naval Institute: Proceedings,* November 2004.
34. Douglas A. Gentile and J. Ronald Gentile, "Violent Video Games as Examplary Teachers: A Conceptual Analysis," *Journal of Youth and Adolescence* 37 (2008): 127-41.
35. Ibid.
36. Daphne Bavelier, C. Shawn Green, Doug Hyun Han, Perry F. Renshaw, Michael M. Merzenich, Douglas A. Gentile, "Brains on Video Games," *Nature Reviews: Neuroscience* 12 (December 2011).

37. Department of Health and Human Services, "Mental Health: A Report of the Surgeon General," report, 155.

38. James Paul Gee, *Good Video Games + Good Learning: Collected Essays on Video Games, Learning, and Literacy* (New York: Peter Lang, 2007), 3.

39. James Paul Gee, presentation, May 20, 2011.

40. Quoted in Rusel DeMaria, *Reset: Changing the Way We Look at Video Games* (San Francisco, CA: Berrett-Koehler, 2007), 16

41. Jenkins, "Reality Bytes."

42. Iona and Peter Opie, *Children's Games in Street and Playground, Vol. 1: Chasing, Catching, Seeking,* 19.

43. Ibid., 21.

44. Brian Sutton-Smith, *The Ambiguity of Play* (Cambridge, MA: Harvard University Press, 1997), 23.

12: THE LUDIC LOOP

1. Eric Jou, "Father Hires In-Game 'Hitmen' to Deter Son From Playing," *Kotaku,* January 2, 2013, http://kotaku.com/5972406/father-hires-in-game-hitmen-to-deter-son-from-playing.

2. Becky Evans, "Chinese Father hires virtual hitman to 'kill' son in online games—so he will get a job," *Mail Online,* October 3, 2014, http://www.dailymail.co.uk/news/article-2258877/Chinese-father-hires-virtual-hitman-kill-son-online-games—job.html.

3. "Stuck in the Machine Zone: Your Sweet Tooth for *Candy Crush,*" *All Things Considered,* National Public Radio, June 7, 2014, http://www.npr.org/blogs/alltechconsidered/2014/06/07/319560646/stuck-in-the-machine-zone-your-sweet-tooth-for-candy-crush.

4. Kaiser Family Foundation, "Generation M2: Media in the Lives of 8-to 18-Year-Olds," report, January 20, 2010, http://kff.org/other/event/generation-m2-media-in-the-lives-of/.

5. Tom Chatfield, *Fun, Inc.: Why Gaming Will Dominate the Twenty-First Century* (New York: Pegasus, 2010), 76.

6. Nick Yee, *The Proteus Paradox: How Online Games and Virtual Worlds Change Us—and How They Don't* (New Haven, CT: Yale University Press, 2014), 37.

7. Ibid., 37-38.

8. Ibid.

9. Weaver, "Irrational Behavior, Episode 5: What Are We Afraid Of?," podcast, *Irrational Games,* May 3, 2010, http://irrationalgames.com/insider/irrational-behavior-episode-5/.

10. Gerard Jones, *Killing Monsters: Why Children Need Fantasy, Super Heroes, and Make-Believe Violence* (New York: Basic Books, 2002), 18.

11. Ibid.

12. Ibid., 11.

13. Eric Schleifer, interview with author, October 3, 2014.

14. Chris Hecker, *Critical Path,* interview, http://criticalpathproject.com/?v=50858919 (accessed November 18, 2014).

15. Jamie Madigan, "The Psychological Appeal of Violent Shooters," *Games Industry International,* April 9, 2013.

16. Scott Rigby and Richard M. Ryan, *Glued to Games: How Video Games Draw Us in and Hold Us Spellbound* (Santa Barbara, CA: Praeger, 2011), 23-24.

17. Lori Takeuchi and Reed Stevens, "The New Co-Viewing: Designing for Learning through Joint Media Engagement," report, Joan Ganz Cooney Center, Fall 2011, 11-12.

18. Rosalind Wiseman, *Masterminds and Wingmen: Helping Our Boys Cope with Schoolyard Power, Locker-Room Tests, Girlfriends, and the New Rules of Boy World* (New York: Harmony Books, 2013), 170.

19. Tom Bissell, "Poison Tree: A letter to Niko Bellic about *Grand Theft Auto V*," *Grantland,* September 25, 2013, http://grantland.com/features /tom-bissell-writes-letter-niko-bellic-grand-theft-auto-v/.

20. Greg Toppo, "Experts Warn of Harm to Kids from Secondhand TV Viewing," *USA Today,* October 23, 2011.

21. Lisa Guernsey, *Into the Minds of Babes: How Screen Time Affects Children from Birth to Age Five* (New York: Basic Books, 2007), 195.

22. Douglas A. Gentile, "Pathological Video Game Use among Youth 8 to 18: A National Study," *Psychological Science,* 2009.

23. *New Scientist* staff and Reuters, "Video games interfere with homework but not family," *New Scientist,* July 3, 2007, http://www.newscientist .com/article/dn12180-video-games-interfere-with-homework-but-not -family.html#.VC8C1vldXTo.

24. Scott Rigby and Richard M. Ryan, "Video Game Addiction: Why They're So Compelling and Five Warning Signs for Assessing Risk," *Written Voices,* http://www.writtenvoices.com/article_display.php?art icle_id=1065 (accessed November 18, 2014).

25. Rigby and Ryan, *Glued to Games,* 170-71.

26. Hilarie Cash and Kim McDaniel, *Video Games & Your Kids: How Parents Stay in Control* (Enumclaw, WA: Issues Press, 2008), 20.

27. Ibid., 67. Emphasis theirs.

28. American Academy of Pediatrics Council on Communications and Media, "Children, Adolescents and the Media," *Pediatrics* (2013): 959 ; originally published online October 28, 2013, http://pediatrics.aappub lications.org/content/132/5/958.full.html.

29. Jesse Schell, *The Art of Game Design: A Book of Lenses* (Burlington, MA: Morgan Kaufman, 2008), 451.

EPILOGUE: GAMES EVERYWHERE

1. Ariana Wyatt, interview with author, May 24, 2014.

2. Ico Bukvic, interview with author, August 20, 2014.

3. Herbert Kohl, *Math, Writing and Games in the Open Classroom* (New York: Random House, 1973), 242.

4. Scot Osterweil, interview with author, October 3, 2014.

INDEX